Consciousness and Self-Regulation
Advances in Research and Theory

VOLUME 4

A Continuation Order Plan is available for this series. A continuation order will bring delivery of each new volume immediately upon publication. Volumes are billed only upon actual shipment. For further information please contact the publisher.

Consciousness and Self-Regulation

Advances in Research and Theory

VOLUME 4

Edited by

RICHARD J. DAVIDSON
University of Wisconsin, Madison
Madison, Wisconsin

GARY E. SCHWARTZ
Yale University
New Haven, Connecticut

and

DAVID SHAPIRO
University of California at Los Angeles
Los Angeles, California

SPRINGER SCIENCE+BUSINESS MEDIA, LLC

Library of Congress Cataloging in Publication Data

Main entry under title:

Consciousness and self-regulation.

 Vol. 3, 4 has subtitle: Advances in research and theory.
 Vol. 3, 4 edited by Richard J. Davidson, Gary E. Schwartz, and David Shapiro.
 Includes bibliographies and indexes.
 1. Consciousness. 2. Self-control. I. Schwartz, Gary E., 1944–   . II. Shapiro, David,
1924–   . III. Davidson, Richard J.
BF311.C64   1976   153   76-8907
ISBN 978-1-4757-0631-4   ISBN 978-1-4757-0629-1 (eBook)
DOI 10.1007/978-1-4757-0629-1

© 1986 Springer Science+Business Media New York
Originally published by Plenum Press, New York in 1986

All rights reserved

No part of this book may be reproduced, stored in a retrieval system, or transmitted
in any form or by any means, electronic, mechanical, photocopying, microfilming,
recording, or otherwise, without written permission from the Publisher

Contributors

BARRY H. COHEN, Department of Psychology, State University of New York, Purchase, New York

BARRY R. DWORKIN, Pennsylvania State College of Medicine, Milton S. Hershey Medical Center, Hershey, Pennsylvania

NINA GOLDMAN, Rutgers—The State University, New Brunswick, New Jersey

CLAUDIA W. HOOVER, Center for Behavioral Medicine, Rockville, Maryland

J. MICHAEL LACROIX, Department of Psychology, Glendon College, York University, Toronto, Ontario

PAUL M. LEHRER, University of Medicine and Dentistry of New Jersey, Rutgers Medical School, Busch Campus, Piscataway, New Jersey

JAMES W. LEWIS, Mental Health Research Institute, University of Michigan, Ann Arbor, Michigan

JOHN C. LIEBESKIND, Department of Psychology, University of California, Los Angeles, Los Angeles, California

LINDA R. NELSON, Department of Psychology, University of California, Los Angeles, Los Angeles, California

DONALD A. NORMAN, Institute for Cognitive Science, University of California, San Diego, La Jolla, California

JAMES W. PENNEBAKER, Department of Psychology, Southern Methodist University, Dallas, Texas

CURT A. SANDMAN, Fairview Hospital, Costa Mesa, California

TIM SHALLICE, Medical Research Council, Applied Psychology Unit, Cambridge, England

YEHUDA SHAVIT, Department of Psychology, University of California, Los Angeles, Los Angeles, California

GREGORY W. TERMAN, Department of Psychology, University of California, Los Angeles, Los Angeles, California

ROBERT L. WOOLFOLK, Rutgers—The State University, New Brunswick, New Jersey

Preface

In the Preface to the third volume, we described the evolution of this Series and the changes that have taken place in the field since the first volume appeared. The contents of the current volume continue the commitment to a broadly based perspective on research related to consciousness and self-regulation which was embodied in the previous three volumes. Chapters are included which consider the role of consciousness in cognitive theory and clinical phenomena. Several of the contributions to this volume are concerned with the nature of self-regulation and the role of conscious processing in the mediation of self-regulated behavior. Most of the authors adopt a psychobiological approach to their subject matter. Our selection of contributors with a bias toward this approach reflects our own views that the psychobiological approach is a very fruitful one and that the "architecture" of the nervous system places important constraints on the types of theories that are possible in this emerging area.

While the subject matter of the chapters in this volume is quite diverse, the contributions are united by their emphasis on the importance of consciousness and/or self-regulation in the understanding of behavior and experience. We have selected what we believe is representative of the best theory and research in the diverse areas which bear on the theme of this series, maintaining a balance between basic and clinical research. We are confident that developments in the field will warrant future volumes in which the outstanding work of the previous two years are selected for extended treatment and review.

RICHARD J. DAVIDSON
GARY E. SCHWARTZ
DAVID SHAPIRO

Overview

The first chapter "Attention to Action: Willed and Automatic Control of Behavior" by Donald A. Norman and Tim Shallice underscores the importance of concepts of consciousness for contemporary cognitive psychology. These theories explain the importance of attentional interventions for certain types of action. Willful attention is required for action associated with the modification of a plan, the implementation of a novel alternative action sequence, or the prevention of an habitual act. Norman and Shallice propose a supervisory attentional system (SAS) which is activated when actions require "deliberate attention." They propose that this system is subserved by the frontal cortex and associate will with this form of attentional process.

The relation between volition and consciousness, a theme introduced in the first chapter, is continued in the second chapter entitled "The Motor Theory of Voluntary Thinking" by Barry H. Cohen. Cohen reviews theories that argue for a central role of motor activity in various forms of conscious processing. He concludes that motor activity (at least the central efferent commands which specify such activity) is necessary only for voluntary thinking. The experience of volition is said to arise from the generation of activity in the motor system. Certain types of perception and imagery of an automatic nature (which are not experienced as volitional) are said not to require the generation of activity in the motor system. Cohen concludes his chapter with the specification of some useful experimental approaches to systematically investigate the question of the necessity of motor activity in the experience of volition.

Curt A. Sandman in his chapter, "Cardiac Afferent Influences on Consciousness," extends the psychophysiological work of the Laceys on cardiac afferent feedback to the brain. Sandman and his colleagues have used novel experimental procedures to probe the influence of cardiac feedback on neurobehavioral processes. For example, he examined brain evoked potentials elicited by stimulii presented at different phases of the cardiac cycle. As would be predicted from the Laceys' theory, responses evoked by stimuli presented at the diastole were more dramatically influenced by cardiac phase compared with stimuli presented at other portions of the cardiac cycle. Hemispheric asymmetries were also noted in the topography of the responses, suggesting that cardiac afferent feedback may be lateralized. Sandman has also used several additional novel experimental procedures to examine other features of cardiac feedback. He concludes the chapter by considering some of the implications of rhythmic fluctuations in physiological activity for certain aspects of consciousness.

The next chapter by James W. Lewis, Linda R. Nelson, Gregory W. Terman, Yehuda Shavit, and John C. Liebeskind entitled "Intrinsic Control Mechanisms of Pain Perception" surveys recent findings on different endogenous mechanisms of pain control. The authors note that stress produced analgesia can operate through both opioid and non-opioid systems. Importantly, these investigators have demonstrated that the type of stressor that releases opioids is both immunosuppressive and produces learned helplessness. They thus have identified a cluster of effects resulting from a specific form of stress. These findings underscore the complex and differentiated nature of stress. Stress-produced analgesia is not a unitary phenomenon. Different neurochemical, neuroanatomical and hormonal substrates appear to exist for different forms of analgesia. Which of these is called into play appears to depend on variations in the parameters of the stress stimulus. One of the parameters that is most important is that of control over the stressor. Stressful stimuli that were least likely to be perceived as controllable are also those that are associated with opioid analgesia, learned helplessness and immunosuppression.

The clinical implications of variations in different aspects of conscious processing is a theme which is taken up next by James W. Pennebaker and Claudia W. Hoover in their chapter "Inhibition and Cognition: Toward an Understanding of Trauma and Disease." They begin their chapter by establishing a relation between early trauma and reports of illness. Those subjects who experienced early trauma, particularly of a sexual nature, had more symptoms of illness. Pennebaker and Hoover also report that those who had sexual trauma were less likely to confide in others about their trauma compared with subjects who had been subjected to other traumatic events. The authors then report the findings of a questionnaire study where they compared subjects who had experienced trauma and confided with those who had experienced comparable trauma but who had not confided. They found that subjects who had not confided were more likely to have illnesses compared with those who had. The authors consider the failure to confide as an example of inhibition. They consider inhibition to require mental work and find that it is itself stressful. The data and theorizing that is presented in this chapter raises several important and fascinating questions concerning the role of verbalization about and consciousness of stressful events in the illness process.

In the next chapter, "Mechanisms of Biofeedback Control: On the Importance of Verbal (Conscious) Processing," J. Michael Lacroix considers the nature of learning in biofeedback. He first reviews Brenner's notions of how learning in the biofeedback situation occurs. Brenner argued that when learning to control autonomic responses, subjects first learn to discriminate and identify interoceptive afferent processes related to the target response. Lacroix's review of the empirical evidence finds little support for this suggestion. Training in biofeedback does not enhance subjects' ability to discriminate changes in the target physiological response. Performance on tests of response discrimination are usually uncorrelated with performance on tests of response control. And, training in biofeedback does not usually lead to greater response specificity as a function of practice. On the basis of these observations, Lacroix argues that a verbally mediated feedforward process can account for most forms of learning within the biofeedback situation. It is only in those relatively rare situations when the "verbal library" cannot access information relevant to the appropriate behavioral programs that learning could be expected to proceed along the lines suggested by Brenner.

The next chapter continues the concern with the nature of learning associated with physiological self-regulation. Barry R. Dworkin, in his essay entitled "Learning and Long-term Physiological Regulation", presents a theory of autonomic self-regulation. The theory assumes the existence of Type II learning of visceral responses. The theory is novel with respect to contemporary treatments of biofeedback in that it emphasizes the interaction between central events and local autoregulatory processes. Dworkin squarely places these phenomena within their appropriate biological contexts. The theory also stresses the notion that the nervous system participates in both short-term dynamic adjustments and long-term or steady state adjustments.

In the final chapter by Paul M. Lehrer, Robert L. Woolfolk, and Nina Goldman entitled "Progressive Relaxation Then and Now: Does Change Always Mean Progress?" the concepts of self-regulation are extended to the clinical domain in a discussion of the efficacy and mechanisms of different relaxation techniques. These authors present a review of recent literature on progressive relaxation, a relaxation technique first developed by Edmund Jacobson in the 1930s. Various procedural variations in the administration of relaxation are evaluated, such as live versus taped instructions, number of sessions required and the number of muscles which are trained simultaneously. Lehrer *et al.* then proceed to a discussion of cognitive and somatic factors in anxiety and its treatment. They build on the theory of cognitive and somatic subcomponents of anxiety that was put forth by Davidson and Schwartz in 1976. Lehrer *et al.'s* review of recent literature supports the Davidson and Schwartz position that cognitive relaxation techniques have a greater effect on cognitive symptoms while somatic techniques, like progressive relaxation, have greater effects on the somatic components of anxiety. The role of suggestion and biofeedback in relaxation training are also considered. The authors conclude that anxiety and relaxation are complex, multifactorial processes. Different procedures, which emphasize different features of relaxation, will have reliably different effects.

Contents

1. **Attention to Action: Willed and Automatic Control of Behavior**   1

    DONALD A. NORMAN AND TIM SHALLICE

    I. Theory   3
        A. Contention Scheduling   5
        B. Determination of Activation Values   6
        C. The Supervisory Attentional System   6
    II. Evidence   8
        A. Evidence for a Distinct Supervisory Attentional System: Neuropsychological Findings   8
        B. Attentional Processes Only Modulate Schema Selection   10
        C. Attentional Resources Are Primarily Relevant for Action Selection   13
        D. Competition between Tasks   13
        E. Will and Deliberate Conscious Control   14
        References   16

2. **The Motor Theory of Voluntary Thinking**   19

    BARRY H. COHEN

    I. Previous Motor Theories   20
        A. The Motor Theory of Consciousness   20
        B. The Motor Theory of Thinking   22
        C. The Motor Theory of Attention   24
    II. Defining the Motor Theory of Voluntary Thinking   26
        A. The Experience of Volition   27

B. Specific Motor Associations   28
C. General Motor Associations   34
III. The Role of Covert Motor Activity in External Attention   38
    A. Voluntary Attention   38
    B. Spontaneous Attention   39
IV. Regulating the Stream of Thought   40
    A. Ordinary States   40
    B. Natural Relaxation   41
    C. Progressive Relaxation and Meditation   43
V. Conclusions   45
    A. Summary   45
    B. Implications for Experimental Research   46
    References   52

3. Cardiac Afferent Influences on Consciousness   55

CURT A. SANDMAN

I. Introduction   55
    A. Consciousness as Cognition and Emotion (Brain and Body)   56
II. Cardiovascular and Baroreceptor Physiology   57
III. Cardiovascular Relations to Behavior   63
    A. Control of Body, Control of Consciousness   63
    B. Effects on Consciousness of Transient Changes in the Cardiovascular System   67
IV. Influence of Cardiovascular System on the Brain   69
    A. The EEG   69
    B. Auditory Event–related Potentials   74
    C. Evoked Vascular Responses (EVRs)   77
V. Conclusions   80
    References   81

4. Intrinsic Control Mechanisms of Pain Perception   87

JAMES W. LEWIS, LINDA R. NELSON, GREGORY W. TERMAN, YEHUDA SHAVIT, AND JOHN C. LIEBESKIND

I. Introduction   87
II. Evidence for Endogenous Mechanisms of Pain Control   88
III. Activation of Endogenous Analgesia Systems: Stress-induced Analgesia   89

CONTENTS

    IV. Opioid and Nonopioid Mechanisms of Stress Analgesia 91
    V. Role of Endocrine Systems in Stress Analgesia   91
    VI. Neurotransmitters Involved in Stress Analgesia   93
    VII. The Neuroanatomy of Stress Analgesia   94
    VIII. Evidence for Two Independent Opioid Forms of Stress Analgesia   95
    IX. Early Experience Influences Stress Analgesia: The Effects of Prenatal Alcohol Exposure   97
    X. Immunosupressive and Tumor-enhancing Effects of Stress 98
    XI. Summary and Conclusions   99
    References   100

5. Inhibition and Cognition: Toward an Understanding of Trauma and Disease   107

JAMES W. PENNEBAKER AND CLAUDIA W. HOOVER

    I. Introduction   107
    II. Personal Traumas and Health   109
    A. Initial Survey   110
    B. *Psychology Today* Sample   112
    C. Medical Psychology Class Survey   115
    III. The Failure to Confide: The Role of Inhibition   118
    A. The Nature of Inhibition   119
    B. Inhibition and Physiological Activity   120
    C. Long-Term Inhibition: Personality Considerations 124
    D. Failure to Confide as Inhibition   128
    IV. Summary and Final Considerations   129
    A. Inhibition and Psychotherapy   130
    B. Cognitive Organization and Self-disclosure   130
    C. Links to Other Theories   131
    D. Summary   133
    References   133

6. Mechanisms of Biofeedback Control: On the Importance of Verbal (Conscious) Processing   137

J. MICHAEL LACROIX

    I. Introduction   137
    II. A Promise Unfulfilled   138

III. The Verbal (Consciousness?) Interface   147
IV. A Two-process Theory   152
   References   159

7. Learning and Long-term Physiological Regulation   163

BARRY R. DWORKIN

   References   181

8. Progressive Relaxation Then and Now: Does Change Always Mean Progress?   183

PAUL M. LEHRER, ROBERT L. WOOLFOLK, AND NINA GOLDMAN

   I. Introduction   183
   II. Pedagogy versus Technology   187
      A. Number of Sessions   188
      B. One Muscle at a Time versus All at Once   188
      C. Live versus Taped Relaxation   189
      D. Conditioned Relaxation   190
      E. The "Pendulum Effect"   191
      F. The Use of Biofeedback   194
   III. Differing Views on Cognitive and Somatic Factors in Emotion and in Treatment   195
   IV. Suggestion   202
   V. Conclusion   209
      References   210

   Author Index   217
   Subject Index   223

Contents of Previous Volumes

Volume 1

1 A Model of Consciousness

E. Roy John

2 Self-Consciousness and Intentionality: A Model Based on an Experimental Analysis of the Brain Mechanisms Involved in the Jamesian Theory of Motivation and Emotion

Karl H. Pribram

3 Self-Regulation of Stimulus Intensity: Augmenting/Reducing and the Average Evoked Response

Monte Buchsbaum

4 Neodissociation Theory of Multiple Cognitive Control Systems

Ernest R. Hilgard

5 Hypnotic Susceptibility, EEG-Alpha, and Self-Regulation

David R. Engstrom

6 Toward a Cognitive Theory of Self-Control

Donald Meichenbaum

7 Physiological and Cognitive Processes in the Regulation of Anxiety

Thomas D. Borkovec

8 Dreaming: Experimental Investigation of Representational and Adaptive Properties

David B. Cohen

9 Biofeedback and the Twilight States of Consciousness

Thomas H. Budzynski

Volume 2

1 The Human Brain and Conscious Activity

A. R. Luria

2 Imagery and Thinking: Covert Functioning of the Motor System

F. J. McGuigan

3 Regulation of the Stream of Consciousness: Toward a Theory of Ongoing Thought

Kenneth S. Pope and Jerome L. Singer

4 Self-Deception, Self-Confrontation, and Consciousness

Harold A. Sacken and Ruben C. Gur

5 Visceroception, Awareness, and Behavior

György Ádám

6 Stimulus-Bound Behavior and Biological Self-Regulation: Feeding, Obesity, and External Control

Judith Rodin

7 Operant Conditioning of Autonomic Responses: One Perspective on the Curare Experiments

Larry E. Roberts

8 Acquired Control of Peripheral Vascular Responses

Uwe Schuri

9 On the Nature of Alpha Feedback Training

Matrin T. Orne and Stuart K. Wilson

10 Passive Meditation: Subjective, Clinical, and Electrographic Comparison with Biofeedback

Charles F. Stroebel and Bernard C. Glueck

Volume 3

1 A Reason for Doubting the Existence of Consciousness

Georges Rey

2 Conscious Contents Provide the Nervous System with Coherent, Global Information

Bernard J. Baars

3 Event-Related Brain Potentials in the Study of Consciousness

Emanuel Donchin, Gregory McCarthy, Marta Kutas, and Walter Ritter

4 Anxiety and Fear: Central Processing and Peripheral Physiology

Peter J. Lang, Gregory A. Miller, and Daniel N. Levin

5 Meditation: In Search of a Unique Effect

Robert R. Pagano and Stephen Warrenburg

1   *Attention to Action*

Willed and Automatic Control of Behavior

DONALD A. NORMAN AND TIM SHALLICE

Much effort has been made to understand the role of attention in perception; much less effort has been placed on the role attention plays in the control of action. Our goal in this chapter is to account for the role of attention in action, both when performance is automatic and when it is under deliberate conscious control. We propose a theoretical framework structured around the notion of a set of active schemas, organized according to the particular action sequences of which they are a part, awaiting the appropriate set of conditions so that they can become selected to control action. The analysis is therefore centered around actions, primarily external actions, but the same principles apply to internal actions—actions that involve only the cognitive processing mechanisms. One major emphasis in the study of attentional processes is the distinction between *controlled* and *automatic* processing of perceptual inputs (e.g., Shiffrin & Schneider, 1977). Our work here can be seen as complementary to the distinction between controlled and automatic processes: we examine action rather than perception; we emphasize the situations in which deliberate, conscious control of activity is desired rather than those that are automatic.

In this chapter we will be particularly concerned with the different ways in which an action is experienced. To start, examine the term *automatic*: it has at least four different meanings. First, it refers to the way that certain tasks can be executed without awareness of their performance (as in walking along a short stretch of flat, safe ground). Sec-

---

DONALD A. NORMAN ● Institute for Cognitive Science, University of California, San Diego, La Jolla, California 92093. TIM SHALLICE ● Medical Research Council, Applied Psychology Unit, 15 Chaucer Road, Cambridge, CB2 2EF England. Research support to D. A. Norman was provided by the Personnel and Training Research Programs, Office of Naval Research under contract N00014-79-C-0323. The collaboration was made possible by a grant from the Sloan Foundation to the Program in Cognitive Science at UCSD. Support was also provided by grant MH-15828 from the National Institute of Mental Health to the Center for Human Information Processing.

ond, it refers to the way an action may be initiated without deliberate attention or awareness (as in beginning to drink from a glass when in conversation). Third, it is used in cases such as the orienting response, in which attention is drawn *automatically* to something, with no deliberate control over the direction of attention. And finally, within contemporary cognitive psychology, the term *automatic* is often defined operationally to refer to situations in which a task is performed without interfering with other tasks. In this situation, *automatic* is principally defined to mean that the task is performed without the need for limited processing resources (Shiffrin & Schneider, 1977), although variations on this theme are prevalent (e.g., Kahneman & Treisman, 1983; Posner, 1978).

It is possible to be aware of performing an action without paying active, directed attention to it. The most general situation of this type is in the initiation of routine actions. Phenomenally, this corresponds to the state that Ach (1905) describes as occurring after practice in reaction time tasks. Over the first few trials, he said, the response is preceded by awareness that the action should be made, but later there is no such awareness unless preparation has been inadequate. In such well-learned tasks the subject does experience the response as proceeding with "an awareness of determination," even if it is not immediately preceded by any experience of intention to act. Awareness of determination can, however, be absent. One example comes from the study of slips of action (Norman, 1981; Reason, 1979; Reason & Mycielska, 1982): one may find oneself doing a totally unexpected set of actions, much to one's own dismay.

In contrast to acts undertaken without active, directed attention being paid to them are those carried out under deliberate conscious control. This distinction corresponds closely to Williams James's (1890) distinction between "ideo-motor" and "willed" acts. To James, "wherever movement follows unhesitatingly and immediately the notion of it in the mind, we have ideo-motor action. We are then aware of nothing between the conception and the execution." He contrasted these with acts which require will, where "an additional conscious element in the shape of a fiat, mandate, or expressed consent" is involved.

Experientially, a number of different sorts of tasks appear to require deliberate attentional resources. These tasks fit within the following categories:

1. They involve planning or decision making
2. They involve components of troubleshooting
3. They are ill-learned or contain novel sequences of actions
4. They are judged to be dangerous or technically difficult

5. They require the overcoming of a strong habitual response or resisting temptation.

The general principle involved is that these are special situations in which the uncontrolled application of an action schema is not desired for fear that it might lead to error.

I. Theory

Our goal is to account for several phenomena in the control of action, including the several varieties of action performance that can be classified as automatic, the fact that action sequences that normally are performed automatically can be carried out under deliberate conscious control when desired, and the way that such deliberate control can be used both to suppress unwanted actions and to enhance wanted ones. In addition, we take note both of the fact that accurate, precise timing is often required for skilled performance and the fact that it is commonly believed that conscious attention to this aspect of performance can disrupt the action. Finally, in normal life numerous activities often overlap one another, so that preventing conflicts between incompatible actions is required.

These phenomena pose strong constraints upon a theory of action. The theory must account for the ability of some action sequences to run themselves off automatically, without conscious control or attentional resources, yet to be modulated by deliberate conscious control when necessary. Accordingly, we suggest that two complementary processes operate in the selection and control of action. One is sufficient for relatively simple or well learned acts. The other allows for conscious, attentional control to modulate the performance. The basic mechanism, *contention scheduling,* which acts through activation and inhibition of supporting and conflicting schemas, is proposed as the mechanism for avoiding conflicts in performance. Precise timing is handled by means of "triggers" that allow suitably activated schemas to be initiated at the precise time required. The mechanisms for contention scheduling and triggers follow those developed by McClelland and Rumelhart (1981) and Rumelhart and Norman (1982).

Start by considering a simple, self-contained, well-learned action sequence, perhaps the act of typing a word upon the receipt of a signal. This action sequence can be represented by a set of schemas, which when triggered by the arrival of the appropriate perceptual event result in the selection of the proper body, arm, hand, and finger movements. Whenever the action sequence is effected, its representation by means

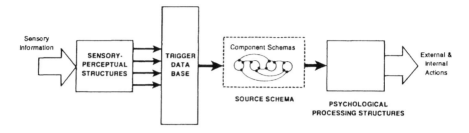

FIGURE 1. A horizontal thread. For well-learned, habitual tasks an autonomous, self-sufficient strand of processing structures and procedures can usually carry out the required activities without the need for conscious or attentional control. Selection of component schemas is determined, in part, by how well the "trigger conditions" of the schema match the contents of the "trigger data base." Such a sequence can often be characterized by a (relatively) linear flow of information among the various psychological processing structures and knowledge schemas involved: a horizontal thread.

of action schemas constitutes a "horizontal thread." The important point is that the processing structures which underlie a horizontal thread can in principle be well specified. The general nature of the processing structure for a simple action sequence is shown in Figure 1.

When numerous schemas are activated at the same time, some means must be provided for selection of a particular schema when it is required. At times, however, there will be conflicts among potentially relevant schemas, and so some sort of conflict resolution procedure must be provided. This is a common problem in any information-processing system in which at any one moment several potential candidates for operation might require access to the same resources or might result in incompatible actions. (McDermott & Forgy, 1978, discuss this issue for production systems and Bellman, 1979, discusses the problem with respect to animal behavior.)

The procedure we propose is constrained by the desire to transmit properties by means of the single variable of amount of activation, a concept consistent with current psychological theory. We propose that the individual schemas of the horizontal threads each have an activation value that is determined by a combination of factors, some that operate among schemas, some that result from special processes that operate upon the schemas.

A schema is selected once its activation level exceeds a threshold. Once selected, it continues to operate, unless actively switched off, until it has satisfied its goal or completed its operations, or until it is blocked when some resource or information is either lacking or is being utilized by some more highly activated schema. The activation value is important primarily in the selection process and when the selected schema must compete either for shared resources or in providing component schemas with initial activation values.

The scheduling is, therefore, quite simple and direct. No direct attentional control of selection is required (or allowed). Deliberate attention exerts itself indirectly through its effect on activation values. All the action, therefore, takes place in the determination of the activation values of the schemas.

A. Contention Scheduling

To permit simultaneous action of cooperative acts and prevent simultaneous action of conflicting ones is a difficult job, for often the details of how the particular actions are performed determine whether they conflict with one another. We propose that the scheduling of actions takes place through what we call *contention scheduling*, which resolves competition for selection, preventing competitive use of common or related structures, and negotiating cooperative, shared use of common structures or operations when that is possible. There are two basic principles of the contention scheduling mechanism: first, the sets of potential source schemas compete with one another in the determination of their activation value; second, the selection takes place on the basis of activation value alone—a schema is selected whenever its activation exceeds the threshold that can be specific to the schema and could become lower with use of the schema.

The competition is effected through lateral activation and inhibition among activated schemas. What degree of lateral inhibition exists between schemas on the model remains an open issue. Schemas which require the use of any common processing structures will clearly need to inhibit each other. Yet the degree of inhibition cannot be determined simply *a priori*. Thus, some aspects of the standard refractory period phenomena can be plausibly attributed to such inhibition between schemas; explanations based upon conflicts in response selection fit the data well (Kahneman, 1973). Unfortunately, it is not always clear how to determine when two tasks use common processing structures. The experimental literature on refractory periods reveals interference between tasks involving the two hands. This suggests that responses involving the two hands may use common processing structures. However, one cannot assume that the two hands inevitably involve a common processing structure, as refractory period effects can disappear if highly compatible tasks are used (Greenwald & Shulman, 1973). On the model, as tasks become better learned, the schemas controlling them could become more specialized in their use of processing structures, reducing potential structural interference and minimizing the need for mutual inhibition among schemas.

B. Determination of Activation Values

We divide activational influences upon a schema into four types: influences from contention scheduling, from the satisfaction of trigger conditions, from the selection of other schemas, and from "vertical thread" influences. Trigger conditions specify under what conditions a schema should be initiated, thus allowing for precise environmental control of performance. How well existing conditions match the trigger specifications determines the amount of activation contributed by this factor.

Selection of one schema can lead to the activation of others. Any given action sequence that has been well learned is represented by an organized set of schemas, with one—the source schema—serving as the highest-order control. The term *source* is chosen to indicate that the other component schemas of an action sequence can be activated through the source. We assume that the initial activation values of component schemas are determined by means of their source schema. For example, when the source schema for a task such as driving an automobile has been selected, all its component schemas become activated, including schemas for such acts as steering, stopping, accelerating, slowing, overtaking, and turning. Each of these component schemas in turn acts as a source schema, activating its own component schemas (braking, changing gear, signalling, and so on).

C. The Supervisory Attentional System

The horizontal thread specifies the organization structure for the desired action sequence. However, a schema may not be available that can achieve control of the desired behavior, especially when the task is novel or complex. In these cases, some additional control structure is required. We propose that an additional system, the Supervisory Attentional System (SAS), provides one source of control upon the selection of schemas, but it operates entirely through the application of extra activation and inhibition to schemas in order to bias their selection by the contention-scheduling mechanisms. (A planning mechanism which performs an analogous function in problem-solving programs has been simulated by various researchers; see, for example, Boden, 1977). The

Attention to Action

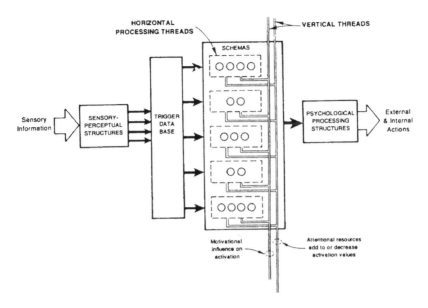

FIGURE 2. The overall system: Vertical and horizontal threads. When attention to particular tasks is required, vertical thread activation comes into play. Attention operates upon schemas only through manipulation of activation values, increasing the values for desired schemas, decreasing (inhibiting) the values for undesired ones. Motivational variables are assumed to play a similar role in the control of activation, but working over longer time periods. To emphasize that several tasks are usually active, with the individual components of each task either being simultaneous or overlapping in time, this figure shows five different horizontal threads. Some means of selecting the individual schemas at appropriate times while providing some form of conflict resolution becomes necessary. The interactions among the various horizontal threads needed for this purpose are indicated by the lines that interconnect schemas from different threads.

overall system is shown in Figure 2. Note that the operation of the SAS provides only an indirect means of control of action. *Attention*, which we will associate with outputs from SAS, controls only activation and inhibition values, not selection itself. Moreover, it is control overlaid on the horizontal thread organization. When attentional activation of a schema ceases, the activational value will decay back to the value that other types of activating input would produce.

In addition, we assume that motivational factors supplement the activational influences of the SAS. We take motivation to be a relatively slow-acting system, working primarily to bias the operation of the horizontal thread structures toward the long-term goals of the organism by activating source schemas (and through their selection component schemas).

II. Evidence

That horizontal thread control of action may be viewed within a schema framework is too well known to need reviewing here (see, e.g., Pew, 1974, Schmidt, 1975). There are four major aspects of the model that require assessment:

1. Actions under deliberate conscious control involve a specific mechanism in addition to those used in automatic actions.
2. Attentional processes can modulate the selection process only by adding activation or inhibition. Attention to action is neither sufficient nor necessary to cause the selection of an action sequence.
3. Attentional processes are primarily relevant to the initiation of actions, not for their execution.
4. Selection between competing action sequences takes place through the mechanism of contention scheduling.

Now let us examine the evidence for these aspects of the model.

A. *Evidence for a Distinct Supervisory Attentional System: Neuropsychological Findings*

A major feature of our model is that for well-learned action sequences two levels of control are possible: deliberate conscious control and automatic contention scheduling of the horizontal threads. Possibly the strongest evidence for the existence of both levels comes from neuropsychology. The functions we assume for the supervisory attentional control—those that require "deliberate attention"—correspond closely with those ascribed by Luria (1966) to prefrontal regions of the brain, thought by Luria to be required for the programming, regulation, and verification of activity. In this view, if the Supervisory Attentional System were damaged the resulting behavior should be similar to that exhibited by patients with prefrontal lesions.

On the model, well-learned cognitive skills and cognitive procedures do not require the higher-level control system. Higher-level control becomes necessary only if error correction and planning have to be performed, if the situation is novel, or temptation must be overcome. It is well known in clinical neuropsychology that lesions confined to prefrontal structures leave the execution of basic skills such as the use of objects, speaking, and writing unaffected (see Walsh, 1978, for review). "Well able to work along old routine lines" is a classical char-

ATTENTION TO ACTION 9

acterization of such patients (Goldstein, quoted by Rylander, 1939). Quantitatively it has, for instance, been shown by McFie (1960) that performance of WAIS subtests is relatively unaffected by lesions to the frontal lobes. The model does predict impairments in the performance of tasks that require error correction or planning, or are in some basic way novel—just the constellation of deficits that are observed clinically in the so-called frontal syndrome (see Walsh, 1978).

Evidence for the contrast in performance in the two types of situations can be obtained from case studies of patients with frontal lobe lesions. A classic study was that carried out by Lhermitte, Derouesne, and Signoret (1972). Their two principal patients could perform certain Verbal and Performance WAIS subtests at normal level (Derouesne, personal communication). These were tasks which require the use of well-learned skills in routine fashion. Thus digit span, which uses maintenance rehearsal schemas, was well performed. When much novel programming of the external and internal action sequence was required, performance was extremely poor. Examples were WAIS Block Design or the reproduction of a complex figure—the Figure of Rey. However, performance could be greatly improved by providing a program for the patient; in the case of the Figure of Rey, this involved breaking down the total design into a series of hierarchically organized subcomponents.

Group studies of neurological patients also provide support. It is well established that patients with frontal lobe lesions have difficulties with error correction. The Wisconsin card-sorting test involves multidimensional stimuli and requires the patient to switch from sorting on one dimension to sorting according to another. In this task, frontal patients show a strong tendency to perseverate in sorting on the previously correct dimension, even when they are told they are wrong (Milner, 1964; Nelson, 1976). Planning, too, has been shown to present difficulties for these patients. The simplest example of such a defect is Gadzhiev's finding (see Luria, 1966) that frontal patients presented with a problem tend to miss out the initial assessment of the situation. Shallice and McCarthy (see Shallice, 1982) showed that patients with left frontal lesions are significantly more impaired than those with lesions in other sites in look-ahead puzzles related to the Tower-of-Hanoi; comparison of performance on this task with that on other tasks suggested that it was the planning component of the task that was affected. Novel learning tasks have also been shown to produce specific difficulties for frontal lobe patients. Petrides and Milner (see Milner, 1982) found that both patients with left frontal and those with right frontal lesions were significantly impaired in learning new arbitrary pairings presented one at a time in a random sequence.

Prediction about the effect of an impairment to the Supervisory

Attentional System can be approached in another way. On the model, the failure of this single mechanism can give rise to the apparent contradiction between increased perseveration and increased distractability, depending on the pattern of trigger–schema relations. What would be expected if behavior is left under the control of horizontal thread structures plus contention scheduling? If one schema is more strongly activated than the others, it will be difficult to prevent it from controlling behavior. By contrast, when several schemas have similar activation values, one should obtain another clinical characteristic of frontal patients: an instability of attention and heightened distractability (see Rylander, 1939; Walsh, 1978). Both types of results are also observed in animals with prefrontal lesions (see Fuster, 1980, for review).

If the properties of the Supervisory Attentional System seem to correspond fairly well with neuropsychological evidence, does the same apply to the properties of contention scheduling? One possible relation is with mechanisms in the corpus striatum of the basal ganglia, often thought to be involved in the selection of actions (see Denny-Brown & Yanagisawa, 1976; Marsden, 1982). The basal ganglia are innervated by one of the major dopamine projections, and dopamine release is in turn facilitated by amphetamine. Robbins and Sahakian (1983) have provided an explanation of the effects of increased doses of amphetamine based on the work of Lyon and Robbins (1975), in terms closely related to ours. The account goes like this: Increased amphetamine results in an increase in the speed with which response sequences are carried out and a decrease in the interval between them. At higher levels "competition for expression via the motor or executive system begins to occur between different sequences with the result that some sequences are aborted and their terminal elements are lost. Eventually, the performance of a complete sequence is drastically attenuated and the stereotype occurs." Robbins and Sahakian argue that increased dopamine release potentiates the activation level of schemas and leads to an increasing number of schemas being activated above threshold. In our terms, if the potentiation becomes too great, the lateral inhibitory control of contention scheduling is broken. Many schemas are selected at the same time, producing a jamming of almost all objects of behavior. Parkinsonism appears to provide a complementary condition.

B. *Attentional Processes Only Modulate Schema Selection*

The motivation for this aspect of the model is that attentional control is probably too slow and unwieldy to provide the high precision of accuracy and timing needed to perform skilled acts. Deliberate conscious control is generally agreed to involve serial processing steps, each step taking on the order of 100 msec or more. Such control would simply be too slow to account for skilled human behavior that requires action sequences to be initiated just when environmental or internal conditions call for them; in some situations they must be accurate to the nearest 20 msec. This is consistent with the general view that deliberate control of skilled performance leads to deterioration of performance. Accordingly, in the model we allow attentional processes only to bias or modulate the operation and selection of schemas. Precise timing is controlled by the fit of stimulus input to that required by the set of trigger conditions for a schema.

Other factors are also involved. Thus, despite one's desire to attend to one set of signals, if the trigger conditions of another are sufficiently well met, the other may be selected in contention scheduling despite the attention directed toward the one: triggering activation can be more powerful than activation from the Supervisory Attentional Mechanisms. A classic example of this difficulty is the Stroop phenomenon. Another set of relevant findings comes from the classical literature on selective attention in which an attempt is made to keep the subject concentrating upon a primary task while other signals are presented. Certain classes of words presented upon a secondary channel can intrude upon or bias primary task performance, such as a word that fits within the context of the primary channel, or that has been conditioned to electric shock, or that has high emotional value. Performance of the other task is impaired when the interrupt occurs (e.g., Treisman, 1960, or in the refractory period paradigm, Helson & Steger, 1962). In terms of our model, these "intrusions" result from data-driven entry of action schemas into the contention-scheduling mechanism, and their selection there is due to the strongly activating properties of such triggers.

Further evidence that attention serves a biasing or modulating role comes from a study by McLean and Shulman (1978) that examined the role of attention on the speed of performance in a letter-matching task. Once a subject's attention had been directed toward a particular expectation, performance remained biased toward that expectation even after the subjects had been told that the expectation was no longer valid. The bias decayed slowly, lasting for around one second, thereby acting more like the decay of activation from a memory structure than of an attentional selection that could be quickly added or taken away. Although the emphasis in this experiment was on perception rather than action, their conclusion that attention acts by means of an activation level on memory units (schemas, in our vocabulary) is support for this aspect of the model.

Possibly the strongest evidence that conscious attentional control is not necessary for the initiation or execution of action sequences comes from the study of slips of action (Norman, 1981; Reason & Mycielska, 1982). In the class of errors known as "capture errors," the person appears to perform the action without either conscious control or knowledge. Capture errors are easily illustrated by an example: one of Reason's subjects described how, when passing through his back porch on the way to get his car out, he stopped to put on his Wellington boots and gardening jacket as if to work in the garden.

Consider what would happen on the model if a routine task is being carried out that does not require continuous monitoring and activation from the Supervisory Attentional System. Its component schemas can be selected using contention scheduling alone, so the Supervisory Attentional System could be directed toward activating some other noncompeting schema (i.e., "thinking about something else"), and the component schemas in the routine action would still be satisfactorily selected by contention scheduling alone. Occasionally, though, a schema that controls an incorrect action could become more strongly activated in contention scheduling than the correct schema and capture the effector systems. The supervisory system, being directed elsewhere, would not immediately monitor this, and a capture error would result.

Findings from the diary study of Reason (1983) provide support for an interpretation of this type of error in terms of the model. The data show that people typically rate themselves as being "preoccupied" and "distracted" in the situations wherein lapses occur. This would correspond in our model to the case in which no activation is being received for the "appropriate" schema from the supervisory system: instead, the supervisory system is activating a different, noncompeting schema. In Reason's data, both captured and capturing actions are rated as occurring "very often" and being "automatic." Moreover, the captured and capturing actions were rated as having very similar stimulus characteristics. These characteristics are all consistent with the model: frequently performed action sequences are apt to have developed sufficient horizontal thread structure that they could be carried out by contention scheduling alone—"automatically." The similarity of the captured and capturing actions is consistent with the suggestion that some data-driven activation of the capturing schema might take place and that trigger conditions appropriate for one sequence are likely to be appropriate for the other as well. All these factors maximize the chance of an incorrect schema's being more activated in contention scheduling than the correct one, thus leading to a capture error.

C. *Attentional Resources Are Primarily Relevant for Action Selection*

One theme of the model is that attentional resources are relevant only at the specific points in an action where schema selection is required. Thus, control of a hand movement in response to a signal will usually require attentional resources twice: once to initiate the schemas that start the motion, once to initiate the schemas that control termination of the motion (see Keele, 1973). This fits with the results of probe studies during movement where responses to probes at the start or end of the movement can be more delayed than those during execution (Posner & Keele, 1969). (The interpretation of probe studies is not straightforward—see McLeod, 1980—but U-shaped functions of the type obtained by Posner and Keele seem unlikely to arise artifactually.) When a simple movement is made to an external stop, the response time to a probe during the movement appears to be no greater than if no movement is being made (Posner & Keele, 1969; Ells, 1973). This suggests that when hand motion can be stopped by an external device the movement can be stopped without initiating an action sequence and without attentional control.

D. *Competition between Tasks*

On the model, the degree to which two tasks will interfere with each other depends upon a number of factors. These include structural factors critical for the contention scheduling mechanism, the balance of activation and inhibition in that mechanism, and the degree of learning which is relevant mainly for the degree of involvement required of the Supervisory Attentional System.

For most task combinations, precise prediction of the degree of interference depends on too many unknown parameters (see Shallice, McLeod, & Lewis, 1985). One obvious prediction is that "parallel" dual task performance should be most easily possible when one or both of the tasks can be performed without attentional control. This fits the experimental literature on monitoring (see Duncan, 1980, for review). When two response streams have to be initiated, the model makes the standard prediction that parallel performance is more likely if subjects are skilled and well practiced (see Allport, Antonis, & Reynolds, 1972; McLeod, 1977; Spelke, Hirst, & Neisser, 1976). Note that even in these situations performance normally deteriorates somewhat when two tasks are combined, even though there appear to be no obvious grounds for structural or attentional interference. We feel this indicates that even when the individual tasks are well learned at times there will be a need for schemas that require vertical thread activation for rapid selection. Thus, as Allport (1980) pointed out, in experiments involving piano playing conducted by Allport, Antonis, and Reynolds (1972), the one subject who showed no interference "was also the most competent of our pianists." The other subjects all found some technical challenge in the music such that "moments of emergency occurred" when recovery required some relatively unpracticed applications of keyboard technique and therefore, on our model, attentional resources.

E. Will and Deliberate Conscious Control

A major goal of our approach has been to produce an explanation for the different types of experience one can have of an action. Consider the types of information the Supervisory Attentional System would require in order to carry out its complex functions. Representations of the past and present states of the environment, of goals and intentions, and of the repertoire of higher-level schemas it could activate would all have to be available. Yet more would be necessary. The system would need to know aspects of the operation of a selected schema or, to be more precise, of those selected schemas which it could potentially activate (source schemas). It would need to know not only which source schemas had been selected but also the action sequences they produced and probably the eliciting triggers as well. Without such information, error correction would be a hopeless task, but it is a key function of the supervisory system.

How an action is experienced is dependent upon what information about it is accessed by the Supervisory Attentional System and upon whether the supervisory system activates source schemas itself and, if so, how strongly. This, therefore, allows a variety of states of awareness of actions to exist.

Consider the different meanings of *automatic* discussed earlier. The first two meanings which refer to automaticity in the initiation and carrying out of an action correspond to the selection and operation, respectively, of a schema without the supervisory system's assessing information relevant to it. In contrast are those occasions when a trigger not only activates a schema strongly and directly but also produces an interrupt in the supervisory system itself. This corresponds to the third, very different, meaning of *automatic*, wherein what is automatic is the attention-demanding characteristics of the stimulus. When the supervisory system does access some aspect of the triggering or selection of schema, or where it monitors the action sequence itself while at the same time providing no attentional activation to assist in schema selection, we have a correspondence for James' ideomotor acts. Schema selection is elicited solely by triggers, but information about the process is accessed at the higher level.

What happens when the supervisory system does produce attentional activation to modulate schema selection? We propose that *will* be this direction of action by deliberate conscious control. This definition is consistent both with the popular meaning of the term and with the discussions of will in the earlier psychological literature (e.g., James, 1890; Pillsbury, 1908). Thus, strongly resisting a habitual or tempting action or strongly forcing performance of an action that one is loathe to perform seem to be prototypical examples of the application of will. The former would appear to result from deliberate attentional inhibition of an action schema, the latter from deliberate activation.

In our view, will varies along a quantitative dimension corresponding to the amount of activation or inhibition required from the supervisory attentional mechanisms. The assumption that this activation value lies on a continuum explains why the distinction between willed and ideomotor actions seems quite clear in considering extreme actions but becomes blurred in considering those that require very little attentional effort. Thus, introspection fails in determining whether will is involved in the voluntary lifting of the arm. But there is no need to make a distinction if this act is simply identified as being near the zero point of the quantitative scale of attentional activation.

The idea that will corresponds to the output of the Supervisory Attentional System has certain other useful consequences. Consider the errors that occur with brief lapses of attention, when there is a failure to sustain will adequately. One type of error results following a decision not to do a step within a habitual sequence of actions. To eliminate the step requires deliberate (willful) inhibition of the relevant schema. If there is a momentary lapse of attention to the deliberate inhibition, the step may get done anyway. Closely related is the error that occurred to one of us, who decided not to take another bite of a delicious but extremely rich dessert; with only a brief lapse of attention, the cake got eaten.

Certain aspects of will require elaboration. In some circumstances an action may seem to require no will at all, yet at other times it will require extreme demands. Thus, getting out of bed in the morning is at times an automatic act and at other times requires great exertion of will. One explanation for this phenomenon is that activation of an action schema by the attentional mechanisms necessarily involves knowledge of consequences. When these are negative, they lead to inhibition of the source schemas which then must be overcome. In some cases, the self-inhibition can be so intense as to prevent or at least make very difficult the intended act. Thus, inflicting deliberate injury to oneself (as in pricking one's own finger in order to draw blood) is a difficult act for many people.

The elicitation of strong activation from the supervisory attentional mechanism is not necessarily unpleasant. Indeed, many sports and games seem to be attractive because they do necessitate such strong activation. In this case *concentration* is perhaps the more appropriate experiential equivalent rather than *will*. In addition, will is not just a matter of attention to actions. As Roy D'Andrade (personal communication) has pointed out, a willed act demands not only strong attentional activation; it also depends on the existence of a "mandated decision," independent of one's attending—a conscious knowledge that the particular end is to be attained. This mandate, in our view, would be required before the supervisory attentional mechanisms will produce their desired activation output. However, the critical point for the present argument is that the phenomenal distinction between willed and ideomotor acts flows from the separation of the supervisory attentional mechanisms from the systems they oversee. The phenomenology of attention can be understood through a theory of mechanism.

ACKNOWLEDGMENTS

We thank members of the Skills group of the Cognitive Science Laboratory at UCSD, especially David Rumelhart, Geoffrey Hinton, Wynne Lee, Jonathan Grudin, and Bernie Baars. We appreciate thoughtful reviews and comments by Roy D'Andrade, Steve Keele, John Long, George Mandler, and Peter McLeod.

REFERENCES

ACH, N. (1905). *Uber die Willenstätigkeit und das Denken*. Gottingen: Vardenhoek.
ALLPORT, D. A. (1980). Attention and performance. In G. L. Claxton (Ed.), *New directions in cognitive psychology*. London: Routledge.
ALLPORT, D. A., ANTONIS, B., & REYNOLDS, P. (1972). On the division of attention: A disproof of the single channel hypothesis. *Quarterly Journal of Experimental Psychology, 24,* 225–235.
BELLMAN, K. (1979). *The conflict behavior of the lizard,* Sceloporus Occidentalis, *and its implication for the organization of motor behavior*. Unpublished doctoral dissertation. University of California, San Diego.
BODEN, M. (1977). *Artificial intelligence and natural man*. New York: Basic Books.

ATTENTION TO ACTION 17

DENNY-BROWN, D., & YANAGISAWA, N. (1976). The role of the basal ganglia in the initiation of movement. In M. D. YAHR (Ed.), *The basal ganglia*. New York: Raven Press.

DUNCAN, J. (1980). The locus of interference in perception of simultaneous stimuli. *Psychological Review, 87*, 272–300.

ELLS, J. G. (1973). Analysis of temporal and attentional aspects of movement control. *Journal of Experimental Psychology, 99*, 10–21.

FUSTER, J. M. (1980). *The prefrontal cortex*: New York: Raven Press.

GREENWALD, A. G., & SHULMAN, A. G. (1973). On doing two things at once. II. Elimination of the psychological refractory period. *Journal of Experimental Psychology, 101*, 70–76.

HELSON, H., & STEGER, J. A. (1962). On the inhibitory effect of a second stimulus following the primary stimulus to react. *Journal of Experimental Psychology, 64*, 201–205.

JAMES, W. (1890). *The principles of psychology*. New York: Holt.

KAHNEMAN, D. (1973). *Attention and effort*. Englewood Cliffs, NJ: Prentice-Hall.

KAHNEMAN, D., & TREISMAN, A. M. (1983). Changing views of attention and automaticity. In R. PARASURAMAN, R. DAVIES, & J. BEATTY (Eds.), *Varieties of attention*. New York: Academic Press.

KEELE, S. W. (1973). *Attention and human performance*. Pacific Palisades, CA: Goodyear.

LHERMITTE, F., DEROUESNE, J., & SIGNORET, J-L. (1972). Analyse neuropsychologique du syndrome frontale. *Revue Neuropsychologique, 127*, 415–440.

LURIA, A. R. (1966). *Higher cortical functions in man*. London: Tavistock.

LYON, M., & ROBBINS, T. (1975). The action of central nervous system drugs: A general theory concerning amphetamine effects. In W. B. ESSMANN & L. VALZELLI (Eds.), *Current developments in psychopharmacology, Vol. 2*. New York: Spectrum.

MARSDEN, C. D. (1982). The mysterious motor function of the basal ganglia. *Neurology, 32*, 514–539.

McCLELLAND, J. L., & RUMELHART, D. E. (1981). An interactive activation model of context effects in letter perception: Part 1. An account of basic findings. *Psychological Review, 88*, 375–407.

McDERMOTT, J., & FORGY, C. (1978). Production system conflict resolution strategies. In D. A. WATERMAN & F. HAYES-ROTH (Eds.), *Pattern-directed inference systems*. New York: Academic Press.

McFIE, J. (1960). Psychological testing in clinical neurology. *Journal of Nervous and Mental Diseases, 131*, 383–393.

McLEAN, J. P., & SHULMAN, G. L. (1978). On the construction and maintenance of expectancies. *Quarterly Journal of Experimental Psychology, 30*, 441–454.

McLEOD, P. D. (1977). A dual task response modality effect: Support for multiprocessor models of attention. *Quarterly Journal of Experimental Psychology, 29*, 651–658.

McLEOD, P. D. (1980). What can probe RT tell us about the attentional demands of movement? In G. E. STELMACH & J. REQUIN (Eds.), *Tutorials in motor behavior*. Amsterdam: North-Holland.

MILNER, B. (1964). Some effects of frontal lobectomy in man. In J. M. WARREN & K. AKERT (Eds.), *The frontal granular cortex and behavior*. New York: McGraw-Hill.

MILNER, B. (1982). Some cognitive effects of frontal-lobe lesions in man. *Philosophical Transactions of the Royal Society of London, Series B., 298*, 211–226.

NELSON, H. (1976). A modified card sorting test sensitive to frontal lobe defects. *Cortex, 12*, 313–324.

NORMAN, D. A. (1981). Categorization of action slips. *Psychological Review, 88*, 1–15.

PEW, R. W. (1974). Human perceptual motor performance. In B. H. KANTOWITZ (Ed.), *Human information processing: Tutorials in performance and cognition*. Hillsdale, NJ: Erlbaum.

PILLSBURY, W. B. (1908). *Attention*. London: Swan Sonnenschein.

POSNER, M. I., & KEELE, S. W. (1969). Attention demands of movement. In *Proceedings of the 16th International Congress of Applied Psychology*. Amsterdam: Swets and Zeitlinger.

POSNER, M. I. (1978). *Chronometric explorations of mind*. Hillsdale, NJ: Erlbaum.

REASON, J. T. (1979). Actions not as planned. In G. UNDERWOOD & R. STEVENS (Eds.), *Aspects of consciousness*. London: Academic Press.

REASON, J. T. (1983). Lapses of attention. In R. PARASURAMAN, R. DAVIES, & J. BEATTY (Eds.), *Varieties of Attention*. New York: Academic Press.

REASON, J. T., & MYCIELSKA, K. (1982). *Absentminded? The psychology of mental lapses and everyday errors*. Englewood Cliffs, NJ: Prentice-Hall.

ROBBINS, T. W., & SAHAKIAN, B. (1983). Behavioral effects of psychomotor drugs: Clinical and neuropsychological implications. In I. CREESE (Ed.) *Stimulants: Neurochemical, behavioral and clinical perspectives*. New York: Raven Press.

RUMELHART, D. E., & NORMAN, D. A. (1982). Simulating a skilled typist: A study of skilled cognitive-motor performance. *Cognitive Science, 6*, 1–36.

RYLANDER, G. (1939). Personality changes after operations on the frontal lobes. *Acta Psychiatrica Neurologica Scandinavica, Supplement no. 30*.

SCHMIDT, R. A. (1975). A schema theory of discrete motor skill learning. *Psychological Review, 82*, 225–260.

SHALLICE, T. (1982). Specific impairments of planning. *Philosophical Transactions of the Royal Society of London, Series B, 298*, 199–209.

SHALLICE, T., MCLEOD, P. D., & LEWIS, K. (1985). Isolating cognitive modules with the dual task paradigm: Are speech perception and production separate processes? *Quarterly Journal of Experimental Psychology* (in press).

SHIFFRIN, R. M., & SCHNEIDER, W. (1977). Controlled and automatic human information processing: II. Perceptual learning, automatic attending, and a general theory. *Psychological Review, 84*, 127–190.

SPELKE, E., HIRST, W., & NEISSER, U. (1976). Skills of divided attention. *Cognition, 4*, 205–230.

TREISMAN,. A. M. (1960). Contextual cues in selective listening. *Quarterly Journal of Experimental Psychology, 12*, 242–248.

WALSH, K. W. (1978). *Neuropsychology: A clinical approach*. Edinburgh: Churchill Livingstone.

2 *The Motor Theory of Voluntary Thinking*

BARRY H. COHEN

The theory proposed in this chapter—the motor theory of voluntary thinking (MTVT)—is not exactly new; its basic elements can be found in the motor theories of Bain (1888), Maudsley (1889), Ribot (1889), Pillsbury (1908), and Washburn (1916) to name just a few. Many of the ideas expressed below were commonplace at the beginning of this century, and the interested reader is encouraged to explore the original sources referenced within this chapter, which frequently contain detailed, anecdotal descriptions and lengthy logical arguments in support of these ideas. To maintain the clarity of my exposition, I will quote only a few examples from the early literature; it is not my intention to present a history of the theoretical formulations concerning the relation between the motor system and attention or thought (a brief history can be found in Smith, 1969). Rather, my purpose in writing the present chapter is to present some of these old ideas in the context of a cohesive theory that is as clear, plausible, and useful as possible.

It is my opinion that the current lack of popularity of motor theories derives from the fact that these theories often contained unnecessarily restrictive or implausible provisions and were often tied to physiological notions based on the limited knowledge of their times. However, I feel that to reject these theories in their entirety is to disregard a host of potentially useful ideas, which appeal to one's common sense and may stand in close agreement with one's own introspections. The MTVT, as expressed herein, is far from complete and should certainly be considered as work in progress. Nonetheless, I feel it is useful to present the theory at this time, especially considering the current increased interest in facial muscle action (Ekman, Friesen, & Ellsworth, 1972; Fridlund & Izard, 1984), in order to encourage the notion that overt or covert

---

BARRY H. COHEN ● Department of Psychology New York University, The development of this paper and the original research were supported, in part, by NIMH pre-doctoral fellowship F31-MH07303-02, and post-doctoral fellowship F32-MH08889-01.

20   BARRY H. COHEN

changes in skeletal muscle activity may be more than just indicators of
mental processes—these motoric activities may play an important me-
diational role.

I. PREVIOUS MOTOR THEORIES

Rather than discuss the details of the various motor theories proposed by particular psychologists, I will separate these theories into
broad categories and then discuss issues common to the theories within
each category.

A. The Motor Theory of Consciousness

In its simplest form, the motor theory of consciousness states that
no perception, no image, no thought—in fact, no mental experience—
is possible without the occurrence of some unique pattern of activation
in the motor system; it is the particular motor activity pattern evoked
directly by some external stimulus or associative process that determines
which mental experience will occur.

The arguments in favor of the motor theory of consciousness can
be quite convincing when applied to aspects of perception in which
motor activity plays a critical role, such as discerning the shape of an
object by scanning its boundaries visually and thus making appropriate
eye movements (Sperry, 1952; Weimer, 1977). Accounting for mental
imagery then becomes a simple matter: reproducing the pattern of
motor activity that has been associated with a particular perception, even
if covertly or only centrally, can, in the absence of the appropriate external object, evoke a pattern of cerebral activity similar to the cerebral
activity accompanying the perception and thus produce a "faint" form
of perception perceived as an image (in this case, a visual image). However, when one considers perceptual distinctions in which motor activity
plays no obvious role, the motor theory of consciousness is far less convincing. For example, the perceptual quality that results from staring at
a red wall is quite different from that which results from staring at a
green wall, yet it is not obvious how the patterns of motor activity associated with each perception would consistently differ. Of course, if
the motor theory of consciousness cannot explain the perceptual differences among colors, it also cannot explain the mental imagery of
colors. In a relatively recent paper arguing in favor of a motor theory
of consciousness, Weimer (1977) deals with the problem of sensory qual-
ities in such a general manner as to offer no concrete explanation at all.

It is undoubtedly such weaknesses that explain the current unpopularity of the motor theory of consciousness. The motor theory of thinking is less encompassing than the motor theory of consciousness but may contain similar weaknesses, as will be discussed in the following section.

At this point it is appropriate to discuss an important issue that affects all types of motor theories: the necessity of peripheral motor feedback, that is, afferent feedback from the contraction of muscles. Theories that require peripheral feedback are susceptible to disconfirmation from studies in which the skeletal musculature of a human volunteer was paralyzed with curare (e.g., Leuba, Birch, & Appleton, 1968; Smith, Brown, Toman, & Goodman, 1947). In the Leuba *et al.* study, the subject was able to solve complex mental problems just as well when paralyzed as when not. Although McGuigan (1978) has amply criticized the curare studies (e.g., most curare studies have not used electrical recordings to establish that total paralysis had occurred), these studies have cast a great deal of suspicion on motor theories in general.

Actually, most proponents of motor theories have suggested that although peripheral feedback may be necessary in the initial stages of internalizing thought, such feedback becomes unnecessary when repeated associations result in "short-circuit" connections within the central nervous system. Dunlap (1927) suggested that this short-circuiting might occur "between cerebellum and cerebrum, with no muscular activity . . . involved" (p. 265). Although it is not likely that the cerebellum plays an indispensable role in cognition, the type of speculation offered by Dunlap does not seem entirely implausible in the light of more recent research on central efferent monitoring and corollary discharge (Evarts, 1971). Since it is unlikely that peripheral feedback is necessary for many types of overt motor acts, it seems even less likely that peripheral feedback would be necessary for thinking. A good example of the extreme central position is contained in the motor theory of consciousness proposed by Sperry (1952): "The core of the perceptual process is not itself a motor pattern. It is more pre-motor or better pre-premotor in nature owing to the hierarchical plan of neural organization" (p. 309).

Motor theories that are formulated exclusively in terms of central motor feedback are difficult to disprove experimentally and are therefore sometimes viewed with suspicion. But although central motor theories may not be easily disconfirmed, they can represent useful approaches to organizing our knowledge of cognitive processes and can suggest valuable experiments. The MTVT, described in subsequent sections, adopts this viewpoint in assuming that only central motor feedback is necessary when motor feedback is necessary at all, and that actual muscle contraction is never necessary for the motor system to influence mental experience.

B. The Motor Theory of Thinking

The motor theory of thinking, in its simplest conception, is just a subset of the motor theory of consciousness. The motor theory of thinking does not propose that motor activity is required for *all* mental experiences, but rather that motor activity is required for mental experience in the absence of external sensation—that is, for images and thoughts. From a commonsense point of view, the motor theory of thinking seems much more plausible than the motor theory of consciousness. Most perceptions do not seem to require motor activity necessarily, and certainly not specific and unique patterns of motor activity. On the other hand, the occurrence of mental images can seem somewhat mysterious—they are like perceptions in some respects, yet they have no obvious cause. The motor theory of thinking provides a reasonable explanation for the generation of mental images.

According to Washburn (1916), kinesthetic images are simply faint kinesthetic sensations: kinesthetic "images" are generated through slight, covert contraction of the appropriate muscles—the afferent feedback from these slight contractions is perceived as an image rather than a perception. It is quite reasonable to assume that one could make such slight contractions without being at all aware of making them and then regard the resulting faint kinesthetic sensation as a purely mental experience. That subjects do, indeed, produce slight muscle contractions when imagining muscular acts was confirmed by the early work of Jacobson (1932).

Jacobson pioneered the use of electromyography (EMG; the amplification and display of the tiny changes in electrical voltage associated with muscle contraction) to demonstrate that when a subject imagined bending one arm, slight contractions occurred in the biceps of that arm, but not the other arm. Moreover, the imaging of rhythmic activities, such as pumping a tire, were associated with a corresponding rhythm of slight muscle contraction and relaxation. Shaw (1938) partially replicated these results by exploring a wide range of motoric activities.

Washburn's explanation of kinesthetic imagery cannot, of course, be applied to other forms of imagery. Kinesthesia is the only modality in which sensations can be produced directly by voluntary action. Images in other modalities may be explained, however, through their association with kinesthetic sensations. The case of speech imagery (auditory images of one's own voice) or "inner speech" is by far the simplest to explain. Associations between one's own voice and kinesthetic sensations from one's speech musculature are very specific, consistent, and frequently repeated. It is a reasonable assumption that eventually the

THE MOTOR THEORY OF VOLUNTARY THINKING
23

kinesthetic sensations produced by slight contractions of the speech musculature can evoke auditory images of one's own voice, even when one is not aware of any kinesthetic sensations or images. As in the case of kinesthetic imagery, there is electromyographic evidence that covert muscle contractions occur in the appropriate area (i.e., the speech musculature) when subjects are asked to imagine speaking; in fact, the evidence is quite extensive (see McGuigan, 1978, for a comprehensive review). The specificity of this covert speech activity was convincingly demonstrated in an experiment by McGuigan and Winstead (1974), in which the EMG was recorded from both the tongue and the lips while subjects read and mentally rehearsed words containing either labial (requiring the lips for pronounciation) or lingual (requiring the tongue for pronounciation) phonemes. As expected, the lip EMG was significantly higher than the tongue EMG when subjects mentally processed the labial words, whereas the reverse was true for lingual words.

The whole notion that kinesthetic feedback can, after frequent association, evoke a particular auditory image is rendered plausible by an experiment conducted by Hefferline and Perera (1963). In this experiment:

> When the subject occasionally emitted an invisibly small thumb twitch (detected electromyographically), he received a tone as a signal to press a key. After several conditioning sessions, the tone was progressively diminished to zero. The subject nevertheless continued to press the key whenever he emitted a thumb twitch, and he reported that he still heard the tone. (p. 835)

It is visual imagery that is the most difficult to explain in terms of motor activity or kinesthetic sensations, especially the imagery of different colors. Only in the case of visual objects that are extremely elongated in one direction or are moving does the possibility of a consistent association between eye movements and visual perception become realistic. In fact, in an early study by Jacobson (1930), eye movements (as indicated by the electrooculogram, or EOG) in the appropriate direction were found to accompany the visual imagination of elongated objects, such as the Eiffel Tower. This finding was confirmed by Totten (1935), who photographed a spot of light reflected off the cornea of her subjects. In the great majority of cases in which subjects formed a visual image of elongated objects, eye movements in the appropriate direction were clearly observable. Instances in which eye movements were not observed generally involved visual images which were "distant" or small. More recent studies have found an association between eye movements and visual images involving motion; these studies are discussed in a later section.

Hebb's (1968) theoretical notions would predict eye movements also in the case of forming a visual image of an object with well-defined boundaries. Hebb wrote:

> It is easy to form a clear image of a triangle or a circle when eye movement is made freely (not necessarily following the contours of the imagined figure), harder to do with fixation of gaze while imagining the eye movement, but impossible if one attempts to imagine the figure as being seen with fixation on one point. Though such informal evidence cannot carry great weight, it does agree with the idea that the motor accompaniments of imagery are not adventitious but essential. (p. 470)

It is not clear whether Hebb would expect eye movements to accompany an amorphous visual image, such as one of an empty blue sky. Hebb also leaves unclear the mechanism involved in imagining eye movements and the conditions under which an individual would be more likely to imagine making eye movements to form a visual image than actually to make them.

It is possible, as I have speculated previously (Cohen, 1978), that the visual imagery of static objects is associated with a characteristic pattern of muscle tension ordinarily associated with focused visual attention (e.g., squinting, including tension in the brows and around the eyes). But it seems unlikely that the motor activity accompanying the visual image of an orange on a table could be distinguished from the motor activity accompanying the visual image of an apple on a table. Therefore, it would appear that any motor theory of thinking which insists that visual images cannot occur without some unique pattern of motor activity or that the content of the visual images is completely determined by the accompanying motor activity must remain unconvincing. The motor theory of voluntary thinking, which I describe below, explicitly avoids this weakness.

C. The Motor Theory of Attention

The motor theory of attention does not assert that motor activity is necessary for the creating of mental experience but that motor activity plays a critical role in emphasizing one aspect of perception or thought over another. Among the earliest expressions of this theory was the view of Bain (1888) that "in selecting a quality out of a complex effect; in maintaining the attention upon one of several images that rise to the view; in a word, in all voluntary control of the thinking trains,—there is a muscular intervention" (p. 373). A distinction is invariably made between spontaneous attention and voluntary attention; the former is drawn automatically by its object with no concomitant sense of effort, whereas the latter is more abstractly motivated and requires the constant application of effort and will. It is generally hypothesized that only voluntary acts of attention require activation of the motor system.

The motor theory of attention does not require specific patterns of motor activation to correspond to particular perceptions, images, or thoughts and thus avoids a major weakness of the motor theories described in the previous two sections. However, the motor theory of attention rests on there being some general relation between motor activity and the direction of attention. Pillsbury (1908) delineates three classes of motor activity related to attention: movements that adapt the sense organs for keener perception; general movements which depend on the nature of the stimulus; and "general overflow effects upon the voluntary muscles which do not depend upon the nature of the stimulus" (p. 12). James (1890/1950) describes motor activation of the first type as follows:

> In attending to either an idea or a sensation belonging to a particular sense-sphere, the movement is the adjustment of the sense-organ, felt as it occurs. I cannot think in visual terms, for example, without feeling a fluctuating play of pressures, convergences, divergences, and accommodations in my eyeballs. The direction in which the object is conceived to lie determines the character of these movements. (p. 300)

Fechner described a difference between attention to external objects and attention to mental images; as quoted by James (1890/1950), Fechner stated:

> I have, when I try to vividly recall a picture of memory or fancy, a feeling perfectly analogous to that which I experience when I seek to apprehend a thing keenly by eye or ear; and this analogous feeling is very differently localized. While in sharpest possible attention to real objects . . . the strain is plainly forwards, . . . the case is different in memory or fancy, for here the feeling withdraws entirely from the external sense-organs, and seems rather to take refuge in that part of the head which the brain fills; if I wish, for example, to recall a place or person it will arise before me with vividness, not according as I strain my attention forwards, but rather in proportion as I, so to speak, retract it backwards. (p. 435–6)

As an example of the second class of attention-related motor activities, Pillsbury refers to those subtle, automatic movements and changes in body posture which can allow a skilled "mind-reader" (or "muscle-reader," as Pillsbury contended) to discern the direction of an object upon which a person is concentrating. Generally, the person concentrating is unaware of performing these tell-tale motor activities, and the "mind-reader" may even be unaware of the source of his information.

The third class of motor activity is associated with all forms of attentional effort, regardless of its direction, and may account in large measure for the experience of effort. Pillsbury mentions the "wrinkled brow" as associated with mental effort. James associated tension in the brow and glottis to feelings of approval and disapproval but added: "in *effort* of any sort, contractions of the jaw muscles and of those of respiration are added to those of the brow and glottis" (p. 301, original emphasis). Ribot (1889), in describing the muscular reactions accompanying intense reflections, concluded that, in addition to more specific reactions, "in all persons and in every case there are modifications in the respiratory rhythm" (p. 27).

The theory I describe in the following section—the MTVT—combines elements from both the motor theory of thinking and the motor theory of attention. Many of the hypotheses I propose occurred to me independently of the works of the early psychologists cited above. However, the elegant writings of these pioneer investigators are helpful in providing rich examples of many of the phenomena to which I refer.

II. Defining the Motor Theory of Voluntary Thinking

The motor theory of voluntary thinking (MTVT) does *not* propose that a specific pattern of motor activity is necessary for the occurrence of each and every mental image or thought. According to the MTVT, any thought or image may occur as an association to a sensation or another thought or image. It seems reasonable that the cerebral processes involved in the experience of one mental image can stimulate the cerebral processes underlying another image without the mediation of any form of motor activity. However, the feedback from motor activity can also evoke thoughts or images according to principles of association. These motor associations can be highly specific, as in the case of inner speech, where the covert reproduction of a specific speech motor pattern can evoke the auditory image of a particular phoneme; or the associations can be much less specific, as will be discussed in a subsequent section. Furthermore, the MTVT does not merely suggest that motor feedback *can* evoke mental images and thoughts; it ascribes to the motor system a very important role in the ordinary thinking process. Patterns of covert motor activity can guide the direction of thought, sometimes very specifically, through the associations they generate. Moreover, it is proposed that motor activity is responsible for the experience of will or volition in thinking—for mental effort—as well as other important aspects of thought to be detailed below.

The basic premise of the MTVT is that all acts of will, or effort, involve activation of the motor system; that central motor activity is the only cerebral activity under direct voluntary control; and that the experience of voluntariness arises only from motor activity, even if only central and not peripherally expressed. Thus, the MTVT parsimoniously explains that the experience of volition that accompanies certain mental acts arises from the same source as the experience of volition accompanying physical acts.

A. The Experience of Volition

The MTVT explains quite simply why some mental images or thoughts are experienced as voluntary (e.g., rehearsing an unfamiliar phone number) and others not (e.g., suddenly experiencing visual memories upon perceiving a particular fragrance); the former images involve motor activation, whereas the latter do not. To be specific, rehearsing a phone number requires a speech motor pattern to be repeated covertly. However, memories can also occur spontaneously through association with other cerebral processes, which may arise in the form of perceptions or may themselves remain out of awareness.

It should be noted that the MTVT does not assert that motor activation must always lead to an experience of voluntariness. Even overt motor acts may become so habitual that they can be performed without any awareness and therefore with no sense of effort. It is possible in the case of some thought patterns that although they arise through association with motor feedback, the covert motor acts with which they are associated are performed automatically—that is, with no sense of effort. For instance, the persistent repetition of the auditory image of a popular song may be the result of a habitual covert motor pattern of which one is unaware, just as one may be unaware of habitually straightening an article of clothing or walking in the wrong direction while engrossed in conversation. Thus a thought may appear to be effortless because no motor activation is involved, or because the motor activity is of an automatic nature.

Whether a covert motor act associated with mental activity is perceived as voluntary or not would be determined by the same principles which determine the degree of voluntariness experienced during overt motor acts. In the preceding chapter, Norman and Shallice describe a theoretical motor mechanism, the "Supervisory Attentional System," the output of which is strongest when motor acts recruit the greatest exercise of attention, as when the motor act is particularly difficult, dangerous, novel, or unpleasant. Norman and Shallice then propose "that *will* be this direction of action by deliberate conscious control" and that "*will* corresponds to the output of the Supervisory Attentional System." The theory they propose is concerned primarily with external actions, but, as they say, "the same principles apply to internal actions—those that involve only the cognitive processing mechanisms." It is also worth noting that the concept of the Supervisory Attentional System is bolstered by the fact, pointed out by Normal and Shallice, that the functions proposed for this mechanism "correspond closely with those ascribed by Luria (1966) to prefrontal regions of the brain, thought by Luria to be required for the programming, regulation, and verification of activity."

B. Specific Motor Associations

The chief assertion of the MTVT is that without the motor system there could be sensation, perception, and even mental images—but no voluntary thought. The critical aspect of this theory is the delineation of the mechanisms by which covert motor activity can explain all aspects of voluntary thinking. One important principle is that the more specific the associations are between patterns of motor activity and the contents of mental experience in a particular modality, the more closely mental experience in that modality can be determined through voluntary motor control. In the case of kinesthetic imagery and inner speech, the associations are simple and direct, as described above in the motor theory of thinking, and therefore these types of imagery should be easy to control. To recall how it feels kinesthetically to row a boat, one need only to activate covertly the appropriate pattern of motor activity. To imagine how it might feel to perform some new motor activity, one would only have to activate covertly the pattern of motor activity that one believes would be necessary, just as one would activate the new pattern overtly if trying the activity for the first time.

1. Inner Speech

In order to rehearse a telephone number one would simply "speak" the numbers covertly—that is, activate the appropriate speech motor patterns, but too slightly to produce audible speech. To take the case of rehearsing a telephone number a step further, consider that the person is being distracted by loud music. Because the music would be competing for his attention, he would have to increase the amplitude of his rehearsal by increasing the speech motor activity, perhaps to the point of making actual lip and tongue movements. Were the music loud enough he might have to speak the numbers aloud so that the numbers would capture enough of his awareness to remain in his short-term memory. McGuigan and Rodier (1968) did indeed find increased speech motor activity (as measured by EMG) in subjects who read during auditory distraction (e.g., white noise, "reverse" speech) as compared to reading in silence.

The person rehearsing the telephone number might also be distracted by his own thoughts or images. For instance, he might be facing an important deadline and find his awareness flooded with verbal thoughts about activities which must be performed as soon as possible. Although it is conceivable that these distracting thoughts could arise spontaneously without accompanying motor activity, it seems more likely that these distracting thoughts would themselves be based on covert speech activity that occurs rapidly and automatically in response to an awareness of the impending deadline. Increasing the speech motor activation associated with the telephone number can probably diminish the distraction of competing thoughts in two ways. First, the telephone number captures an increasing amount of awareness (this would work against any distractor, whether music or thought). Second, to the extent that the distracting thoughts require activation of the speech motor system in their own service, attempting to monopolize the speech system with the telephone number allows less access to the distracting thoughts. At this point it should be considered that thoughts are not likely to require full speech motor patterns to reach awareness. Partial patterns can probably be activated very rapidly, intertwining two or more thoughts in such a way that they seem virtually simultaneous. However, it also seems clear that the strong and rapid repetition of one particular thought can greatly diminish the expression of competing thoughts. Rehearsing a telephone number is just the type of thinking that is very likely to require voluntary thinking in every case and, therefore, speech motor activity, against an inevitable background of distracting thoughts and images.

2. Visual Imagery

The case of voluntary visual imagery is less straightforward than the case of inner speech, but its explanation presents no great problem for the MTVT. Visual imagery represents the case in which the relation between motor activity and mental content is not highly specific, yet some degree of voluntary control is still possible. First, it must be made clear that the MTVT does not posit a one-to-one correspondence between patterns of motor activity and the contents of visual images. Consequently, it cannot be contended that specific visual images are evoked by activating the appropriate motor pattern. However, even if visual images cannot be directly evoked by motor activity, they can to some extent be suppressed, enhanced, or moved by the appropriate motor pattern. In the case of visual imagery, the appropriate motor activity very likely involves the extraocular muscles, which control the movements of the eye, and the musculature which surrounds the eye, including the muscles which draw down the brow to aid in squinting.

Eye movements seem to play an important role in supplying motion to visual images. Antrobus, Antrobus, and Singer (1964) found that subjects exhibited significantly more eye movements when forming visual images involving motion (e.g., a tennis match) than when forming static images (e.g., an orange on a table). Several experiments have confirmed that most subjects produce noticeable, rhythmic horizontal eye movements when visually imagining a moving pendulum (Brown, 1968; Deckert, 1964; Lenox, Lange, & Graham, 1970). Those subjects not producing measurable eye movements may yet have been producing the same central oculomotor activity, but at a level insufficient to move the eye.

It should be noted at this point that the lack of useful proprioception from the extraocular muscles, which has been convincingly demonstrated (e.g., Matin, Pearce, Matin, & Kibler, 1966), does not weaken this part of the MTVT. Central feedback from motor activity plays an important role in visual perception and may play an important role in visual imagery as well. To those who are skeptical of the involvement of eye movements or oculomotor commands in the motion of visual images, the following demonstration is recommended:

> Imagine that you are standing on the roof of a tall building and looking across the street at a building that is even twice as tall. On the roof of the opposite building, just near the edge, is a colorful beach ball (you must look upward to see it). At this point in the demonstration, the reader must actually move his eyes upwards as high as it is physically possible, without inducing pain (obviously, the reader will have to read the demonstration through once before actually trying it, unless it is being read to him). Then, while maintaining your eyes in this upward position as firmly as possible, imagine that a slight breeze has caused the beach ball to fall off the edge of the opposing roof. Without allowing your eyes to move down even slightly from their extreme upward position, imagine the beach ball falling slowly downward. You must actually "see" the beach ball as a visual image, as vividly as you can. The beach ball begins its descent above you, but it is soon level with your position, as it continues to fall. Remembering not to allow your eyes to lower even slightly, continue to "see" the beach ball fall downwards until it bounces on the street below you.

When this demonstration was read to a group of more than 30 experimental psychologists and graduate students, the majority felt a

THE MOTOR THEORY OF VOLUNTARY THINKING   31

strong tendency to move their eyes along with the visual image and felt
that the image was marred if they did not succumb to this tendency.
Many felt they simply could not "see" the beach ball fall without moving
their eyes. I devised this demonstration as a visual analog of a demonstration described by James (1890/1950) and attributed to Stricker. In
the Stricker demonstration the subject must imagine hearing a word
such as *bubble*, while keeping his mouth partly open. Some people find
their auditory images disturbed, at least initially, because of the incom-
patibility between the feedback from a partially opened mouth and the
feedback that would occur in pronouncing the word.

If eye movements can be effective in "moving" a visual image, they
can, perhaps, play a role in suppressing unwanted visual images by
"moving" them to the periphery, or even past the boundaries of the
mental visual field. Consistent with this hypothesis is the finding by
Singer and Antrobus (1965) that eye movements were significantly
greater when a subject was trying to suppress rather than maintain an
image, whether the subject's eyes were open or covered with a trans-
lucent surface.

To increase the vividness of visual images, some individuals may
activate the motor pattern that produces squinting, as this is the motor
activity most closely associated with trying to enhance visual perception.
In my own research, I have obtained some evidence which suggests that
subjects who generate greater corrugator (brow) tension relative to lip
or arm tension experience more vivid visual imagery than subjects
whose brow tension is less prominent. After performing two different
cognitive tasks, all subjects rated the vividness of their visual imagery
and inner speech for each task. Only 7 out of the 22 subjects gave higher
ratings generally for their use of visual, as compared to speech, imagery.
These subjects were considered a separate "group" in an ANOVA which
included muscle area as a within-subject factor. The interaction between
imagery group and muscle area was on the borderline of significance,
$F(1.63, 32.53) = 3.37$, $p < .06$ (the degrees of freedom were adjusted
according to the method of Geisser and Greenhouse [1958] to account
for the lack of homogeneity of covariance). As can be seen in Figure 1,
the two groups do not differ in total muscle tension during cognitive
performance, but rather in the way that the tension is distributed.

So far I have described how motor activity may modify a visual
image that already exists in awareness. However, there are times when
one voluntarily produces visual images in order, for example, to recall
a previous vacation or to imagine a future one. If, according to the
MTVT, visual images do not directly correspond to patterns of motor
activity, it must be explained how they can be voluntarily evoked. The
explanation is that they are evoked only indirectly by association, but

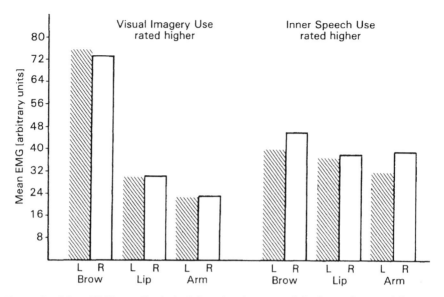

FIGURE 1. Mean EMG amplitude in left and right areas of the brow, lips, and forearms during cognitive performance for two subgroups of subjects differing in reported imagery use (see text).

that some of these associations are under direct, voluntary control. The strong association between words and visual images should be apparent to anyone who has read a novel, especially one in which visual aspects of the setting played an important role. If one closes one's eyes and thinks the word *elephant*, it is difficult not to get some visual impression of a bulky animal with a trunk, etc. To voluntarily produce a visual image, then, one need only name the object in question or describe it with inner speech (in fact, there are extreme visualizers who cannot think any word, even an abstract one, without immediately experiencing some kind of image), which in turn requires the activation of speech motor patterns. Some individuals must close their eyes to experience a clear image, whereas others tend also to squint. Still others claim that they never experience clear visual images. The MTVT does not attempt to explain these differences in visual imagery ability; the theory simply asserts that all visual images are evoked by association (not necessarily to inner speech; perhaps kinesthetic images or sensations can evoke visual images, for instance), more easily for some than for others.

It should be noted that the MTVT does not propose that eye movements are necessary to form vivid, static images or nonelongated images. In fact, it may be helpful to suppress large eye movements in order to minimize disruptive movement of the image. This principle may explain the results of Ehrlichman and Barrett (1983) who recorded fewer eye movements when subjects solved spatial problems (presumably using some visual imagery) than when they solved verbal problems, whether in a dark or lighted environment. These investigators were somewhat puzzled by their results because they expected imagery disruption to be a factor only in a lighted environment due to movements of the external visual field; they did not consider movements of the images *per se*. It should be mentioned that Stoy (1930), who used very different spatial problems, obtained the opposite results. Whether imagery *movement* helps or hinders the solving of a spatial problem may depend on the details of the particular problem.

An experiment by Marks (1973) suggests yet another role for eye movements during visual imagery: scanning for detail. In Marks' study, two groups of subjects were selected on the basis of the subjective ratings they had given to the vividness and clarity of visual images called for by a questionnaire. Eye movement rates were measured for both the "vivid" and "poor" visualizers while they viewed complex visual stimuli and while they attempted to answer questions concerning the visual details of what they had seen several seconds before. Marks found that the vivid visualizers not only recalled more visual details but also exhibited fewer eye movements during recall than did the poor visualizers. This result might be difficult to explain for a theory that requires eye movements for all visual imagery, but it is consistent with the MTVT. The vivid visualizer is such because visual images appear to him more quickly and completely when he thinks about the image. The poor visualizer, in an attempt to answer questions about details he could not easily visualize, may have needed to scan repeatedly his vague and incomplete image. The vivid visualizer, on the other hand, had all the details he needed at once before his mind's eye.

Cuthbert and Lang (1984) obtained a result seemingly inconsistent with the findings of Marks. They found that subjects whose imagery was below average on vividness as reported on a questionnaire were less likely than the remaining subjects to exhibit eye movements during recall of a moving visual display. However, both results are consistent with a theory which posits specific functions for eye movements during visual imagery but does not contend that eye movements are necessary to create a vivid visual image. Subjects with a vivid image in the Cuthbert and Lang study could be expected to use eye movements to set the image in motion (the MTVT posits that even the best visualizer cannot voluntarily visualize objects in motion without producing eye movements), whereas subjects with a poor image would not be able to produce a noticeable effect on their image with eye movements. Quite likely it is hard to notice a clear pattern of motion when one's image is hazy and unstable to start with. Because changes in visual imagery due to eye movements would not be clear, such movements would not be reinforced. Cuthbert and Lang's result replicates a similar finding by Brown (1968) who used a moving pendulum. In summary, it is suggested that subjects with vivid visual imagery, as compared to those reporting poor imagery, would be more likely to produce eye movements when imaging a moving object but would produce fewer eye movements in searching for details because the details would be more easily and quickly noticed.

The notion that visual images can be controlled only indirectly is not a weakness of the MTVT. On the contrary, this principle can explain some important differences between visual imagery and inner speech. First, it should be noted that nearly all undergraduate respondents to a questionnaire reported clear experiences of inner speech, whereas experience with visual imagery varied widely (Cohen & Jonas, 1978). Second, for most individuals, visual imagery is harder to control than inner speech; it is relatively easy to compose a novel sentence, but for some individuals it is quite difficult to combine diverse visual elements into a novel visual image. Third, when associations occur spontaneously as during daydreams or night dreams, visual images are likely to exhibit combinations that are more bizarre and less logically structured than verbal imagery; the visual images are combining according only to the laws of association, whereas verbal images tend to retain the structure of language.

3. Other Modalities

Other modalities of imagery (e.g., smells, tastes) can be accounted for in a manner similar to the explanation of visual imagery. To form the image of a taste, one might think the appropriate words, while covertly activating tongue or jaw movements. For an olfactory image, some form of covert sniffing would likely accompany an internal verbal description. Auditory images other than the sound of one's own voice represent an interesting case that has been surprisingly neglected. From my own introspection, I find that to imagine the sound of a musical instrument I subvocally mimic the sound of the instrument and "sing" or "hum" the tune mentally, while my memory fleshes out the sound. As in the case of visual imagery, these other modalities are under less direct control than inner speech and rely principally on a combination of inner speech and the appropriate sensory memories.

C. General Motor Associations

In addition to evoking specific thoughts and images, and their immediate associations, covert motor activity may play a more general role

THE MOTOR THEORY OF VOLUNTARY THINKING   35

in the deployment of attention. There is a great deal of research demonstrating that experimentally induced muscle tension can, up to some optimal tension level, improve performance on a variety of mental tasks (see Cohen, 1983, Appendix B, for a recent review). There is also suggestive evidence that the mental performance increments associated with induced tension are due to the increased cortical arousal produced (e.g., Pinneo, 1961). That proprioceptive stimuli can be highly effective in producing cortical arousal was shown directly in cats and monkeys by Bernhaut, Gellhorn, and Rasmussen (1953). In addition, Gellhorn (1958) found the reverse effects in cats; muscle relaxation produced by curare paralysis was accompanied by a marked reduction in cortical arousal and responsiveness to painful stimulation. Thus it may be supposed that individuals increase the tension in their muscles globally, or according to idiosyncratic patterns, in order to increase their level of arousal and thus improve their mental performance. This response, however, can become maladaptive if the individual is already aroused above his optimal level for the mental task in question.

Covert motor activity may also serve in a general way to focus attention. There may be some motor patterns that are activated whenever the individual expends mental effort, regardless of the type of imagery or thought engaged in, or the nature of its content. Each individual may have his own idiosyncratic tension pattern that he activates whenever he concentrates (i.e., focuses his attention). However, some motor elements may have nearly universal association with mental concentration. In particular, brow contraction appears to be closely related to the process of focusing attention.

Rather than being mere by-products of mental effort, these general tension patterns may serve an important short-term mnemonic function that aids the individual in maintaining the direction of his attention. If a certain motor pattern has often been associated with mental effort in a particular individual, feedback from that motor activity could serve to remind the individual that he is presently involved in some attentive act from which he has become distracted. Although the feedback would not tell the individual where his attention should be, it would cause him to search his immediate memory. This mechanism could act as a mental "string around the finger" in the following manner. Suppose an individual is concentrating on some mental problem while tensing his muscles in a characteristic pattern. His attention wanders off the problem, but within seconds he becomes aware of motor feedback from his "concentration" activity. He then quickly searches his immediate memory to recall the particular problem he had been working on. This shifting of attention back and forth could occur very quickly and frequently, especially if the problem were not intrinsically interesting.

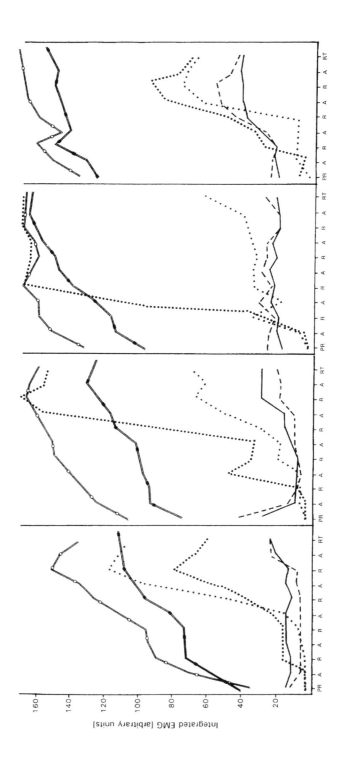

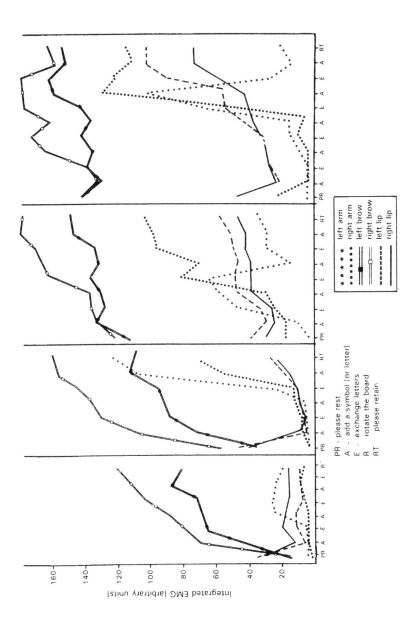

FIGURE 2. Integrated EMG from left and right areas of the brow, lips, and forearms for one subject during four trials of a mental rotation task followed, after a brief rest break, by four trials of a letter transformation task.

It could be suggested that the individual would soon adapt to the constant feedback from his concentration activity, which would then be rendered ineffective. One solution to this problem of adaptation would be for the individual to increase continuously the intensity of his concentration activity during the period of focused attention. This increasing motor activity could be expected to produce a rising tension gradient in at least some of the individual's muscles. Such tension gradients have indeed been found during experiments involving continuous attention (Bartoshuk, 1956; Wallerstein, 1954). In my own research (Cohen, 1983), I observed that for some subjects brow tension did not decrease appreciably within or between trials but would rise higher with each succeeding trial until a rest period was given (after each block of four trials). These gradients were much less pronounced and considerably more variable in the lip and forearm areas. Trials consisted of a series of aurally presented instructions describing progressively more difficult mental rotations or transformations of a string of letters. These instructions were cumulative within a trial and the subject did not respond until the end of a trial. Figure 2 presents data for two blocks of trials for one subject who exhibited prominent brow tension gradients.

III. The Role of Covert Motor Activity in External Attention

A. Voluntary Attention

Mental effort accompanies not only the focusing of attention upon purely mental experiences such as images or thoughts; a sense of mental effort can also be experienced in attending to one of several competing external stimuli. The classic example is the "cocktail party phenomenon", in which the listener is bombarded with several simultaneous conversations and must attend to one of them, at least long enough to understand its meaning. Moreover, the conversation selected need not be the loudest. An explanation consistent with the MTVT is that the listener would "shadow" the selected conversation (i.e., repeat it covertly) to keep his attention oriented toward it. However, covert motor activity may aid in selective attention by an additional mechanism in this case, and this additional mechanism may account, in part, for the sense of effort and volition involved in selectively attending to one of many external stimuli. This additional mechanism consists of producing a pattern of covert motor activity to represent symbolically one of the competing inputs. For example, if one conversation originates from the listener's left and the other from his right, to select the leftmost conversation the listener may produce a bodily posture subtly oriented toward the left. This posture may be expressed solely in tensional adjustments without producing any actual body movements. In the case of several conversations originating from diverse locations, the tensional adjustments would likely be less specific and less helpful, but nonetheless could aid in the listener's spatial orientation. This mechanism could be applied analogously for other perceptual modalities. The MTVT asserts that the experience of effort that sometimes arises during external attention is due entirely to motor activation, whether in the form of postural adjustments, sensory organ adjustments, or inner speech. Symbolic postural adjustments may also play a role in directing attention to one thought or image as opposed to another, but in the case of internal attention, spatial orientation is less likely to be a useful factor, and inner speech probably assumes the major burden in determining direction.

B. Spontaneous Attention

James (1980/1950) described two forms of "sensorial attention": one that is "active and voluntary" (as described in the previous section) and one that is "passive, reflex, non-voluntary, effortless" (p. 416). The latter form of attention, which I prefer to call *spontaneous*, may be *immediate*, drawn to stimuli by virtue of their force or intrinsic interest, or *derived*, that is, drawn to stimuli by virtue of their association with objects of immediate attention. In psychophysiological research, the type of attention described by James as "passive immediate sensorial" has been evoked experimentally by visual stimuli depicting, for instance, attractive nudes or repulsive accident scenes; passive derived sensorial attention has been evoked by presenting warning signals for trials involving aversive events, or fast reaction. Both types of passive sensorial attention have been associated with significant decreases in heart rate, usually associated with lowered arousal; other arousal indicators simultaneously changed in the direction of heightened arousal (e.g., Libby, Lacey, & Lacey, 1973; Obrist, Webb, & Sutterer, 1969). This paradoxical divergence of arousal indicators has been called *directional fractionation* (Lacey, 1967).

On the basis of a series of experiments which demonstrated that heart rate reductions to warning stimuli were accompanied by reductions in various aspects of somatic activity (e.g., chin tension, respiration, eyeblinks), Obrist, Webb, Sutterer, and Howard (1970) proposed that both the cardiac and somatic activity reductions are due to a global inhibition of bodily activity in order to reduce neural noise which might otherwise compete with the perception of the external stimulus. Thus, it appears that spontaneous external attention may involve increased activation in specific cortical areas (which may correlate with observed increases in, for example, electrodermal activity), coupled with an active inhibition of somatic activity. This phenomenon is easily understood within the context of the MTVT. Ordinarily, the perception of external stimuli would stimulate associations, which would lead to a series of covert motor responses and their accompanying mental images, as this is how normal thinking is posited to proceed. However, if it is important to maintain attention to the environment, it would be best to minimize thinking, and motor inhibition would serve this purpose (in addition to reducing the distraction of extraneous bodily activity *per se*). Because mental effort is not required for this type of attention—both perception and cortical activation are stimulated directly by the environmental and cognitive situation—motor activity is not required (and can actually be a hindrance). However, I suspect that in spontaneous attention, although there is a global reduction in bodily activity, including muscle tension, there may be increased activity in certain muscle areas, especially the brow. Tension in selected regions, not sufficient to offset the global reduction in bodily activity, may be activated automatically to aid in the focusing of attention. Considering the nature of spontaneous attention, any muscle tension that accompanies this state would probably remain in a fixed pattern and at an unusually steady level.

The two types of attention, described in the previous two sections as voluntary and spontaneous, correspond to some degree with the processes of controlled search and automatic detection, respectively, as postulated by Shiffrin and Schneider (1977). The former requires mental effort, often in the form of covert verbal rehearsal, and should therefore be accompanied by significantly more muscle tension than the latter, which may benefit from motor inhibition. (Automatic detection, as described by Shiffrin and Schneider, more specifically corresponds to James's definition of passive derived sensorial attention since it must be learned.) Moreover, the amount of muscle tension generated during controlled search would likely be a function of the "load" as defined in the Shiffrin and Schneider paradigm.

IV. REGULATING THE STREAM OF THOUGHT

A. *Ordinary States*

In Volume Two of this series, Pope and Singer (1978) presented a paper entitled "Regulation of the Stream of Consciousness" in which they described the major factors that determine the contents of one's daily mental experience. Among their excellent descriptions of different styles of consciousness regulation, Pope and Singer include a hypothetical case of a person who pushes away distracting thoughts while reading a book about mathematics but indulges in free association while reading poetry. This example was chosen by Pope and Singer to illustrate that "we are able . . . to adopt temporary, situation-specific 'plans' for mental processing" (p. 126). These investigators, however, do not describe any mechanism by which such plans could be enacted.

The MTVT, not surprisingly, can describe a mechanism which can account for this important aspect of consciousness regulation. According to the MTVT, the person pushes away distracting thoughts while reading by increasing the covert speech motor activity which he uses to represent the words he is reading. He may also increase tension in the muscles associated with visual perception and the control of eye movements, including the extraocular muscles, and the muscles of the brow and neck. Finally, he may increase the tension in his skeletal musculature generally, but especially in those muscles with which he associates the act of concentrating. On the other hand, to allow the ideas evoked by his reading to distract him from the reading process, he need only relax his motor activity somewhat and refrain from engaging in the types of motor activity which would direct his attention to his primary task.

In such a manner as described above, the MTVT can explain a very salient experiential dimension of ordinary consciousness—the feeling of voluntariness with respect to mental activity. These are times during the course of ordinary daily activities when we seem to be struggling with our thoughts—trying to push unwanted thoughts from our mind, or perhaps repeating particular thoughts in the attempt to find some elusive solution to a problem. There are other times, for instance, sitting idly on a bus or train, when our thoughts seem to flow quite by themselves, and we feel more that we are observing them than creating them. According to the MTVT, the feeling of effort and will associated with some instances of thinking is due to the deliberate engagement of the motor system during such instances in the service of guiding or controlling the direction of thought. When thoughts seem to flow effortlessly, it is because the motor system has not been voluntarily enlisted in the thinking process. A state in which one is absorbed by an exciting train of thought can be described as spontaneous internal attention. Any motor activity (overt or covert) occurring during such a state would be of an automatic nature, not involving the highest cortical control.

B. Natural Relaxation

An obvious prediction from the MTVT is that states of global motor quiescence should be accompanied by free-flowing, nonvolitional mentation. This prediction does not apply to states in which muscular relaxation is induced pharmacologically, as with curare, because there would still be the possibility of considerable central motor activity. Nor does it apply to the case of spontaneous external attention during which the decrease in motor activation appears to be the result of an active inhibition coupled with high cortical arousal. It is when reduced motor activation occurs due to fatigue, and the environment does not draw attention, that attention is likely to turn inward. However, this state differs from spontaneous internal attention because cortical arousal is likely to be lower than normal. It is more a state of reduced attention. During such drowsy states, the MTVT predicts that images would flow more according to principles of free association than logical requirements because of the reduction in motor control. Even when the individual is not drowsy, a natural reduction in motor activity should allow ideas to flow more freely by association. This principle can account for the finding of psychoanalysts that lying on the couch tends to encourage free association.

Antrobus *et al.* (1964) interrupted subjects during periods of naturally occurring ocular motility or relative quiescence. The subjects rated their mental content as it was just preceding the interruption. Ocular quiescence tended to be associated with more reports of daydreamlike mentation than did ocular motility. If ocular quiescence is indicative of reduced motor activation, this finding fits well with the predictions of the MTVT. Singer (1975) reported the results of personal, introspective experiments involving interruptions of his own stream of thought: "The impression I gained . . . was that under relaxed, slightly drowsy conditions, one's brain is not geared to producing an orderly sequence of thought. Personalized visual imagery intruded upon me quite regularly" (p. 44). From the viewpoint of the MTVT, spontaneous bursts of visual imagery during relaxed states are quite understandable. As Singer notes, such imagery is likely to involve a memory sequence which flows according to well-worn associations. Much less likely in such a state would be to "hear" an auditory image of one's own voice composing a complex essay.

States of profound relaxation, such as occur just prior to the onset of sleep, are often accompanied by increasingly bizarre combinations of thoughts and images. If, as the MTVT implies, motor activity is required for organizing images and thought into analytical and logical progressions, then it is not surprising to find images evoking other images according to primitive principles of association when the motor system is inactive. It is, perhaps, no coincidence that the state of normal consciousness most closely associated with bizarre, illogical mentation is the state accompanied by the most profound facial motor inhibition—namely, rapid eye movement (REM) sleep.

Creative thinking often involves a stage of free-flowing mentation during which ideas can combine in new ways that may even seem illogical during ordinary states of thinking. Often a creative episode is preceded by a period of ordinary mental effort during which some problem is considered along with proposed logical solutions. However, the novel, creative solution to the problem often occurs when the individual has stopped thinking about the problem and has relaxed his motor activity. It is in such a state that ideas are more likely to flow by free association.

C. Progressive Relaxation and Meditation

The MTVT allows that thoughts can arise either by association with sensations or previous thoughts, or by association with the feedback from motor activity. At this point, I would like to propose tentatively that without sustained motor activity any train of associations would quickly fade away, that it is only the maintenance of motor activity that can prolong a train of thought indefinitely. In this regard, it should be recalled that, according to the MTVT, thoughts may arise through association with spontaneous or habitual motor activity. Together, these two notions—that some motor activity is necessary for sustained thought and that spontaneous motor activity is sufficient for thought—have some interesting implications. One implication is that very deep relaxation of the entire motor system should result in the cessation of thought, but not necessarily of consciousness. Another implication is that the cessation of thought is impossible without the relaxation of all thought-evoking motor activity.

The above hypotheses explain why most people find it impossible to stop their flow of thoughts for more than a very few seconds. Some of the motor activity which is capable of evoking thoughts occurs habitually and may be motivated by the same relentless forces that maintain various nervous habits, such as nail biting. In order to eliminate a habit, one must first be made aware of performing the habitual act. But unlike nail biting, habitual covert motor activity may have no readily observable consequences other than the thoughts it produces. Still, in principle, it should be possible to gain voluntary control over any particular pattern of motor activity; the results of EMG biofeedback experimentation lend much support to this principle (Basmajian, 1979). The possibility of using EMG biofeedback to gain control of specific thought patterns seems remote at present. However, two global procedures offer some promise towards the goal of reducing or even eliminating habitual thought. Jacobson (1938) observed that many individuals exhibited a good deal of residual muscle tension of which they were unaware when they were lying down and supposedly relaxing. Typically, a person asked to relax further would "try" to do so and thus increase, rather than decrease, his tension. Through his experimentation, Jacobson discovered that subjects could relax residual tension in a particular muscle more completely when they became aware of the proprioceptive sensations arising from tension in that muscle. To improve his subjects' ability to perceive muscle tension and thus relax it, Jacobson devised the technique of progressive relaxation. In this technique, a subject systematically tenses and relaxes all of the major muscles, noting the feeling of tension in each, and the feeling of relaxation, of "letting go." Subjects are encouraged to continue letting go even after the point at which they believe the muscle has been completely relaxed. Particular attention is paid to the muscles most closely associated with thought, those involved with speech and control of visual perception. Remarkably, Jacobson found that well-trained subjects could attain a state of muscular relaxation so profound that all images and thoughts would cease, leaving the subject awake and alert but with his consciousness devoid of any particular object. Thus, Jacobson believed that his technique could eliminate habitual thinking, at least temporarily, during total relaxation. He also believed that the effects of progressive relaxation would generalize to daily life and minimize excessive rumination or worrying.

The state Jacobson described, in which a subject's mind was alert but "blank," is similar to the state of "pure awareness" or "pure consciousness" that is said to be the goal of many forms of meditation. Meditative techniques can be divided into two types depending on whether they involve active or passive forms of concentration (Naranjo & Ornstein, 1971). This active-passive distinction is similar to the one drawn by James in discussing attention. In active concentration, mental effort is used to direct the focus of attention; in passive concentration, the attention is left free to be drawn by any mental object, though usually some focal object, such as the act of breathing or a mantra (a Sanskrit word that is usually easy to articulate but may have no meaning to the user), is used as a point of departure. It can be shown, within the context of the MTVT, how passive mantra meditation can lead, by a complementary route, to the same state of thought-free alertness described by Jacobson.

According to the technique of transcendental meditation (TM), a form of passive mantra meditation popularized by Maharishi Mahesh Yogi (Bloomfield, Cain, & Jaffe, 1975), one is to return one's attention to the mantra whenever one becomes aware that his attention has wandered, but one is not to use mental effort to maintain the mantra in awareness. The effect of "trying" to think of the mantra without expending effort is that one becomes increasingly aware of the effort exerted in producing any thought. According to the MTVT, the effort involved in producing a thought is nothing more than the effort exerted to create the motor activity that evokes the thought. By becoming increasingly aware of producing very subtle motor activity, the individual may gain the ability to relax such motor activity, including the motor activity responsible for habitual thinking. Thus, it may be possible through both passive mantra meditation and progressive relaxation to become aware of and relax away the spontaneous covert motor activity underlying habitual thought.

The alleged benefits of progressive relaxation (Jacobson, 1964) and transcendental meditation (Bloomfield *et al.* 1975) with respect to reduced anxiety and increased energy and efficiency may be due in large part to the reduction of habitual thinking that may be produced by both techniques. Habitual thinking may be harmful not only as a consistent waste of energy but as a mediator of stress reactions.

V. CONCLUSIONS

A. Summary

The central assertion of the MTVT is that the experience of acting voluntarily arises solely from activity in the motor system, whether the voluntary act is physical or purely mental. However, not all activity in the motor system produces an experience of volition; only activity that requires deliberate conscious control produces this experience. Because the ordinary perception of one's environment does not appear to require any volitional act or to give rise to any sense of effort, the MTVT, unlike the motor theory of consciousness, does not posit the necessity of motor activity for the emergence of conscious perceptions. Similarly, some mental images seem to arise spontaneously by association with a perception or another image. The MTVT does not posit that these mental experiences require motor activity either, although the possibility is raised that images which seem to arise spontaneously may actually be associated with habitual or automatic motor activity.

The MTVT does assert that all images and thought produced or guided in a voluntary manner are associated with motor activity. Deliberately imagined kinesthetic imagery is evoked by covert motor activity directly corresponding to the imagined activity. Similarly, all deliberate inner speech is based on the appropriate covert activity in the speech musculature. Visual imagery, however, cannot be controlled so closely or directly because there is no one-to-one correspondence between visual perception and motor patterns. Similarly, imagery in the other modalities is not directly controlled, nor are shifts in external attention.

The MTVT asserts that all mental acts which involve the experience of voluntariness must be accompanied by some distinct pattern of motor activity. But it is conceded that it is not presently possible to state for all modalities the exact types of motor activation involved, nor can the possibility of significant individual differences be ignored. However, reasonable speculations can be offered. Inner speech appears to play a major role in evoking and controlling imagery in other modalities. Inner speech may be accompanied by motor patterns associated with perception as appropriate for each modality. Thus, visual imagery may be accompanied by squinting and, if the images require motion or scanning, eye movements in the appropriate direction. The voluntary imaging of tastes or smells may be accompanied by covert oral or nasal adjustments. Attending to some types of imagery or some aspects of the external environment may be aided by directional adjustments in bodily posture. In the most general case, overall increases in bodily tension or, just in certain idiosyncratically preferred muscles, may aid any form of mental effort. On the other hand, motor activity may be deliberately inhibited during states of spontaneous attention, in order to reduce internal distractions. In such states, only a few muscles may be contracted, and these contractions would be maintained steadily.

Conversely, during the marked reduction of motor activity produced by fatigue, the organizing effects of motor activity upon thought would decrease, and the stream of thought would tend to flow more by free association than according to logically structured, purposeful plans. Finally, spontaneous thinking, which may seem virtually impossible to eliminate voluntarily, may be the result of habitual covert motor activity. Both progressive relaxation and certain forms of meditation hold the promise of allowing the individual to gain greater awareness of the habitual motor activity that produces incessant thoughts and thereby to gain greater control of his consciousness.

B. Implications for Experimental Research

1. The Issue of Necessity

In its present form, the MTVT would not be easy to prove or disprove experimentally. Because the MTVT posits that only central motor activity is actually necessary to produce the experience of volition during mental activity, attempts to block muscle contraction peripherally are irrelevant. Even if data were collected showing that for at least a few subjects no measurable EMG changes could be found during a period when the subjects were expending great mental effort and not receiving any paralytic drugs, it could be argued that these subjects were producing tension in idiosyncratic muscle areas not measured. Alternatively, it could be argued that these subjects were generating motor activity sufficient to generate useful central feedback, but not sufficient to produce measurable changes in muscle contraction.

To block central motor activity by artificial means is not possible at the present stage of neurophysiology, and considering the difficulty of defining motor activity as opposed to other forms of neural activity within the central nervous system, this means of disconfirming the MTVT may never be possible. However, there are nonpharmacological methods for reducing central motor activity that can be considered. For instance, if biofeedback procedures are employed to ensure that a subject maintains a state of relaxation in a certain muscle region, it can be assumed that this relaxation is the result of a reduction in central motor commands directed at that region. This was the approach adopted by Hardyck and Petrinovich (1970); these investigators found that subjects who kept their laryngeal region relaxed while reading a difficult essay exhibited worse comprehension than subjects who kept their forearms relaxed, or nonrelaxed control subjects. The group that maintained relaxation in their forearms was included to control for the distracting effects of trying to keep the EMG biofeedback signal off (i.e., keeping the EMG amplitude below some threshold value). The effectiveness of this control procedure can be questioned. The tendency for forearm tension to rise while reading is far less than the tendency for laryngeal tension to rise (this was even confirmed within the Hardyck and Petrinovich study, for the nonrelaxation group), so keeping forearm tension at baseline levels is probably the easier and less distracting condition. Therefore, distraction cannot be ruled out as an explanation for the impaired reading comprehension in the laryngeal relaxation group.

The optimal design for using the biofeedback-relaxation strategy is to select two different mental tasks which are associated with muscle tension in two different areas; four conditions are employed such that in two conditions subjects are relaxing "necessary" muscles and in the remaining two conditions relaxing "irrelevant" muscles. Unfortunately, demonstrating that the relaxation of necessary muscles impairs mental task performance significantly more than the relaxation of irrelevant muscles would still not prove the necessity of motor activity for mental performance. It could always be argued that the tendency to produce tension in one muscle region as opposed to others is invariably greater for a particular task, even though that tension is not necessary or even helpful. Because the degree of distraction associated with keeping a muscle relaxed is likely to increase with the tendency to activate the muscle during a particular task, distraction could never be ruled out as the sole cause for the relevant performance decrements. One would strongly prove the association between motor activation *tendencies* and particular mental tasks, but not the absolute necessity of motor activation. However, the stronger and more reliable these motor tendencies are proven to be, the more useful and important it becomes to delineate the exact relation between mental content and motor pattern, as will be discussed further below.

On the other hand, Cole and Young (1975), using the laryngeal biofeedback-relaxation technique, claimed to have demonstrated that subvocalization (i.e., covert speech motor activity) is not necessary for nonsense syllable memorization. Subjects receiving EMG feedback were compared to a control group which had no relaxation requirement at all. Although feedback subjects produced significantly more errors than the control group, Cole and Young attributed this impairment entirely to the effects of distraction. These investigators argued that the occurrence and type of errors in each group was unaffected by the presence or absence of subvocalization on any given trial. However, a serious flaw in Cole and Young's experimental design greatly weakens the force of their arguments. The EMG was recorded only from the laryngeal area, and this was the only area that subjects were ever required to relax. The larynx, though, is not the only area that is activated during audible speech or covert speech motor activity; according to McGuigan (1978) the tongue and lips, in that order, are the most sensitive indicators of inner speech. In fact, the bulk of speech information is encoded in the form of lip, tongue, and mouth movements; lip readers lose rather little information even without perceiving the speaker's laryngeal activity. It is quite possible that feedback subjects quickly learned to "mouth" covertly the nonsense syllables while suppressing laryngeal activity. Indeed, subjects may actually have compensated for laryngeal suppression with an increase in covert tongue and lip activity. Cole and Young's conclusions would have been far more compelling had they ruled out the above objection by additionally recording the EMG from the tongue and/or lips and including a group of subjects required to maintain relaxation in several speech areas simultaneously.

To prove that a pattern of motor activity is necessary for a particular mental event to occur, one must show not only that the motor pattern is exhibited whenever the mental event occurs but also that preventing the motor pattern's occurrence also prevents the occurrence of the par-

THE MOTOR THEORY OF VOLUNTARY THINKING   49

ticular mental event. It seems safe to state that, at present, the necessity of motor activity has not been proven with respect to any class of mental events. Moreover, for the reasons discussed above, it does not seem likely that the necessity of motor activity will be proven in the near future. However, although proving the necessity of motor activity for certain mental experiences would be of enormous theoretical interest, failing to prove necessity does not render worthless the vast wealth of data demonstrating the association between motor manifestations and various mental contents.

2. Applications of Research in Covert Motor Activity

There are at least two important reasons for studying the motor correlates of mental states even if those motor correlates are totally unnecessary. First, if patterns of motor activity are correlated in a highly specific and reliable way with certain aspects of mental experience, the motor patterns may serve as useful indicators of the type of mental content. These motor patterns, which can be measured through the use of several simultaneous EMG recordings, can provide clues concerning a subject's cognitive strategy at times when verbal report may be inconvenient, distracting, unreliable, or simply unavailable (e.g., aphasic patients). Second, the motor activity accompanying mental effort, whether helpful or not, can have psychological and physiological consequences that are of practical importance. In extreme cases, the muscle tension generated during mental concentration may produce a debilitating degree of discomfort.

In regard to the use of EMG patterns as indicators of cognitive strategy, the recent work of Cacioppo and Petty (1981) should be noted. These researchers monitored lip EMG during several cognitive tasks which differed in their expected demand on the use of inner speech The relative amounts of lip tension generated by the different tasks conformed well with theoretical predictions. The EMG was also recorded from the left forearm to rule out the possibility that changes in general arousal, rather than inner speech, could account for the task differences in lip tension. Forearm EMG did not differ significantly between conditions, confirming the specificity of the observed changes in lip tension. The Cacioppo and Petty experiment represents an excellent example of the way measurements of covert motor activity can be measured and used as a tool to explore cognitive processes. However, one improvement should be mentioned. By using forearm EMG as a comparison to control for the effects of general arousal, Cacioppo and Petty implicitly assumed that the forearm would be as responsive—or at least nearly so—as the lips to changes in general arousal. This need not be so. It is quite possible, as has been argued before (Cohen, 1983), that some muscles, such as the orbicularis oris (which manipulates the lips), or the corrugator (which pulls down the brow), are far more responsive than other muscles to changes in general arousal. The use of additional simultaneous EMG recordings to measure more comprehensively the tension patterns that accompany the performance of cognitive tasks would expand the usefulness and render more conclusive the results obtained by Cacioppo and Petty.

The design of the Cacioppo and Petty experiment was based on the great volume of research (a large portion of which was conducted by McGuigan and his associates) which has established the reliable and specific relation between the use of inner speech and the covert activation of the speech musculature. Further research involving the motor correlates of other types of mental activity is needed to expand the usefulness of covert motor activity as an indicator of cognitive strategy. For example, the motor correlates of visual imagery should be studied more thoroughly, using EMG recordings from several facial areas, particularly around the eyes, in addition to the EOG for measuring eye movements. The visual imagery tasks used in these experiments should be designed so as to control more carefully various aspects of the images subjects are expected to form, such as the size of the image and the direction of any required motion or scanning. Research involving imagery in other modalities, though less useful in the exploration of higher cognitive processes, would be of considerable theoretical importance, as the results could refine and clarify our conception of the MTVT.

Much research effort has recently been directed towards the classification of facial expressions associated with distinct emotions, and the use of facial EMG as an indicator of specific affect (Fridlund and Izard, 1983). The bulk of this research has focused on affective states that are typically regarded as highly emotional; little attention has been paid to the affective state known as "interest." However, because interest often accompanies and blends with various emotions, and because for many individuals interest may be present by itself more frequently than any other affective state, it would seem worthwhile to explore the motor correlates of mental states involving relatively pure interest. It should be noted, however, that these motor correlates may vary according to the general direction in which the interest is deployed. For instance, interest stimulated by the environment may be associated with a somewhat different facial expression (and other motor manifestations) from interest in one's own mental imagery. Moreover, interest involving audition may differ motorically from interest in the visual field. During the early phases of research into the motor correlates of interest, investigators should be careful to note the exact conditions by which the state of interest was evoked and to record from as wide a representation of muscle areas as possible.

It would be very helpful if the motor correlates of specific types of attention proved to be universal, exhibiting similar motor patterns from one individual to the next; assumptions could then be made about individuals whose motor patterns had not yet been observed in controlled circumstances. However, it would also be useful if individuals fell into well-defined categories based on their motor patterns during mental work; these categories might then be found to represent important and consistent individual differences with respect to cognitive style. But even if the motor correlates of mental activity were highly idiosyncratic— differing considerably between any two individuals—as long as these patterns were consistent within each individual over time, they could still be useful. One form of attention, the motor correlates of which could be expected to be rather idiosyncratic, is attention which is directed to one of several similar-sounding auditory stimuli distributed widely in space. Different individuals may employ a different set of motor patterns to aid their efforts in directing attention to a particular spatial location. One individual might control his attention in this situation by the position of his eyes, whereas a second individual might adjust the position of his jaw. (In the initial stages of this experimentation, many channels of simultaneous EMG recordings, as well as EOG and visual observation, would have to be employed to cover the many possible motor strategies that could arise.) If an individual maintained such a motor strategy consistently throughout an experiment, this information could be useful in subsequent experimental sessions with the same individual, in which the individual might be induced, for instance, to switch his attention rapidly between two inputs the spatial location and separation of which could be systematically varied. Just to observe the different motoric strategies of several experimental subjects as they switch the direction of their attention could be a useful first step in this research program.

The second reason mentioned above for studying the motor activity accompanying mental work involves the consequences of such motor activity. Regardless of whether such motor activity serves any useful function, it can result in high levels of muscle tension. There is evidence that muscle tension in some bodily areas, particularly the forehead, can rise continuously during sustained mental performance. More research is needed to determine whether the tension in these areas can eventually produce enough discomfort to interfere with mental performance. It is likely that individuals who are prone to having tension headaches would show steeper forehead tension gradients during mental work. Other individuals may show similar gradients in other muscles, perhaps in the jaw or neck. Even among those who rarely experience pain from muscular tension headaches, tension levels may reach high enough levels to produce distraction and diminish mental concentration. The possibility ought to be explored that individuals could be trained to increase their span for concentration by learning to relax certain muscles during mental performance. This was the hope of Jacobson (1938) in devising the concept of differential relaxation.

Finally, the possibility of reducing or eliminating extraneous and even debilitating thoughts through refined techniques of relaxation is too intriguing to be ignored. The potential benefits of such relaxation for mental health are enormous. Although numerous studies have been conducted using EMG biofeedback and abbreviated forms of progressive relaxation, such studies have not focussed on the relation between covert motor activity and the intensity of concurrent mental activity. Perhaps mental devices for relaxation can be validated and refined through the use of multichannel EMG measurement. Such experimentation could be capable of combining the benefits of ancient wisdom concerning meditation practices with modern technology in order to approach the highest goal of self-control: control of consciousness itself.

REFERENCES

ANTROBUS, J. S., ANTROBUS, T. S., & SINGER, J. L. (1964). Eye movements accompanying daydreaming, visual imagery and thought suppression. *Journal of Abnormal and Social Psychology, 69*, 244–252.

BAIN, A. (1888). *The emotions and the will.* London: Parker.

BARTOSHUK, A. K. (1956). EMG gradients and EEG amplitude during motivated listening. *Canadian Journal of Psychology, 10*, 156–164.

BASMAJIAN, J. V. (1979). *Muscles alive: Their functions revealed by electromyography.* Baltimore: Williams & Wilkins.

BERNHAUT, M., GELLHORN, E., & RASMUSSEN, A. T. (1953). Experimental contributions to the problem of consciousness. *Journal of Neurophysiology, 16*, 21–35.

BLOOMFIELD, H. H., CAIN, M. P., & JAFFE, D. T. (1975). *Transcendental meditation: Discovering inner energy and overcoming stress.* New York: Delacorte.

BROWN, B. B. (1968). Visual recall ability and eye movements. *Psychophysiology, 4*, 300–306.

CACIOPPO, J. T., & PETTY, R. E. (1981). Electromyographic specificity during covert information processing. *Psychophysiology, 18*, 518–523.

COHEN, B. H. (1978, September). *Role of the motor system in visual imagery.* Paper presented at the annual meeting of the American Psychological Association, Toronto, Canada.

COHEN, B. H. (1983). *Electromyographic patterns associated with cognition and affect.* Unpublished doctoral dissertation, New York University.

COHEN, B. H., & JONAS, C. (1978, November). *A closer look at the visualizer: Habit or vividness?* Paper presented at the second annual convention on the Imagery and Fantasy Process, Chicago.

COLE, R. A., & YOUNG, M. (1975). Effect of subvocalization on memory for speech sounds. *Journal of Experimental Psychology: Human Learning and Memory, 1*, 772–779.

CUTHBERT, B. N., & LANG, P. J. (1984). Eye movements in visual imagery. *Physiology, 21*, 574.

THE MOTOR THEORY OF VOLUNTARY THINKING 53

DECKERT, G. H. (1964). Pursuit eye movements in the absence of a moving visual stimulus. *Science, 143,* 1192–1193.

DUNLAP, K. (1927). The short-circuiting of conscious responses. *Journal of Philosophy, 24,* 263–267.

EHRLICHMAN, H., & BARRETT, J. (1983). 'Random' saccadic eye movements during verbal-linguistic and visual-imaginal tasks. *Acta Psychologica, 53,* 9–26.

EKMAN, P., FRIESEN, W., & ELLSWORTH, P. (1972). *Emotion in the human face.* New York: Pergamon Press.

EVARTS, E. V. (1971). Feedback and corollary discharge: A merging of the concepts. *Neurosciences Research Program Bulletin, 9,* 86–112.

FRIDLUND, A. J., & IZARD, C. E. (1984). Electromyographic studies of facial expressions of emotions and patterns of emotions. In J. T. CACIOPPO & R. E. PETTY (Eds.), *Social psychophysiology: A sourcebook,* New York: Guilford Press.

GEISSER, S., & GREENHOUSE, S. W. (1958). An extension of Box's results on the use of the F distribution in multivariate analysis. *Annals of Mathematical Statistics, 29,* 885–891.

GELLHORN, E. (1958). The influence of curare on hypothalamic excitability and the electroencephalogram. *Electroencephalography and Clinical Neurophysiology, 10,* 697–703.

HARDYCK, C. D., & PETROVICH, L. F. (1970). Subvocal speech and comprehension level as a function of the difficulty of reading material. *Journal of Verbal Learning and Verbal Behavior, 9,* 647–652.

HEBB, D. O. (1968). Concerning imagery. *Psychological Review, 75,* 466–477.

HEFFERLINE, R. F., & PERERA, T. B. (1963). Proprioceptive discrimination of a covert operant without its observation by the subject. *Science, 139,* 834–835.

JACOBSON, E. (1930). Electrical measurements of neuromuscular states during mental activities. III. Visual imagination and recollection. *American Journal of Physiology, 95,* 694–702.

JACOBSON, E. (1932). Electrophysiology of mental activities. *American Journal of Psychology, 44,* 677–694.

JACOBSON, E. (1938). *Progressive relaxation* (2nd ed.). Chicago: University of Chicago Press.

JACOBSON, E. (1964). *Anxiety and tension control: A physiologic approach.* Philadelphia: Lippincott.

JAMES, W. (1890). *The principles of psychology.* New York: Holt. (Reprinted: New York: Dover, 1950).

LACEY, J. I. (1967). Somatic response patterning and stress: Some revisions of activation theory. In M. H. APPLEY & R. TRUMBULL (Eds.), *Psychological stress: Issues in research.* New York: Appleton-Century-Crofts.

LENOX, J. R., LANGE, A. F., & GRAHAM, K. R. (1970). Eye movement amplitude in imagined pursuit of a pendulum with the eyes closed. *Psychophysiology, 6,* 773–777.

LEUBA, C., BIRCH, L., & APPLETON, J. (1968). Human problem solving during complete paralysis of the voluntary musculature. *Psychological Reports, 22,* 849–855.

LIBBY, W. L., JR., LACEY, B. C., & LACEY, J. I. (1973). Pupillary and cardiac activity during visual attention. *Psychophysiology, 10,* 270–294.

LURIA, A. R. (1966). *Higher cortical functions in man.* London: Tavistock.

MARKS, D. F. (1973). Visual imagery differences in eye movements in recall of pictures. *Perception and Psychophysics, 14,* 407–412.

MATIN, L., PEARCE, D., MATIN, E., & KIBLER, G. (1966). Visual perception of direction in the dark: Roles of local signs, eye movements and ocular proprioception. *Vision Research, 6,* 453–469.

MAUDSLEY, H. (1889). *The physiology of mind.* New York: D. Appleton.

MCGUIGAN, F. J. (1978). *Cognitive psychophysiology: Principles of covert behavior.* New Jersey: Prentice-Hall.

McGUIGAN, F. J., & RODIER, W. I., III. (1968). Effects of auditory stimulation on covert oral behavior during silent reading. *Journal of Experimental Psychology, 76*, 649–655.

McGUIGAN, F. J., & WINSTEAD, JR., C. L. (1974). Discriminative relationship between covert oral behavior and the phonemic system in internal information processing. *Journal of Experimental Psychology, 103*, 885–890.

NARANJO, C., & ORNSTEIN, R. E. (1971). *On the psychology of meditation.* New York: Viking.

NORMAN, D. A., & SHALLICE, T. (1985). Attention to action: Willed and automatic control of behavior. In R. J. DAVIDSON, G. E. SCHWARTZ, & D. SHAPIRO (Eds.), *Consciousness and self-regulation: Advances in research and theory, Vol. 4.* New York: Plenum Press.

OBRIST, P. A., WEBB, R. A., & SUTTERER, J. R. (1969). Heart rate and somatic changes during aversive conditioning and a simple reaction-time task. *Psychophysiology, 5*, 696–723.

OBRIST, P.A., WEBB, R. A., SUTTERER, J.R., & HOWARD, J. L. (1970). The cardiac-somatic relationship: Some reformulations. *Psychophysiology, 6*, 569–587.

PILLSBURY, W. B. (1908). *Attention.* New York: Macmillan.

PINNEO, L. R. (1961). The effects of induced muscle tension during tracking on level of activation and on performance. *Journal of Experimental Psychology, 62*, 523–531.

POPE, K. S., & SINGER, J. L. (1978). Regulation of the stream of consciousness: Toward a theory of ongoing thought. In G. E. SCHWARTZ & D. SHAPIRO (Eds.), *Consciousness and self-regulation: Advances in research and theory. Vol. 2.* New York: Plenum Press.

RIBOT, T. A. (1889). *The psychology of attention.* New York: Humboldt.

SHAW, W. A. (1938). The distribution of muscular action potentials during imaging. *Psychological Record, 2*, 195–216.

SHIFFRIN, R. M., & SCHNEIDER, W. (1977). Controlled and automatic human information processing: II. Perceptual learning, automatic attending, and a general theory. *Psychological Review, 84*, 127–190.

SINGER, J. L. (1975). *The inner world of daydreaming.* New York: Harper & Row.

SINGER, J. L., & ANTROBUS, J. S. (1965). Eye movement during fantasies. *Archives of General Psychiatry, 12*, 71–76.

SMITH, M. O. (1969). History of the motor theories of attention. *Journal of General Psychology, 80*, 243–257.

SMITH, S. M., BROWN, H. O., TOMAN, J. E. P., & GOODMAN, L. S. (1947). The lack of cerebral effects of d-tubocurarine. *Anesthesiology, 8*, 1–14.

SPERRY, R. W. (1952). Neurology and the mind–brain problem. *American Scientist, 40*, 291–312.

STOY, E. G. (1930). A preliminary study of ocular attitudes in thinking of spatial relations. *Journal of General Psychology, 4*, 379–385.

TOTTEN, E. (1935). Eye movement during visual imagery. *Comparative Psychology Monographs, 11*, No. 3.

WALLERSTEIN, H. (1954). An electromyographic study of attentive listening. *Canadian Journal of Psychology, 8*, 228–238.

WASHBURN, M. F. (1916). *Movement and mental imagery.* New York: Houghton Mifflin.

WEIMER, W. B. (1977). A conceptual framework for cognitive psychology: Motor theories of the mind. In R. SHAW & J. BRANSFORD (Eds.), *Perceiving, acting, and knowing.* Hillsdale, NJ: Erlbaum.

3 Cardiac Afferent Influences on Consciousness

CURT A. SANDMAN

I. INTRODUCTION

The separation of reality from our experience of it has intrigued, confused, and consumed the greatest thinkers of our civilization. Philosophical treatises have been devoted to its analysis, dualistic religions have deified it, and theoretical physics has become its current harbinger. Although it is inviting to plunge impulsively into debate of the issue, instead a framework or paradigm will be erected (or resurrected) for merging mentalistic with psychobiological constructs. Within this framework the separation of reality from its experience had its most obvious expression in the posthumous "debates" of Walter Cannon and William James. The focus of these debates was the necessary ingredients of experience.

In the analysis developed by Cannon (1929), sensory input triggered a predetermined pattern of action or experience. The output of the system (effector system) was graded in terms of its magnitude or level of arousal (the "bang" theory of emotion) and was controlled solely by the central nervous system. Larger responses were assumed to relate to more intense stimuli (experiences), but qualitative differences in consciousness were not accommodated. This reflexive theory still guides most modern-day physiological studies of consciousness.

A radically different view was proposed by James (1892). He suggested that the experience of reality was a product of visceral and autonomic communication with the brain. Perception (or the experience of reality) gained meaning in the context (apperception) in which it was experienced. The peripheral nervous system, coupled with the environment, provided this context. Thus, the viscera, the muscles, and the

---

CURT A. SANDMAN ● Fairview Developmental Center, Costa Mesa, California 92626; Department of Psychiatry and Human Behavior, University of California Irvine Medical Center, Orange, California, 92668.

endocrine system provided information to the brain and thereby participated in the determination of behavior, thoughts, and consciousness. The notion that "we are afraid because we run" derives from this view. The intuitive appeal of this formulation is evident in our everyday activity. Imagine driving down a residential street when all of a sudden a small child darts in front of your car. It is likely that you immediately step on the brakes and, assuming you have missed the child, sit there and ponder your close call. All of a sudden you begin to shake, your heart beats faster, your palms become moist, and your emotional state climaxes. This scenario illustrates that often we first act and then, as the consequences of physiological and psychological action become "conscious," we experience an emotion.

A. Consciousness as Cognition and Emotion (Brain and Body)

Stimulated by the work of Lazarus (1966; Lazarus, Speisman, Mordkoff, & Davidson, 1962, 1966) indicating predictable relationships between the focus of attention and emotion, evidence secured in my laboratory (Sandman, 1971, 1975) suggested that the views of both Cannon and James have merit. Physiological and behavioral responses to stressful, neutral, and pleasant stimuli in subjects with distinctive perceptual or attentional styles were compared. One group, the field-independent subjects, use visceral or bodily information more readily than others and are able to make accurate judgments about the environment even though they may be presented with distracting perceptual information. They evidence qualitative differences in physiological response profiles and apparently enjoy richer emotional existence. Further, they provide more accurate information about their physiological state. The second group, field-dependent subjects, base their perceptual judgments primarily upon external information. Since they utilize environmental, rather than internal, information to assess their emotional or conscious state, they can be misled by nonveridical or distracting environmental stimulation. They tend to have minimal emotional complexity and may respond to stimuli with differing degrees of arousal (Witkin, Dyk, Fattuson, Goodenough, & Karp, 1962).

In my studies (Sandman, 1971, 1975), these two groups of subjects responded differently to the emotionally charged stimuli. Specifically, field-independent subjects displayed different profiles of physiological responses to the different classes of stimuli. Further, they provided more accurate self-reports about their physiological state and evidenced remarkable concordance between how they said they felt, the length of time they viewed the stimulus, and their physiological profiles. Field-dependent persons failed to exhibit different patterns of physiological responses to the affective stimuli and responded with differing degrees of arousal. Moreover, there was no relationship among their physiological responses, their ratings of the stimuli, and their viewing time.

These data indicated that perceptual or attentional style influenced emotional experience or consciousness. The field-independent subjects, with easy access to visceral and autonomic input, responded to environmental stress as predicted by James. The field-dependent group, with limited access to peripheral information and greater reliance upon environmental cues, evidenced a pattern of response characterized by arousal as predicted by Cannon. It is conceivable that these two pervasive theories of consciousness simply describe two distinctive cognitive or perceptual strategies partially reflected by field dependence or independence. Of greatest interest, and a theme developed in this chapter, was the subsequent finding that cognitive strategy, perhaps the "guide" to consciousness, could be modified by learned control of the peripheral nervous system (McCanne & Sandman, 1976). Lest these speculations be viewed as fanciful, the following is a brief review of the mechanisms underlying the interaction of the peripheral nervous system (specifically the cardiovascular system) with the central nervous system.

II. Cardiovascular and Baroreceptor Physiology

The existence of pressure-sensitive receptors (baroreceptors) in the carotid sinus and aortic arch is well established. Nerves from the carotid sinus and aortic arch join the vagus and the glossopharyngeal nerves, terminate in the lower brainstem, and assist in providing homeostatic control of blood pressure to ensure survival of the organism. The baroreceptors increase their firing rates during transient blood pressure increases and decrease their rate of discharge as blood pressure falls. Studies with spontaneous hypertensive rats indicated that the central nervous system was responsible for setting the operational pressure-sensitive range for the baroreceptors (Judy & Farnell, 1979). Participation of the central nervous system in this homeostatic process complements the role of the cardiovascular system.

However, the baroreceptors have functions in addition to those classified as homeostatic (see Figure 1). In 1929 Tournade and Malmejac found that stimulation of the carotid sinus nerve diminished muscle tone in anesthetized animals. Shortly thereafter, Koch (1932) found that increased pressure in the carotid sinus of a dog led to decreased motor activity and even prolonged sleep. These two reports were among the first to suggest that baroreceptor activity influenced higher levels of the

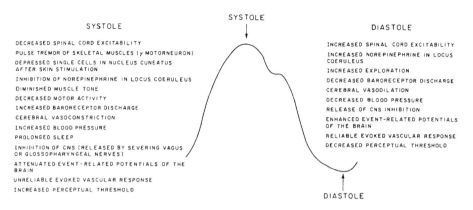

FIGURE 1. Relationships of physiological, biochemical, electrophysiological, and behavioral phenomena with phase (systole/diastole) of carotid pulse-pressure gradient.

nervous system than those needed to maintain cardiovascular homeostasis and that these influences were inhibitory rather than excitatory.

In an ingenious study, Bonvallet, Dell, and Hiebel (1954) distended the carotid sinus of cats and produced an experimental analog of increased pressure. They discovered that increased pressure shifted electrocortical activity from low-voltage fast activity to high-voltage slow activity. Thus, when the baroreceptors in the wall of the carotid sinus detected increased pressure, the electrocortical activity was inhibited. Decreased blood pressure released the cortex from this inhibitory influence. Indeed, Bonvallet *et al.* (1954) discovered that if one severed the vagus and glossopharyngeal nerves the inhibitory influence dissipated.

More recent experiments have demonstrated significant baroreceptor input to areas of the brain remote from those previously associated with cardiovascular control. In fact, contemporary cardiovascular physiologists have suggested that the "vasomotor center" be expanded to include a number of areas superior to the brainstem (Joy, 1975). In an investigation of baroreceptor input to the hypothalamus, Adair and Manning (1975) illustrated the importance of these supramedullary connections by recording evoked potentials in the posterior hypothalamus as early as 10 msec following stimulation of the carotid sinus. Moreover, when these hypothalamic areas were stimulated, a 65% reduction in single-unit firing occurred in medullary neurons responsive to baroreceptor activation. Thus, even before reaching the vasomotor center, baroreceptor activity was detected by the hypothalamus and subsequently channeled to a number of supramedullary structures.

One supramedullary structure which is responsive to vasomotor activity is the locus coeruleus. A series of dramatic studies by Svensson (Svensson & Thoren, 1979; Persson & Svensson, 1981) indicated that peripheral blood volume receptors participated in control of norepinephrine (NE) in the locus coeruleus (LC) and in behavior. Blood was withdrawn (experimental hemorrhage) or fresh blood loaded into conscious rats. After blood loading (increased pressure) behavioral depression and inhibition of NE and neuronal firing rate was observed in the LC. Conversely, hemorrhage resulted in increased exploration and activation of NE and firing rate in the LC. Earlier, Coleridge, Coleridge, and Rosenthal (1976) found that distension of the carotid sinus caused prolonged depression of activity of pyramidal tract cells in the motor cortex. This depression ranged from a 15% reduction in firing to complete cessation of activity and lasted approximately 85 sec after the distension ceased. Similarly, human spinal cord excitability has been shown to vary directly with the cardiac pulse. Forster and Stone (1976) demonstrated that the "physiological tremor" of normal skeletal muscles was a function of cardiovascular modulation, presumably through y-motorneurons. These authors speculated that the rising phase of systolic pressure might alter neuronal excitability by a piezoelectric effect on motor neuron membrane. They offered an equally intriguing alternative possibility that neuronal firing rate changes were a function of microcirculatory, oxygen—carbon dioxide tension during the cardiac cycle.

Sensory processes also are influenced by baroreceptor activity. Gahery and Vigier (1974) showed that stimulation of baroreceptor afferents depressed the responses of single cells in the nucleus cuneatus after stimulation of the skin. These data emphasized that baroreceptors play an important role in sensory and motor functions as well as in the control of blood pressure.

Thus, neurophysiological evidence suggested that increased blood pressure detected by baroreceptors were transmitted through the vagus and the glossopharyngeal nerves to the area of the brainstem maintaining homeostasis and to other areas which may serve to inhibit cortical, autonomic (except cardiovascular), and muscular activity. Accordingly, increased blood pressure was part of an inhibitory or restraining process rather than an activating process. Conversely, decreased blood pressure released this inhibition, resulting in lowering of sensory thresholds and prolongation of stimulus impact.

The importance of the cortical inhibitory influence of the baroreceptors may have adaptive significance for the organism. For instance, the heart and even the baroreceptors (Obrist, Light, McCubbin, Hutcheson, & Hoffer, 1979) respond to environmental stimulation. These changes are detected in bulbar structures of the brain. Thus, cardiovascular responses to external events generate a direct inhibitory influence on the central nervous system. Further, cells firing with a cardiac rhythm have been recorded in the bulbar areas (Humphrey, 1967; Smith & Pearce, 1961), and coagulation in this region prolonged the effects of a stimulus. J. I. Lacey (1967) has suggested that the functions of this area, rich with cardiovascular representation, may be to "control the duration of an episode of stimulus produced in the brain" (p. 27).

The complexities and problems associated with this explanation have not gone unrecognized (Lacey & Lacey, 1970). One problem arises as a result of the fact that the carotid sinus is not purely passive. It has its own properties, and Peterson (1962) has shown that the stiffness of the carotid sinus wall, one determinant of baroreceptor sensitivity, is affected by acetylcholine and norepinephrine. It seems clear that other nervous system activity may alter the stiffness of the wall and the sensitivity of the baroreceptors. Thus, the inhibition thought to be determined solely by baroreceptor activity may be determined in part by other activity of the nervous system affecting the wall of the carotid sinus.

It is not surprising, therefore, that inhibitory effects do not occur every time blood pressure increases. It is clear that other processes modify the cardiovascular—central nervous system relationship. Exercise, for example, will not necessarily lead to inhibitory effects on the organism. The inhibition is subject to modification by higher levels of the central nervous system, not only from the level of the wall of the carotid sinus itself to the area of the brain it ultimately reaches, but also from the area of the brain back to the effector processes where inhibition is observed.

Another limitation is the fact that there are many baroreceptors throughout the body in addition to those in the aortic arch and carotid sinus. It would be naive to assert that only those in the aortic arch and carotid sinus bear any relationship to the central nervous system and behavior. Undoubtedly, there are complex interactions at many levels of the nervous system, among various baroreceptor systems that are scattered throughout the body. For instance, recently Thompson and his colleagues (1979, 1980, 1983) have mapped rapidly responding venous afferents from femoral and brachial veins to the motor-sensory cortex of cats. Venous afferents were stimulated with 200 msec current pulses while recordings were made from the pial surface of the cortex. Stimulation of forelimb and hindlimb venous afferents resulted in unique topographic distribution of the cortical evoked response. The authors suggested that cardiovascular control may be accomplished either by very rapid response to venous pressure or anticipation of circulatory challenge. Recently (1983), these authors have used perfusion distension and mechanical stretch of femoral-saphenous vein, within physiological limits, and recorded cord dorsum potentials. Thus, unique topographic patterns in the CNS can be measured in response to cardiovascular changes distal from the carotid artery which are within physiological limits.

The temporal sequence of baroreceptor discharge poses another problem. Frequency of baroreceptor firing with changes in blood pressure may be slightly out of phase measured from different locations. Furthermore, little is reported concerning the interaction between tonic levels of blood pressure and phasic changes in blood pressure even at the level of the baroreceptors.

Finally, the significance of cerebral blood flow in this inhibitory process is unclear. When carotid baroreceptors are stimulated, there is a decrease in arterial blood pressure which may lead to a significant fall in cerebral blood flow (Purves, 1972). Diminished cerebral blood flow causes a decrease in oxygen available to the tissues, which might account for neuronal inhibition. Although the widely accepted view is that cerebral blood flow is autoregulatory and not subject to any significant neurogenic control (see Purves, 1972, for a review), there are data to indicate that cerebral vasoconstriction occurs when systemic blood pressure is raised and that this vasoconstriction is related specifically to baroreceptor activity (Ponte & Purves, 1974). Stimulus-linked response in localized pulsatile flow has been measured from the thalamus, hypothalamus, and globus pallidus (Birzis & Tachibana, 1964; Tachibana, Kuramoto, Inanaga, Ikemi, 1967). Such rapid blood flow changes probably are not the result of local regulatory mechanisms (i.e., metabolic end-products such as carbon dioxide) but may be neurally mediated events which increase or decrease the availability of essential metabolic substrates (e.g., oxygen, glucose) in anticipation of altered demands. The recent description of a cerebral evoked vascular response (Sandman, O'Halloran, and Isenhart, 1984) supports the coupling of neuronal activity and cerebral blood flow (Ingvar, 1972).

The evolving relationship among the electrical and vascular activity of the brain, the phase of the heart, and behavior is illustrated in Figure 2. Each ventricular contraction of the heart propagates a bolus of blood through the vascular system which is detected as a resonating pulse. Carotid systolic pressure begins to ascend with ventricular contraction and reaches a peak value several milliseconds later. The firing rate of the baroreceptors is related both to transient changes in pressure and heart rate, but the precise nature of their interaction is unknown. Increased pressure also corresponds to slowing or inhibitory patterns of EEG activity. With decreased pressure the inhibitory pattern is released resulting in lower voltage, faster activity. Finally, as will be discussed

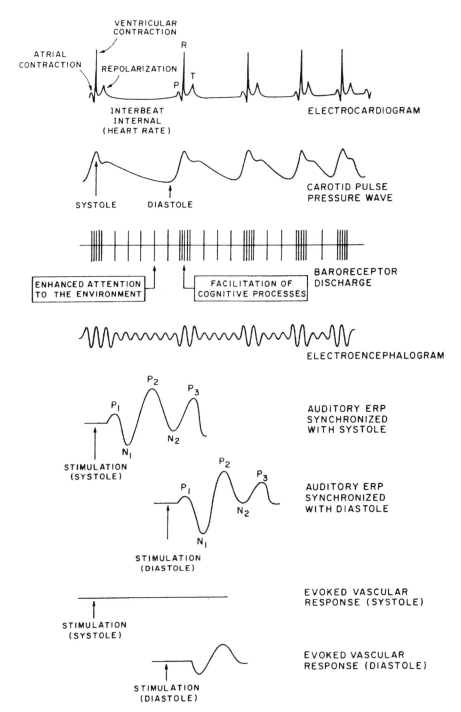

FIGURE 2. Schematized view of the relationships among the cardiovascular system, central nervous system, and behavior.

CARDIAC AFFERENT INFLUENCES ON CONSCIOUSNESS

in detail below, these patterns are coupled with unique psychological states and event-related patterns of the EEG.

III. CARDIOVASCULAR RELATIONS TO BEHAVIOR

In a series of tasks ranging from those requiring attention to the external environment (i.e., detection of flashes) to those in which attention to the environment may interfere with performance of the task (i.e., mental arithmetic) it was discovered that heart rate and blood pressure were the physiological responses which best differentiated cognitive-perceptual processes (Lacey, 1959, 1967; Lacey, Kagan, Lacey, & Moss, 1963). Heart rate decreased during tasks requiring environmental attention, whereas tasks demanding "mental concentration" or "rejection of the environment" were related with heart-rate acceleration.

Further, as discussed above, studies from our laboratory (Sandman, 1971, 1975; Walker & Sandman, 1977) and others (Hare, 1973; Libby, Lacey & Lacey, 1973) indicated that heart rate decelerated while subjects were viewing unpleasant stimuli. This response was surprising since heart rate acceleration commonly is believed to be an aspect of the overall sympathetic nervous system response to stressful stimuli. However, stressful stimuli can invoke a strong attentional demand with obvious evolutionary significance.

In a refined analysis of this issue Cacioppo and Sandman (1978) presented subjects with stressful visual stimuli (pictures of accident victims) and stimuli which were equated with the pictures of accident victims on the dimension of unpleasantness but required "cognitive effort." These latter stimuli included arithmetic problems, anagrams, and strings of digits to be memorized. Consistent with previous studies, heart rate decelerated during stressful stimuli but increased for the equally stressful stimuli which required mental effort. Thus, it appeared that heart rate reflected the type and perhaps the level of processing required by the task but did not reflect its affective components (see Table 1).

A. *Control of Body, Control of Consciousness*

Among the most exciting implications of the relationships among the brain, behavior, and the body is the possibility that specific alterations in physiology may be linked to discrete changes in behavior. Several studies conducted in our laboratory provided support for this possibility. The first two studies (McCanne & Sandman, 1974, 1976) indicated that perceptual threshold and selectivity of externally directed

TABLE 1
Relationships Between Heart Rate and the Brain and Behavior

Lowered heart rate	Elevated heart rate
Slower reaction time in cognitive task	Faster reaction time in cognitive task
Faster reaction time in attentional task	Slower reaction time in attentional task
Decreased perceptual threshold	Increased perceptual threshold
Enhanced ERP	Attenuated ERP
Lower resistance to persuasion	Greater resistance to persuasion

attention could be enhanced when subjects learned to decelerate their hearts. These somewhat straightforward findings were explored in a third study (Cacioppo, Sandman, & Walker, 1978).

One of the implications of narrowed external attention, related to controlled deceleration, may be the sacrifice of reflection and judgment. This possibility was investigated in a study of the influence of learned heart rate control on resistence to persuasion. Resistence to persuasion is, in part, a function of the number of counterarguments subjects can generate to rebut an issue. Evidence indicates that the greater the number of reasons (counterarguments) subjects develop to reject a message, the less likely it is that they will be persuaded by the message (Petty & Cacioppo, 1977). We reasoned that increases in heart rate would enhance cognitive processing. Accordingly, increased heart rate should result in more counterarguments and lowered susceptibility to persuasion. Conversely, subjects may become more susceptible to persuasion during lowered heart rate as their ability to process information is compromised. Thus, control of heart rate could influence attitudes.

As predicted, during cardiac acceleration subjects generated more counterarguments and were less willing to endorse the persuasive message. However, during reinforced heart rate deceleration, subjects provided fewer counterarguments and were much more susceptible to persuasion. Thus, during high heart rate, cognitive elaboration may be facilitated and self-convincing arguments can be generated against a persuasive message. However, during lowered heart rate our cognitive functioning may give way to environmental attention and the demands of the environment prevail. These studies and others, most notably those from David Shapiro's laboratory (see Shapiro & Reeves, 1982), suggested that influences on the brain and behavior may be exerted by controlling the body.

The successful clinical application of this "Clockwork Orange" possibility was reported with a case of a child-molestor (Nolan & Sandman, 1978). This behavioral aberration (pedophilia) has remained immune from most forms of treatment and the consequences both for the patient and society justify a radical approach. We introduced the method "biosyntonic therapy" to consider jointly the synchrony among physiological systems and the correspondence between thoughts or attitudes and the physical state of the organism. That is, we were concerned with the syntony among verbal (mental), physiological, and gross behavioral aspects of the human experience. A major assumption of our approach was that attitudes, emotions, and behavior were intimately related to physiological state. From this perspective, the work of the therapist was carefully to identify (diagnose) the physiological state of the individual in specific situations before attempting to intervene. Once the relationship between mental and physical activity was observed in nonproblem areas, then the problem areas were searched for evidence of disharmony. The goal was to target physiological systems in the problem area that appeared disparate with the patterns of responses in the more normal areas of the client's life. Once diagnosed, the biosyntonic position implies that if the physiological pattern changes, a change in attitude, emotions, or overt behavior will follow.

Mr. J., a 32-year-old blue-collar worker, had a history of numerous sexual experiences with children (nearly all females) dating from his teens. Fearful of the personal and legal consequences of the discovery of his experiences with a female child, he consented to the procedures described below as a last resort. Traditional approaches had been tried without success.

Preliminary diagnostic information indicated extreme sexual attraction for prepubescent females, although Mr. J. maintained an adequate sexual relationship with his wife. An extensive pretreatment physiological assessment was conducted by attaching electrodes for the measurement of heart rate, peripheral vasomotor activity, respiration, and skin potential. Mr. J. reclined in a comfortable chair and viewed a standard sequence (Sandman, 1975) of pictures presented on a screen in front of him. The series included sexually arousing, neutral, and highly distressing (e.g., mutilated corpses) slides. He rated each of them on a pleasure—stress scale while a physiological recording was done.

Mr. J. exhibited differential physiological responses to pleasurable, neutral, and unpleasurable stimuli only in heart rate. We focused on heart rate in a discriminate conditioning paradigm used throughout 16 sessions; the conditioning was designed to alter his physiological responses to female children without disrupting his responses to adult females.

Initially, four sets (male and female adults and male and female children) of six stimuli each were chosen. Mr. J. was asked to bring in pictures of preadolescent girls that he found arousing to varying degrees. Prevalent among the most arousing stimuli were pictures taken from mail-order catalogues of girls modeling underwear. Upon request he also brought comparable pictures of preadolescent boys, though he claimed that none of these were highly arousing. He selected adult male and female stimuli from a group of slides available at the treatment center. Mr. J. rated the stimuli in each of the four sets in terms of his perceived sexual arousal to them. Ratings were based on the 9-point pleasure–stress scale described earlier.

The most striking feature of his physiological response pattern was the extremely elevated heart rate response to the pictures of the semi-clothed female children. However, unlike his response to nude adult females, his verbal report of arousal to the slides of children was not consistent with his physiological response to them. Neither his verbal nor his physiological responses suggested arousal to male children or male adults. Therapy was therefore designed to accomplish both the reduction of the inappropriate arousal to female children and improvement of the congruity between the patient's verbal and physiological responses to such children.

Treatment was conducted in three phases. In phase 1, aversive stimulation (4–6 mA shock) was delivered each time Mr. J.'s heart rate exceeded a criterion in response to pictures of young girls. After several sessions, a significant reduction in heart rate was observed. Further, Mr. J. reported that during his daily activities he felt a sharp pain in his index finger (where shock was applied) aborting his "automatic arousal" to young girls he encountered. New, provocative stimuli were introduced and elements of Mr. J.'s response reemerged.

In phase 2, a more powerful approach was initiated. In addition to punishment for increased heart rate during exposure to young girls, positive reinforcement (monetary incentive) was provided for heart rate increases to pictures of adult women. This approach was successful, but the potential contamination and lack of generalizability of aversive procedures dictated phase 3. In this final phase, positive reinforcement remained contingent upon heart rate acceleration to adult females and was also presented for inhibition of acceleration to pictures of young girls. This procedure produced robust discrimination and was continued for several sessions after which therapy was terminated.

Six months after treatment ended, Mr. J. reported that he had not experienced any incidents of child molesting. He remarked that when he was in a situation formerly considered provocative, he still experienced some pain in his index finger. Of more importance, he consciously avoided compromising situations, indicating that he was able to control his behavior much more efficiently than before. It was of interest to learn

CARDIAC AFFERENT INFLUENCES ON CONSCIOUSNESS 67

that Mr. J. attended X-rated moves at a far higher rate than he had before therapy. Thus, a socially condoned activity had apparently replaced his psychopathic and deviant behavior.

This report indicates that processes ascribed to the brain, thoughts, attitudes, and behavior, can be accessed by control of the body. The three experiments from our laboratory, the case report, and the growing body of biofeedback research and treatment indicate that consciousness has many components, one of which is the interaction between the brain and the body.

B. Effects on Consciousness of Transient Changes in the Cardiovascular System

In addition to the purely correlative studies and to those relating control of physiological systems to behavior, there has been a series of reports of changes in awareness or perception synchronized with the naturally occurring rhythms of the body. As reviewed earlier, similar baroreceptor discharge occurs during changes in heart rate and pulsatile pressure waves, both of these mechanisms cooperate in providing homeostatic control of blood pressure and may exert similar influences on behavior. Even though the Laceys (1967, 1970, 1974) and others (Birren, Cardon, & Phillips, 1963; Callaway & Layne, 1964; Saari & Pappas, 1976) reported that attention was enhanced when stimuli were synchronized with each component (i.e., the P wave) of the EKG, other investigators (Delfini & Campos, 1972; Elliot & Graf, 1972; Thompson & Botwinick, 1970) have not found a significant relationship between these transient events and behavior. In an attempt to unravel the differences among these studies and to provide a link with our studies of heart rate, we (Sandman, McCanne, Kaiser, & Diamond, 1977) constructed a paradigm (see Figure 3) in which tachistoscopic stimuli were synchronized with the P, R, and T wave of the EKG or with decelerating, midrange, and accelerating heart rate.

As summarized in Table 1, we discovered that stimuli presented during the P wave or during decelerating heart rate were perceived more accurately than stimuli presented during the T wave or during accelerating heart rate. In a second study (Sandman, Walker, & Berka, 1982) subjects were shown either a circle or a square synchronized with cardiovascular events and instructed to depress a telegraphic key when the circle appeared. In this case, with a decisional paradigm, we expected that cognitive processes would be facilitated with accelerating heart rate.

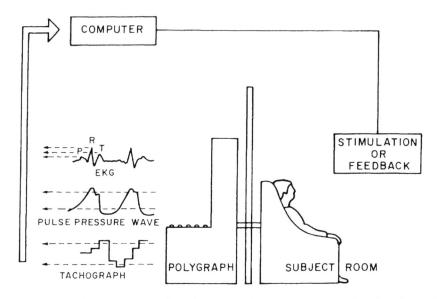

FIGURE 3. Paradigm used in studies of transient changes in heart rate, interbeat interval, and pulse-pressure phase on the brain and behavior.

The findings indicated that during accelerating heart rate, reaction time decreased (thus decision making was facilitated) and, conversely, during decelerating heart rate, reaction time slowed. However, contrary to our studies of stimulus detection, there was no corresponding influence of the cardiac cycle on choice reaction time. These differences may be due to (1) the imperfect coupling of heart rate and cardiac phase influences on the brain (2) the comparative insensitivity of reaction time compared with stimulus detection or (3) the robust influence of heart rate compared with the seemingly delicate impact of events during the cardiac cycle.

In any case, a significant array of evidence has accrued linking behavior to the cardiovascular system. In addition to the data reviewed above, other evidence from our laboratories (Cacioppo & Sandman, 1978; Kaiser & Sandman, 1975; Sandman & Walker, 1985; Walker & Sandman, 1977), as well as volumes dedicated to this subject (Cacioppo & Petty, 1982; Obrist, Black, Brener, & DiCara, 1974) attest to the growing acceptance and importance of these observations. These data are increasingly difficult to reconcile with classical views ascribing all attributes of consciousness to the brain and require that we reevaluate the mind–body debate. However, despite the overwhelming evidence of the influence of the cardiovascular system on behavior very few experimental studies have investigated the impact of the heart on the brain.

IV. Influence of Cardiovascular System on the Brain

A. The EEG

The relationship of the cardiovascular system to the electrical activity of the brain in human subjects has been well documented. The early report of Obrist and Bissell (1955) suggested that changes in posture compromised cerebral blood flow and was reflected in the EEG. The studies of Ingvar (1972) extended these principles and demonstrated that increased perfusion was related to increased arousal of EEG patterns. The early studies of Callaway (Callaway & Buchsbaum, 1965; Callaway & Layne, 1964) demonstrated synchronous relations between the ventricular contractions of the heart and the "ascending" wave of the alpha rhythm. More recently a fascinating influence of cardiovascular disease on the brain has been reported. Sotaniemi (1980) observed 100 consecutive righthanded patients referred for valvular replacement surgery. Preoperatively, neurological and EEG findings were significantly more frequent in the left hemisphere. However, postoperatively the right hemisphere was compromised significantly more frequently.

B. Visual Event–Related Potentials

In order to probe the influence of the heart on the brain, we (Walker & Sandman, 1979) studied event–related potentials (ERPs) of the brain. The ERP is electrical activity recorded from the scalp which is time-locked to a specific stimulus. In order to obtain an evoked response, flashes of light, brief tones, or electrical shock are delivered to subjects while the electroencephalogram (EEG) is measured. The electrocortical responses to each stimulus are summed and the activity which is not related to the stimulus is random and equals approximately zero. The components of the wave which are evoked by the stimulus are then clearly identifiable against this background. The form of the ERPs recorded in our laboratory are presented in Figure 4. Different components have been associated with discrete behaviors. The early aspect of the wave, the primary response, is related to the dimension of the stimulus and is usually unchanged by psychological or physiological interventions. The secondary components (occurring approximately 100 and 200 msec after the stimulus) are sensitive to changes in attention and perception. Larger $P1$ and $P2$ waves are usually related to improved attentional or perceptual processing. The waves occurring approximately 300 msec after the stimulus are termed endogenous because they are related to complex cognitive activity and not the physical characteristics of the stimulus.

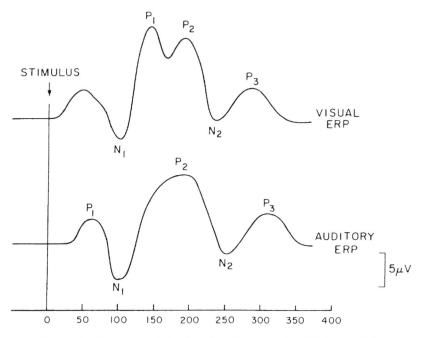

FIGURE 4. Examples of visual and auditory event–related potentials.

In our first experiment (Walker & Sandman, 1979) brief flashes of light were presented to the subject during fast, slow, and midrange heart rates (as in earlier experiments, Figure 3), while ERPs were recorded from the right and left hemispheres of the brain. This paradigm relates most directly to changes in early exogeneous components since the subjects were not required to think or make any behavioral response.

The results indicated that the heart exerted dramatic influences on the ERPs of the right but not the left hemisphere (Figure 5). Furthermore, the amplitudes of $P1$ and $P2$ were larger when flashes of light were synchronized with low heart rate than with high heart rate. Although it may be peculiar to the paradigm we used, it was apparent that the influence of the heart on the brain was lateralized.

As discussed earlier, each ventricular pulse of the heart sends a bolus of blood rushing through the arteries. The bolus of blood is received as a transient shift in pressure and is reflected as a pulse pressure wave. At the peak of the wave (systolic pressure), pressure is the greatest and the baroreceptors increase their firing rate. During the lowest point of the wave (diastolic pressure) the baroreceptors are relatively quiescent. Since pulse pressure is intricately tied to the pumping action of the heart, systolic and diastolic pressure coincide with electrical com-

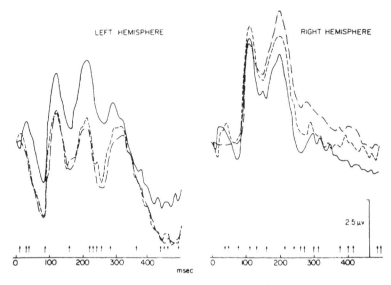

FIGURE 5. Event-related potentials recorded from the left and right hemisphere of the brain when visual stimulation was synchronized with accelerating and decelerating heart rate. Arrows indicate points of statistical preparation as determined by stepwise discriminant function analysis. Key: (---) high heart rate; (-·-) midrange heart rate; (——) low heart rate.

ponents of the electrocardiogram (ECG). From Figure 2 it is apparent that diastolic pressure coincides with the early components of the EEG (P wave) and systolic pressure coincides with the T wave. Therefore, as with the earlier studies (Sandman et al., 1977; 1982) the influence of transient changes in pulse pressure on the ERP was measured. Since similar (but not identical) pressure changes are detected by the baroreceptor during low heart rate and diastolic pressure and during high heart rate and systolic pressure, similar influences on the brain were expected in this study as with the study of heart rate. We reasoned that the effects of pulse pressure changes on the brain were "time-locked" and displacement of stimulation in time may alter the impact of the heart on the brain. Therefore, flashes of light were synchronized with changes in pulses in the brain (occurring approximately 30 msec after carotid pulse changes) and the finger (occurring approximately 180 msec after carotid pressure changes; Walker & Sandman, 1982).

ERPs synchronized with the diastolic phase of the pulse pressure waves recorded from the carotid and cephalic placements were differentiated only in the right hemisphere (Figure 6). Components occurring 200-300 msec after stimulation were enhanced when synchronized with diastole. However, the major effect of stimulus synchronization with

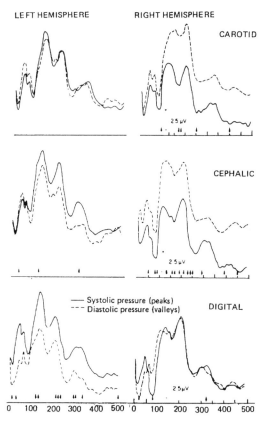

FIGURE 6. Event-related potentials to visual stimuli synchronized with systole and diastole records from the carotid, opthalmic, and digital arteries.

digital placements was observed in the left hemisphere, and augmentation of the ERP occurred during the systolic pulse. The finding that the ERP was altered when stimuli were presented at different phases of the cardiac cycle argued for the importance of the temporal relations between cardiovascular events and the brain. Cardiovascular changes detected by pressure receptors in the carotid artery, and possibly the vasculature of the brain, sensitized the brain to environmental stimulation within very narrow time limits. Further, with the paradigm employed, this sensitization was lateralized in the right hemisphere of the brain during stimulation synchronized with diastole. This effect shifted to the left hemisphere when stimuli were triggered by systole in distal placements.

The heart rate and pulse pressure wave experiments suggested similar effects of these interdependent cardiovascular processes on the

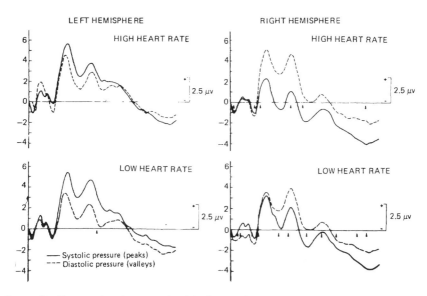

FIGURE 7. Event-related potentials of the brain when visual stimulation was synchronized with changes in heart rate and pulse pressure phase.

brain. For instance, stimulation during both lowered heart rate and diastole resulted in amplification of early components of the ERP. Further, the major influence of these cardiovascular events was unique to the right hemisphere of brain. The remarkable similarity between the findings of the heart rate and pulse pressure experiments prompted a third experiment (Walker & Sandman, 1982), to examine the effects on the ERP of the interaction between heart rate and pulse pressure waves. This experiment was identical to the previous experiments except that presentation of the stimulus was contingent upon changes of heart rate and the pulse pressure wave.

As in the previous experiments, the major effects of stimuli synchronized with heart rate and pulse pressure changes were observed in the right hemisphere of the brain (Figure 7). Only during accelerating heart rate, in the right hemisphere, was the difference between systole and diastole reflected in the ERP. The most significant difference among components during accelerating heart rate was enhancement of *P1* during stimuli synchronized with diastole. A similar, but not significant, trend was apparent during low heart rate.

The results of this study indicated that complex relations exist between heart rate and the pulse pressure wave. These components do not appear to be simply additive. Indeed, if they were additive, the ERP would be maximal for stimuli synchronized with diastole and low heart rate. This was not found. Instead, suppression of the ERP was observed during high heart rate and systole (although only in the right hemisphere). The major finding (that maximal separation of systole and diastole was observed only during elevated heart rate) suggested that during elevated heart rate, maximal (or near maximal) activity of the baroreceptors is achieved during each beat of the heart (Sandman *et al.*, 1982). It is possible that this barrage "exhausts" the cells temporarily, resulting in significant quiescence during diastole. Thus, the greatest contrast between systole and diastole may be during elevated heart rate.

The lateralized influence of stimuli synchronized with diastole or systole may not be surprising. For instance, there is evidence that simple attentional tasks selectively impact the right hemisphere and as the complexity of the task increases the left hemisphere is engaged (Dustman, Schenkenberg, & Beck, 1976; Jutai, 1984). Similarly, the early components of the ERP reflect exogenous or stimulus-related dimensions, whereas the later components are thought to be excited by increasing the work load (Donchin, 1979). This complementary relationship also pertains to the cardiovascular system since acceptance of the environment (attention) is related to lowered heart rate or diastolic components of pulse pressure waves and cognitive processing is facilitated by increases in heart rate or during systole. Consistent with these independent observations, our findings indicate that during simple tasks the early components of the ERP are enhanced in the right hemisphere when stimuli are synchronized with the diastolic phase of the pulse pressure wave. As the task demands are increased, later components of the ERP are augmented in the left hemisphere when stimuli are synchronized with systole.

Rogers, Battit, McPeek, and Todd (1978) provided dramatic physiological evidence of the lateralization of cardiac control. Stellate ganglion blocks of 17 patients indicated that the right stellate ganglion had a much greater influence on heart rate than does the left stellate ganglion. Further, since the cerebral blood vessels are innervated by adrenergic fibers originating in superior cervical and stellate ganglion (Purves, 1978), a lateralized influence may be favored. Coupled with the report of Sotaniemi (1980), already discussed and the findings of Carmon and Gombus (1970) that blood from the heart reaches the right carotid faster than the left, these findings provide a plausible (but untested) explanation for the findings of lateralized influence of the heart on the electrical activity of the brain.

C. *Auditory Event–Related Potentials*

In a recent study (Sandman, 1984) with a design identical to that of the previous studies of the visual evoked potential, auditory evoked

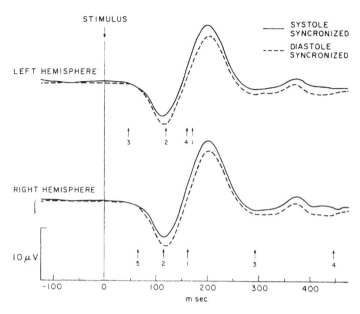

FIGURE 8. Auditory event–related potentials of the brain synchronized with pulse pressure phase.

responses were collected during stimuli synchronized with systolic and diastolic phases of the cerebral pulse pressure wave. Furthermore, attentional demands were assessed by comparing a passive condition with a condition in which subjects counted and reported the number of stimuli they detected. The EEG was measured from C3 and C4 referenced to linked mastoids. Stimuli presented during the diastolic phase of the pulse pressure wave elicited a significantly larger N1 component of the ERP than presentations during systole (Figure 8), a finding which was perfectly consistent with the results for the visual event–related potential.

The subjects were divided into correct and incorrect responders based upon the accuracy of their report. Presumably, subjects who reported accurately were more attentive than subjects who offered incorrect responses. This analysis confirmed that N1 was augmented in correct responders and during diastole. However, stimuli synchronized with systole resulted in a larger N2 component than stimuli synchronized with diastole. Further, a complex interaction indicated that N2 was generally suppressed in the right hemisphere of accurate responders when stimuli were synchronized with diastole.

As reviewed by Picton and Hillyard (1974) and Picton, Hillyard, Krausz, and Galambos (1974), the N1 and P2 components of the auditory

ERP reflected selectivity of attention. Although Picton and Hillyard did not differentiate $N1$ from $P2$, and indeed suggested that they accrued from similar neural assemblies, the results of the current study suggested that they may reflect subtly different processes. For instance, robust changes were seen in $N1$ but not $P2$ when stimuli were synchronized with different phases of the pulse pressure wave. Consistent with their impression was the recent report of Hansen and Hillyard (1983) indicating a protracted negativity (Nd) beginning at $N1$ and continuing for several hundred msec associated with selective attention and cognitive processing.

Although the suppression of $N2$ in accurate responders was consistent with the analysis made by Picton et al., (1974), the significance of cardiac phase on $N2$ in the left hemisphere in the subjects who reported accurately was not immediately obvious. These investigators suggested that $N2$ is influenced by the subject's state of alertness, such that it was attenuated in alert subjects compared with subjects who were drowsy. As such, suppression of $N2$ may represent cortical activation. Thus, attentive subjects evidenced a cortical index of activation for stimuli synchronized with diastole. The suppression of the $N2$ component in the right hemisphere during diastole complemented the findings of enhanced early components in the right hemisphere. It is remarkable that ERP components thought to be related to dimensions of consciousness were altered by internal events in such a consistent manner. These findings lend further support to the proposal that a continuum of consciousness may be regulated by covariation of the cardiovascular system and the brain.

These data suggest that awareness of the environment is partially regulated by the interactions of the brain and the heart. Although it is probable that many visceral and somatic systems "tune" the brain through their afferent pathways, the results of the present study provide direct information of this tuning by the cardiovascular system. One speculative conclusion implied by these findings is that a modest portion of environmental awareness or attention is "hard-wired." For instance, with a task chosen purposefully for its simplicity, a reliable influence on the ERP was observed. Even when attentional demands were imposed, or in subjects who either were attentive or inattentive, the same effect on the ERP was evident. Thus, a portion of the variance (10–20% based on the present data) relating to attention (Sandman et al., 1977), or to the components of the ERP, may be accounted for by peripheral physiological systems (or any background activity) which may be inviolably linked to the brain.

Another speculative conclusion derived from these data is that there are optimal physiological "windows" for enhancing perception or attention and that these windows are cyclic. Certainly, the data from the present study and others (Sandman et al., 1977; Saari & Pappas, 1976; Birren et al., 1963; Walker & Sandman, 1979, 1982) indicated that there are precise periods during the cardiac cycle or the carotid pressure gradient that optimize perception and the impact of stimulation on the brain. It is conceivable that the window of optimal performance is the result of either fortuitous or purposeful synchrony among physiological systems. Although resolution of this cause-and-effect question must be deferred, the findings clearly indicate that there are cyclic physiological states which modulate the impact of external stimuli.

D. Evoked Vascular Responses (EVRs)

Data reviewed earlier indicated that changes in the cerebral vasculature covary with electrical activity recorded from the scalp. Klivington and Galambos (1967) estimated that blood contributes 10% to the conductivity of the cortex. This estimate agrees with the 10–20% augmentation observed in our studies of cardiovascular phase influences on the ERP. Increasingly sophisticated studies indicate predictable relationships between cerebral flow or metabolic activity and behavior. For instance, Willison et al. (1980) reported that patients with elevated venous hematocrit (VH) do poorly on simple tests of alertness. When the VH was lowered in these same subjects, performance improved. Since elevated VH relates to increased blood viscosity, decreased cerebral blood flow (CBF) results (confirmed by Xenon-133 inhalation).

With a more invasive procedure, LeDoux et al. (1983) mapped metabolically active (increased blood flow) areas of the rat brain. Using a rapid index (146-iodoantidyrine metabolized in 30–40 seconds compared with 30–45 minutes for 2-deoxy-D-glucose required with positron emission tomography), these authors reported changes in brain structures associated with primary processing of stimuli as well as areas reflecting conditioned emotional responses. Thus, discrete and significant changes in brain metabolism occur during processing of environmental events. The relationship of these changes to the ERP was investigated in our laboratory (Sandman et al., 1984) with the rheoencephalogram (REG; an impedance-based measure of blood volume). Phasic changes in blood volume elicited by auditory stimulation were measured with the REG and adapted to our ERP procedures. The pulse pressure wave from the REG was averaged in response to auditory stimuli and compared with the pulse-pressure wave occurring just prior to the stimulus. These two values were subtracted on a trial-by-trial basis resulting in a wave representing the stimulus-induced response (Figure 9).

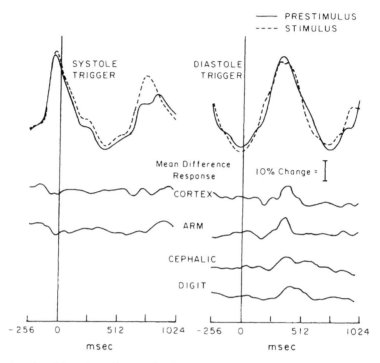

FIGURE 9. Top: Wave form from individual subject indicating prestimulus and stimulus waves. Bottom: Averaged difference waves for stimuli synchronized with systole and diastole.

During diastole four temporally adjacent factors of the REG were identified by principal component analysis. The first factor (which accounted for the most variance) comprised the sampling epoch between 300 and 540 msec. The second (40 to 100 msec), third (100 to 200 msec) and fourth (200 to 300 msec) factors completed the description of the wave form. These factors are consistent with the average of the individual subject waves (Figure 10). The factor structure was not interpretable for waves evoked during systole. Thus, the evoked vascular response (EVR) can be characterized by factor analytic procedures when synchronized with diastole but not with systole.

This is the first report of evoked changes in a measure of the cerebral vasculature from conscious human subjects. The EVR was evident only when stimulation was synchronized with the diastolic phase of the ophthalmic artery. Its latency defies the time course of previously described vascular changes in response to altered metabolic activity. Thus,

VASCULAR EVOKED RESPONSE

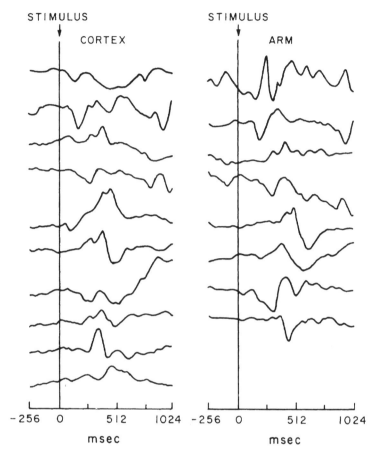

FIGURE 10. Average difference bioimpedance waveforms in cortex ($N = 10$) and arm ($N = 8$). Only diastole synchronized waves are presented.

this response may be a neurogenically mediated vascular event in preparation for altered metabolic demand.

Enhancement of the EVR during diastole is consistent with our previous reports and indicates that rapid changes in blood volume occur according to a similar schedule and of similar proportion to the ERP. The temporal similarities between response of the cerebral vasculature and the electrical response of the brain may suggest common generating mechanisms. For instance, decreased baroreceptor activity (as during diastole) is associated both with increased cerebral blood flow and release from neuronal inhibition. The EVR may prove to be a neurally mediated phenomenon that not only yields clinically relevant information regarding the integrity of vasomotor systems but also may provide new information of brain metabolism related to detecting and processing external information in real time.

V. Conclusions

This program of research indicated that: (1) there are relationships between the cardiovascular system and behavior; (2) control of cardiovascular system alters behavior; (3) predictable relationships exist between the heart and the brain, and (4) one possible mechanism for heart–brain interaction is cerebrovascular dynamics. These findings provide preliminary support for the radical neo-Jamesian proposal that consciousness *is* the interaction among physiological systems. This proposal is short of the heretical views of Kennedy (1959). Kennedy proposed that synchronous brain activity was an artifact induced by the mechanical energy from the ventricular contraction of the heart (Bering, 1955). This "pulse," applied to a gelantinous mass (the brain), in a limited, closed container (the skull) initiated and sustained brain activity by means of the cerebrospinal fluid. Consciousness, or the frequency of oscillation, was related to the "consistency" of the brain and modified by the cerebral vasculature. Thus, during attention, the brain was engorged with blood, detuning the oscillators and blocking synchronous activity. This provocative proposal has not been tested thoroughly, but the studies reviewed above suggest that even transient changes in the oscillator can alter consciousness.

If, as Kennedy implies, there are rhythms in the body which are subservient to, or are driven by, other rhythms, one is left with the question, What is the basic rhythm? Rephrased, the question may become, Is consciousness ultimately regulated by the lowest common denominator? Bentov (1977) proposed five basic rhythms including undetectable (or unnoticeable) body rhythms which were kindled, entrained, or driven by the basic rhythm of the planet Earth. The rhythms we commonly suspect as the carriers of consciousness, Bentov believed, derived from these primitive sources. Supportive observations by Corner (1977) indicated that primitive activity bursts coupled with the EEG dominated the behavior of lower organisms. Corner believed these relationships were vestigial in higher nervous systems and were expressed during early ontogenesis and perhaps during states of lowered consciousness such as sleep (when muscle bursts and EEG are tightly coupled). Thus, when consciousness is lowered, patterns of ancient phylogenetic origin can be expressed.

Recent, but limited, observations in our laboratory extended this thesis. A variation of our ERP procedure is simply to turn the stimulus off and observe the relationship between the pulse pressure gradient and the electrical activity of the brain (Sandman *et al.*, 1982). In normal subjects, there was no evidence of coupling. However, in six depressed patients a striking relationship was observed between the cardiovascular system and the brain. A 9 Hz wave (alpha rhythm) was perfectly coupled with the pulse pressure wave. The ascending (positive-going) wave of the alpha rhythm was synchronized with systole and the decending wave was related to diastole. A very similar finding was reported recently by Walker and Walker (1983) for normal subjects selected for high levels of synchronous (alpha) activity.

Even though this analysis suggests that the hierarchy of consciousness may be a function of a family of rhythms, the issue may not be that obvious. The passive synchronization of physiological rhythms appears to be pathological, and as the lowest driving rhythm is achieved, consciousness follows. However, as we have shown, there are temporal windows in these rhythms which, when properly probed, raise awareness or consciousness. Further, the temporal parameters governing this process exquisitely channel the influence of the heart between liberating and suppressing the left and right hemispheres of the brain. Thus, there are active synchronicities which are adaptive and precise and which ensure optimal performance. Perhaps the task of phylogenesis and ontogenesis is decoupling the passive process. Only as the organism becomes free of primitive "rhythms" or passive synchronization will higher or optimal states be achieved. Thus, reality becomes experienced as filtered through the waves and rhythms of our potential.

REFERENCES

Adair, J. R., & Manning, J. W. (1975). Hypothalamic modulation of baroreceptor afferent unit activity. *American Journal of Physiology, 229,* 1357–1364.

Bentov, I. (1977). Micromotion of the body as a factor in the development of the nervous system. Appendix to *Stalking the wild pendulum*. New York: Dutton.

Bering, E. A. (1955). Choroid plexus and arterial pulsation of cerebral fluid. *Archives of Neurology and Psychiatry, 73,* 165–172.

Birren, J., Cardon, P., & Phillips, S. (1963). Reaction time as a function of the cardiac cycle in young adults. *Science, 140,* 195–196.

Birzis, L., & Tachibana, S. (1964) Local cerebral impedance and blood flow during sleep and arousal. *Experimental Neurology, 9,* 269.

Bonvallet, M., Dell, P., & Hiebel, G. (1954). Tonus sympathétique et activité électrique corticale. *Electroencephalography* and *Clinical Neurophysiology, 6,* 119.

Cacioppo, J. T., & Petty, R. E. (1982). *Perspectives in cardiovascular psychophysiology.* New York: Guilford Press.

CACIOPPO, J. T., & SANDMAN, C. A. (1978). Physiological differentiation of sensory and cognitive tasks as a function of warning, processing demands and reported unpleasantness. *Biological Psychology, 6*, 181–192.

CACIOPPO, J. T., SANDMAN, C. A., & WALKER, B. B. (1978). The effects of operant heart rate conditioning on cognitive elaboration and attitude change. *Psychophysiology, 15*, 330–338.

CALLAWAY, E., & BUCHSBAUM, M. (1965). Effects of cardiac and respiratory cycles on averaged visual evoked potentials. *EEG and Clinical Neurophysiology, 19*, 476–480.

CALLAWAY, E., & LAYNE, R. (1964). Interaction between the visual evoked response and two spontaneous biological rhythms: The EEG alpha cycle and the cardiac arousal cycle. *Annals of the New York Academy of Sciences, 112*, 424–431.

CANNON, W. B. (1929). *Bodily changes in pain, hunger, fear and rage: An account of recent researches into the function of emotional excitment.* New York: Appelton.

CARMON, A., & GOMBUS, G. M. (1970). A physiological vascular correlate of hand preference: Possible implications with respect to hemispheric cerebral dominance. *Neuropsychologia, 8*, 119–128.

COLERIDGE, H. M., COLERIDGE, J. C. G., & ROSENTHAL, F. (1976). Prolonged inactivation of cortical pyramidal tract neurons in cats by distension of the carotid sinus. *Journal of Physiology, 256*, 635–649.

CORNER, M. A. (1977). Sleep and the beginnings of behavior in the animal kingdom: Studies of ultradian motility cycles in early life. *Progress in Neurobiology, 8*, 279–295.

DELFINI, L., & CAMPOS, J. (1972). Signal detection and the "cardiac arousal cycle." *Psychophysiology, 9*, 484–491.

DONCHIN, E. (1979). Event-related brain potential: A tool in the study of human information processing. In H. BEGLEITER (Ed.), *Evoked brain potentials and behavior.* New York: Plenum Press, pp. 13–88.

DUSTMAN, R. E., SCHENKENBERG, T., & BECK, E. C. (1976). The development of the evoked response as diagnostic and evaluative procedure. In R. KARRER (Ed.), *Developmental psychophysiology of mental retardation.* Springfield, IL: Charles C. Thomas.

ELLIOTT, R., & GRAF, V. (1972). Visual sensitivity as a function of phase of cardiac cycle. *Psychophysiology, 9*, 357.

FORSTER, A., & STONE, T. W. (1976). Evidence for a cardiovascular modulation of central neuronal activity in man. *Experimental Neurology, 51*, 141–149.

GAHERY, Y., & VIGIER, D. (1974). Inhibitory effects in the cuneate nucleus produced by vaga-aortic afferent fibers. *Brain Research, 75*, 241–246.

HANSEN, J. C., & HILLYARD, S. A. (1983). Selective attention to multidimensional auditory stimuli. *Journal of Experimental Psychology: Human Perception and Performance, 9*, 1–19.

HARE, R. D. (1973). Orienting and defensive responses to visual stimuli. *Psychophysiology, 10*, 453–464.

HUMPHREY, D. R. (1967). Neuronal activity in the medulla oblongata of cat evoked by stimulation of the carotid sinus nerve. In P. KEZDI (Ed.), *Baroreceptors and hypertension.* New York: Pergamon Press.

INGVAR, D. H. (1972). Patterns of thought recorded in the brain. *Totus Homo, 4*, 98–103.

JAMES, W. *Psychology.* (1892). New York: Henry Holt.

JOY, M. D. (1975). The vasomotor center and its afferent pathways. *Clinical Science and Molecular Medicine, 48*, 253s–256s.

JUDY, W. V., & FARNELL, S. K. (1979). Arterial baroreceptor reflex control of sympathetic nerve activity in the spontaneously hypertensive rat. *Hypertension, 1*, 605–614.

JUTAI, J. W. (1984). Cerebral asymmetry and the psychophysiology of attention. *International Journal of Psychophysiology, 1*, 219–226.

KAISER, D. N., & SANDMAN, C. A. (1975). Physiological patterns accompanying complex problem solving during warning and nonwarning conditions. *Journal of Comparative and Physiological Psychology, 89*, 357–363.

KENNEDY, J. L. (1959). A possible artifact in electroencephalography. *Psychological Review, 66*, 347–352.

KLIVINGTON, K. A., & GALAMBOS, R. G. (1967). Resistence shifts accompanying the evoked cortical response in the cat. *Science, 157*, 211–213.

KOCH, E. (1932). Die Irradiation der pressoreceptorischen Krieslaufreflexe. *Klinische Wochenschrift, 11*, 225–227.

LACEY, B. C., & LACEY, J. I. (1974). Studies of heart rate and other bodily processes in sensorimotor behavior. In P. A. OBRIST, A. H. BLACK, J. BRENER, & L. V. DICARA (Eds.), *Cardiovascular psychophysiology.* Chicago: Aldine.

LACEY, J. I. (1959). Psychophysiological approaches to the evaluation of psychotherapeutic process and outcome. In E. A. RUBINSTEIN & M. B. PARLOFF (Eds.), *Research in psychotherapy.* Washington, DC: American Psychological Association.

LACEY, J. I. (1967). Somatic response patterning and stress: Some revisions of activation theory. In M. H. APPLEY & R. TRUMBULL (Eds.), *Psychological stress: Issues in research.* New York: Appleton.

LACEY, J. I., KAGAN, J., LACEY, B. C., & MOSS, H. (1963). The visceral level: Situational determinants and behavioral correlates of autonomic response patterns. In P. H. KNAPP (Ed.), *Expression of emotions in man.* New York: International Universities Press.

LACEY, J. I., & LACEY, B. C. (1970). Some autonomic-central nervous system interrelationships. In P. BLACK (Ed.), *Phsysiological correlates of emotion.* New York: Academic Press.

LAZARUS, R. S. (1966). *Psychological stress and the coping process.* New York: McGraw-Hill.

LAZARUS, R. S., SPEISMAN, J. C., MORDKOFF, A. M., & DAVIDSON, L. A. (1962). A laboratory study of psychological stress produced by a motion picture film. *Psychological Monograph, 76*.

LEDOUX, J. E., THOMPSON, M. D., IADECOLA, C., TUCKER, L. S., & REIS, D. J. (1983). Local cerebral blood flow increases during auditory and emotional processing in the conscious rat. *Science, 221*, 576–578.

LIBBY, W. L., LACEY, B. C., & LACEY, J. I. (1973). Pupillary and cardiac activity during visual attention. *Psychophysiology, 10*, 270.

McCANNE, T. R., & SANDMAN, C. A., (1974). Instrumental heart rate responses and visual perception: A preliminary study. *Psychophysiology, 11*, 283–287.

McCANNE, T. R., & SANDMAN, C. A. (1976). Operant autonomic conditioning and Rod-and-Frame Test performance. *Journal of Personality and Social Psychology, 34*, 821–829.

NOLAN, J. M., & SANDMAN, C. A. (1978). "Biosyntonic" therapy: Modification of an operant conditioning approach to pedophilia. *Journal of Consulting and Clinical Psychology, 46*, 1133–1140.

OBRIST, P. A., LIGHT, K. C., McCUBBIN, J. A., HUTCHESON, J. S., & HOFFER, J. L. (1979). Pulse transit time: Relationship to blood pressure and myocardial performance. *Psychophysiology, 16*, 292.

OBRIST, P. A., BLACK, A. H., BRENER, J., & DICARA, L. V. (Eds.). (1974). *Cardiovascular psychophysiology.* Chicago: Aldine.

OBRIST, W. D., & BISSELL, L. E. (1955). The electroencephalogram of aged patients with cardiac and cerebral vascular disease. *Journal of Gerontology, 10*, 315–330.

PERSSON, B., & SVENSSON, T. H. (1981). Control of behavior and brain noredrenaline neurons by peripheral blood volume receptors. *Journal of Neural Transmission, 53*, 73–82.

PETERSON, L. H. (1962). The mechanical properties of the blood vessels and hypertension. In J. G. CORT, V. FENCL, Z. HEJL, & J. JIRKA (Eds.), *The pathogenesis of essential hypertension.* Prague: State Medical Publishing House.

PETTY, R. E., & CACIOPPO, J. T. (1977). Forewarning, cognitive responding and resistance to persuasion. *Journal of Personality and Social Psychology, 35*, 645–655.

84 CURT A. SANDMAN

PICTON, T. W., & HILLYARD, S. A. (1974). Human auditory evoked potentials. II: Effects of attention. *EEG and Clinical Neurophysiology, 36*, 191–199.

PICTON, T. W., HILLYARD, S. A., KRAUSZ, H. I., & GALAMBOS, R. (1974). Human auditory evoked potentials. I: Evaluations of components. *EEG and Clinical Neurophysiology, 36*, 179–190.

PONTE, J., & PURVES, M. J. (1974). The neural control of cerebral blood vessels. In *The Physiology of the cerebral circulation*. London: Cambridge University Press.

PURVES, M. J. (1972). The neural control of cerebral blood vessels. In *The physiology of the cerebral circulation*. London: Cambridge University Press.

PURVES, J. J. (1978). Do vasomotor nerves significantly regulate cerebral blood flow. *Circulation Research, 43*, 485–493.

ROGERS, M. C., BATTIT, G., MCPEEK, B., & TODD, D. (1978). Lateralization of sympathetic control of the human sinus node: ECG changes of stellate ganglion block. *Anesthesiology, 48*, 139–141.

SAARI, M., & PAPPAS, B. (1976). Cardiac cycle and phase and movement and reaction times. *Perceptual and Motor Skills, 42*, 767–770.

SANDMAN, C. A. (1971). *Psychophysiological parameters of emotion*. Unpublished doctoral dissertation. Louisiana State University.

SANDMAN, C. A. (1975). Physiological responses during escape and non-escape from stress in field independent and field dependent subjects. *Biological Psychology, 2*, 205–216.

SANDMAN, C. A. (1984). Augmentation of the auditory event–related potential of the brain during diastole. *International Journal of Psychophysiology, 2*, 111–119.

SANDMAN, C. A., MCCANNE, T. R., KAISER, D. N., & DIAMOND, B. (1977). Heart rate and cardiac phase influences on visual perception. *Journal of Comparative and Physiological Psychology, 91*, 189–202.

SANDMAN, C. A., O'HALLORAN, J. P., & ISENHART, R. (1984). Is there an evoked vascular response? *Science, 224*, 1355–1357.

SANDMAN, C. A., WALKER, B. B. (1985). Cardiovascular relationship to attention and thinking. In V. RENTAL, S. A. CARSON, & B. R. DUNN (Eds.), *Psychobiology of reading*. New York: Pergamon Press.

SANDMAN, C. A., WALKER, B. B., & BERKA, C. (1982). Influence of afferent cardiovascular feedback on behavior and the cortical evoked potential. In J. T. CACIOPPO & R. E. PETTY (Eds.), *Perspectives in cardiovascular psychophysiology*, pp. 189–222. New York: Guilford Press.

SHAPIRO, D., & REEVES, J. L. (1982). Modification of physiological and subjective responses to stress through heart rate biofeedback. In J. T. CACIOPPO & R. E. PETTY (Eds.), *Perspectives in cardiovascular psychophysiology*. New York: Guilford Press, pp. 127–150.

SMITH, R. E., & PEARCE, J. W. (1961). Microelectrode recordings from the region of the nucleus solitarius in the cat. *Canadian Journal of Biochemical Physiology, 39*, 933.

SOTANIEMI, K. A. (1980). Brain damage and neurological outcome after open-heart surgery. *Journal of Neurology, Neurosurgery and Psychiatry, 43*, 127–135.

SVENSSON, T. H., & THOREN, P. (1979). Brain noradrenergic neurons in the locus coeruleus: Inhibition by blood volume load through vagal afferents. *Brain Research, 172*, 174–178.

TACHIBANA, S., KURAMOTO, S., INANAGA, K., & IKEMI, Y. (1967). Local cerebrovascular responses in man. *Confinia Neurologica, 29*, 289.

THOMPSON, F. J., LERNER, D. N., FIELDS, K., & BLACKWELDER, A. (1980). Projection of limb versus afferents to the feline motor-sensory cortex. *Journal of the Autonomic Nervous System, 2*, 39–45.

THOMPSON, F. J., YATES, B. J., FRANZEN, O., & WALD, J. R. (1983). Lumbar spinal cord responses to limb vein distension. *Journal of the Autonomic Nervous System, 9*, 531–546.

THOMPSON, F. J., & BARNES, C. D. (1979). Projection of low threshold venous afferents to the spinal cord. *Brain Research, 177*, 561–565.

THOMPSON, L. W., & BOTWINICK, J. (1970). Stimulation in different phases of the cardiac cycle and reaction time. *Psychophysiology, 7*, 57–65.

TOURNADE, A., & MALMÉJAC, J. (1929) Diversité des actions réflexes qui déclenche l'excitation du sinus carotidien et de son nerf. *Comptes Rendus des Séances de la Société de Biologie, 100*, 708–711.

WALKER, B. B., & SANDMAN, C. A. (1977). Physiological response patterns in ulcer patients: Phasic and tonic components of the electrogastrogram. *Psychophysiology, 14*, 393–400.

WALKER, B. B., & SANDMAN, C. A. (1979). Relationship of heart rate on the visual evoked potential. *Journal of Comparative and Physiological Psychology, 93*, 717–729.

WALKER, B. B., & SANDMAN, C. A. (1982). Visual evoked potentials change as heart rate and carotid pressure change. *Psychophysiology, 19*, 520–527.

WALKER, B. B. & WALKER, J. M. (1983) Phase relations between carotid pressure and ongoing electrocortical activity. *International Journal of Psychophysiology, 1*, 65–73.

WILLISON, J. R., DuBOULAY, G. H., PAUL, E. A., RUSSELL, R. W. R., THOMAS, D. J., MARSHALL, J., PEARSON, T. C., SIMON, L. & WETHERLEY-MEIN, C. (1980). Effect of high haematocrit on alertness. *Lancet, 1*, 846–848.

WITKIN, H. A., DYK, R. B., FATTUSON, H. F., GOODENOUGH, D. R., & KARP, S. A. (1962). *Psychological differentiation: Studies of development.* New York: Wiley.

4   *Intrinsic Control Mechanisms of Pain Perception*

JAMES W. LEWIS, LINDA R. NELSON,
GREGORY W. TERMAN, YEHUDA SHAVIT,
AND JOHN C. LIEBESKIND

I. INTRODUCTION

Through the course of evolution, the brain has become increasingly able to respond adaptively to the ever-changing internal and external sensory world. To do so, it must continually monitor the environment through specialized sensory systems. One might imagine that the brain passively receives environmental inputs, processes them, and responds accordingly. We are learning instead that some sensory information can be modulated before it reaches the brain by the activation of centrifugal paths descending from higher central nervous system stations to lower ones in the brain, in the spinal cord, and even in the periphery. Thus, it appears to be important, at least at certain times, that some inputs never reach the brain or arrive only after considerable modification.

Evidence supporting this dynamic model of the brain controlling its own input comes from early studies of several sensory systems (for review see Livingston, 1959). Perhaps the clearest and most dramatic example of such centrifugal control, however, comes from more recent studies of pain perception. In the past fifteen years, a great deal of evidence has accumulated indicating the existence of an endogenous pain-modulating substrate originating in the medial brain stem. Pathways descend from the brain stem to the dorsal horn of the spinal cord where the transfer of nociceptive information from the periphery to as-

---

JAMES W. LEWIS ● Mental Health Research Institute, University of Michigan, Ann Arbor, MI 48109.   LINDA R. NELSON, GREGORY W. TERMAN, YEHUDA SHAVIT, AND JOHN C. LIEBESKIND ● Department of Psychology and Brain Research Institute, University of California, Los Angeles, CA 90024.   The research outlined in this chapter is supported by NIH grant NS 07628 and a gift from the Brotman Foundation. James W. Lewis is supported by NIDA Postdoctoral Fellowship F32DA05221.

cending sensory tracts destined for the brain can be greatly reduced or even blocked completely. The major objective of our chapter is to review this evidence of a centrifugal system of pain suppression. We will focus on recent findings addressing the important question of what natural circumstances call this system into play. Stress appears to be one natural stimulus activating pain suppressive mechanisms, and our studies of stress-induced analgesia in the rat will be summarized and related to similar work by others. Finally, we will describe briefly our most recent work indicating that although analgesia can be viewed as an adaptive response to stress, in certain circumstances stress can also prove maladaptive in that it suppresses the immune system and enhances tumor development.

II. EVIDENCE FOR ENDOGENOUS MECHANISMS OF PAIN CONTROL

Ample evidence indicates that intrinsic to the brain and spinal cord are neural systems the normal function of which is the inhibition of pain. Reynolds (1969) was first to demonstrate that electrical stimulation of a portion of the medial brain stem, the periaqueductal gray matter (PAG), produced analgesia in the rat so profound as to permit surgery without anesthesia. Subsequently, Mayer et al. (1971) and many others have elaborated upon this original observation. Stimulation-produced analgesia (SPA), measured in a variety of standard analgesiometric tests, is as potent as that obtained using moderate to high doses of morphine (e.g., Dennis, Choiniere, & Melzack, 1980; Giesler & Liebeskind, 1976; Mayer et al., 1971). This analgesia appears to represent a true pain suppression and is not secondary to changes in other sensory or motor systems (Mayer et al., 1971). In fact, SPA has proven to be useful in the therapeutic treatment of some forms of intractable pain in man (Hosobuchi, Adams, & Linchitz, 1977; Richardson & Akil, 1977; Young et al., 1984). In general, this descending or centrifugal pain suppression system appears to take origin in the medial diencephalon and PAG, to descend from there to the nucleus raphe magnus (NRM) and thence to the cord by way of the dorsolateral funiculus (Fields & Basbaum, 1979; Lewis, Stapleton, Castiglioni, & Liebeskind, 1982; Watkins & Mayer, 1982). The ultimate locus of pain inhibition deriving from stimulation of any of these areas appears to be the dorsal horn of the spinal cord. Here lie the first central nociceptive neurons, and it is these neurons preferentially whose activity is blocked by analgesic brain stimulation (e.g., Oliveras et al., 1974).

Akil, Mayer, and Liebeskind (1972; 1976b) reported that administration of naloxone, the specific opiate antagonist, significantly reduced SPA in the rat. This finding suggested that SPA results from the liberation of endogenous opiatelike substances, a hypothesis that gained considerable support with the discovery of the opioid peptides (e.g., Hughes *et al.*, 1975; for recent review see Akil *et al.*, 1984). Several other lines of evidence also indicate a significant role for opioid peptides in pain inhibition. SPA manifests tolerance with repeated administration and cross-tolerance with morphine (Mayer & Hayes, 1975). Opiate binding sites and opioid peptide-containing cell bodies or fiber terminals are found in brain areas supporting SPA, areas where analgesia may also be elicited by microinjections of opioid peptides and opiate drugs (e.g., Hökfelt *et al.*, 1977; Watson, Akil, & Barkas, 1979; Yaksh & Rudy, 1978). Lesions in this descending system block SPA and opiate analgesia (Basbaum, Marley, O'Keefe, & Clanton, 1977). In addition, SPA and analgesic doses of morphine or opioid peptides have a similar excitatory electrophysiological action on cellular activity within this medial brain stem substrate (e.g., Oleson, Twombly, & Liebeskind, 1978; Urca & Liebeskind, 1979).

However, it is becoming clear that not all intrinsic mechanisms of pain inhibition rely on this opioid path; rather, multiple mechanisms exist involving separate or partly separate neurochemical and anatomical substrates. For example, shortly after the original report by Akil *et al.* (1976b), several papers appeared describing failures to replicate naloxone antagonism of SPA (e.g., Pert & Walter, 1976; Yaksh, Yeung, & Rudy, 1976). A possible explanation for this discrepancy is suggested by the work of Cannon, Lewis, Weinberg, and Liebeskind (1982), who find that neurochemically discrete SPA substrates appear to exist within the midline PAG. Stimulation within and below ventral PAG provoked SPA that is sensitive to naloxone blockade, whereas more dorsal PAG stimulation caused SPA that was unaffected by this drug. Thus, opioid and nonopioid forms of SPA appear to exist in anatomically discrete regions of the midbrain.

III. Activation of Endogenous Analgesia Systems: Stress-Induced Analgesia

A great deal of recent effort has been given to the search for natural, physiological triggers of the brain's intrinsic analgesia systems. Recently, it has been shown that exposure to a variety of stressors in the rat elicits clear pain suppression lasting for at least several minutes (e.g., Amir & Amit, 1978; Bodnar *et al.*, 1978a, 1978b; Chance, White, Krynock, & Rosecrans, 1977; Chesher & Chan, 1977; Hayes, Bennett, Newlon, &

Mayer, 1978a; Jackson, Maier, & Coon, 1979; Lewis, Cannon, & Liebeskind, 1980a; Madden Akil, Patrick, & Barchas, 1977; Watkins and Mayer, 1982). Such findings have suggested that although pain is an important warning signal, under certain emergency or stress conditions, pain suppression may be yet more adaptive. Thus, stress may be an important natural input to the endogenous analgesia systems of the brain at times when feeling pain could disrupt appropriate coping behaviors (Liebeskind, Giesler, & Urca, 1976).

Akil *et al.* (1976a) and Hayes, Bennett, Newlon, and Mayer (1976) were first to report that exposure to stress causes potent analgesia in rats. These studies differed, however, in one very important regard: Akil *et al.* found that naloxone antagonized stress analgesia suggesting opioid involvement, whereas Hayes, Bennett, Newlon, & Mayer found that it did not. Subsequently, other investigators demonstrated stress analgesia in response to a host of stressors, but the question of opioid involvement remained controversial. To demonstrate clearly a role for opioid peptides in stress analgesia, several criteria must be satisfied: stress analgesia should be blocked by the opiate antagonist drug, naloxone; it should develop tolerance with repeated administration; and it should show cross-tolerance with opiate analgesia. When these criteria were applied to stress analgesia, some investigators obtained evidence of opioid involvement (Amir & Amit, 1978; Bodnar *et al.*, 1978a; Chesher & Chan, 1977; Madden *et al.*, 1977), but others did not (Bodnar, Kelly, Steiner, & Glusman, 1978c; Chance & Rosecrans, 1979a, 1979b; Hayes *et al.*, 1978a).

It was at this time that our studies of stress analgesia began. Because qualitatively and quantitatively different stressors had been used in prior studies to produce analgesia (e.g., rotation, oscillation, cold water swims, restraint, conditioned fear, and different parameters of footshock), integration of these findings was difficult. Our goal was to investigate the phenomenon of stress analgesia systematically and to clarify what role, if any, was played by the opioid peptides. To this end, a single stressor, inescapable footshock, was selected and the parameters of its administration were varied. This procedure allowed precise experimental control over the stressful stimulus and obviated the problems introduced by using qualitatively different stressors. Also, it should be noted that a variety of pain sensitivity tests have been employed in the assessment of stress analgesia (e.g., hot-plate, tail-flick, formalin test), and the particular test used may importantly affect the results obtained (e.g., Dennis & Melzack, 1980). We have chosen to use the tail-flick test (D'Amour & Smith, 1941) and have defined analgesia as an increase in latency to respond to radiant heat.

IV. Opioid and Nonopioid Mechanisms of Stress Analgesia

We found that inescapable footshock of constant intensity can elicit qualitatively different analgesic responses depending upon the temporal parameters of its application (Lewis *et al.*, 1980a). Exposure to prolonged, intermittent footshock (2.5 mA, on 1 sec every 5 for 20–30 min) causes analgesia that is blocked by naloxone in doses as low as 0.1 mg/kg (Lewis *et al.*, 1980a, 1980b). By contrast, brief, continuous footshock of the same intensity applied for 3 minutes causes a roughly equipotent analgesia that is unaffected by even high doses of naloxone.

These results suggest the existence of at least two forms of stress analgesia, one that is mediated by opioid peptides and another that is not. The naloxone-sensitive analgesic response to prolonged, intermittent footshock satisfies two other criteria of opioid involvement. It shows tolerance after 14 stress exposures (Lewis, Sherman, & Liebeskind, 1981c; see also Madden *et al.*, 1977), and it is reduced (cross-tolerance) in morphine-tolerant rats (Lewis *et al.*, 1981c). Once again, brief stress analgesia appears independent of opioid mechanisms in that it shows no evidence of tolerance or cross-tolerance with morphine (Lewis *et al.*, 1981c). Yet another indication of the independence of these two forms of stress analgesia is the lack of cross-tolerance development between them. Thus, animals rendered tolerant to prolonged (opioid) footshock stress display normally robust analgesia in response to brief (nonopioid) footshock, and the analgesic response to prolonged footshock is unaffected in animals previously exposed to 14 brief stress sessions (Terman, Lewis, & Liebeskind, 1983a). Taken together, these results indicate the existence of multiple endogenous analgesia systems selectively accessed by different parameters of the stressful experience.

V. Role of Endocrine Systems in Stress Analgesia

The pituitary-adrenal and the sympatho-adrenal axes have long been recognized for their important roles in the adaptive response to stress (Selye, 1956). If pain suppression may be thought of as an adaptive response to certain stress conditions, participation of these hormonal systems in stress analgesia seems likely. Several lines of evidence suggest that pituitary hormones contribute importantly to the mediation of stress analgesia. First, the pituitary is a rich source of β-endorphin (e.g., Guillemin *et al.*, 1977), thought to be the most potent analgesic of the opioid peptides. Stress has been shown to cause the release of pituitary opioids (e.g., Guillemin *et al.*, 1977; Millan *et al.*, 1981). Finally, we and others have reported that stress analgesia (particularly those forms sensitive to naloxone blockade) is attenuated in hypophysectomized animals (Amir & Amit, 1979; Bodnar *et al.*, 1979; Lewis, Chudler, Cannon, & Liebeskind, 1981b; Millan, Przewlocki, Holt, & Herz, 1980). Hypophysectomy, however, has been found ineffective in reducing some opioid forms of stress analgesia (Terman *et al.*, 1984; Watkins *et al.*, 1982b) and most nonopioid forms (Chance, 1980; Lewis *et al.*, 1981b; Watkins, Cobelli, Newsome, & Mayer, 1982b).

Another peripheral source of opioid peptides is the adrenal medulla. The adrenal medulla contains enkephalin-like peptides that are stored and coreleased with catecholamines in response to sympathetic activation or trauma (see Viveros & Wilson, 1983). Although the precise physiological function of these peptides remains to be determined, we have suggested that they are importantly involved in the analgesic response to certain forms of stress. Opioid, but not nonopioid, stress analgesia is markedly reduced by adrenalectomy, adrenal demedullation, or denervation of the adrenal medulla via celiac ganglionectomy (Lewis, Tordoff, Sherman, & Liebeskind, 1982c). Because demedullation and ganglionectomy have as great an effect as removal of the entire adrenal gland, and because both basal and stressed adrenocortical function was unimpaired in adrenal denervated animals, yet these rats failed to manifest opioid stress analgesia, we concluded that this form of stress analgesia is dependent on adrenal medullary, not cortical, function (cf., however, MacLennan *et al.*, 1982). Moreover, it appears to be the enkephalin-like peptides, not catecholamines, that are involved in mediation of this form of stress analgesia. A dose of reserpine known to deplete catecholamines while increasing the adrenal content and stimulation-induced release of enkephalins (Viveros, Diliberto, Hazum, & Chang, 1980) significantly augments opioid stress analgesia (Lewis *et al.*, 1982c). This increased analgesia appears to reflect increased release of enkephalin-like peptides by stress rather than a nonspecific drug effect in that the analgesia is still virtually eliminated by an opiate antagonist.

These behavioral observations correlate very well with biochemical data we have obtained in a collaborative study with Dr. O. H. Viveros. The amount of opiate-like material in the adrenal medulla was significantly reduced by prolonged (opioid), but not brief (nonopioid), footshock. Medullary enkephalin-like peptide content was dramatically increased in reserpine-treated rats, and this new elevated content was also reduced by exposure to prolonged stress. Finally, rats made tolerant to prolonged footshock analgesia no longer showed depletion of adrenal enkephalin-like peptides after stress (Lewis, Tordoff, Liebeskind, & Viveros, 1982b). These converging lines of evidence strongly implicate adrenal enkephalin-like peptides in opioid stress analgesia. Several important questions, however, such as the locus of the opiate receptor mediating this analgesia, remain to be answered before this hypothesis can be fully accepted. In this regard, Maixner and Randich (1984) recently showed that an opioid form of footshock stress analgesia apparently similar to the adrenal medulla-dependent form we have studied (Lewis *et al.*, 1982c) is attenuated by vagotomy. They suggested that adrenal enkephalins might bind peripherally and thereby activate vagal afferents to central pain-inhibitory circuits.

VI. Neurotransmitters Involved in Stress Analgesia

That opioid peptides functioning as hormones appear critical for some forms of stress analgesia in no way precludes the involvement of central opioids as well. In fact, there is considerable evidence to indicate that stressors causing analgesia alter one or another index of brain opioid activity (e.g., Chance, White, Krynock, & Rosecrans, 1978; Lewis, Cannon, Liebeskind, & Akil, 1981a; Madden *et al.*, 1977; Millan *et al.*, 1981; Rossier *et al.*, 1977; Rossier, Gruillemin, & Bloom, 1978). Undoubtedly, a number of other central neurotransmitter substances are also involved in the mediation of opioid and nonopioid forms of stress analgesia. For example, our work has demonstrated an important role for acetylcholine in opioid stress analgesia (Lewis, Cannon, & Liebeskind, 1983a). We find that opioid, but not nonopioid, stress analgesia is reduced by scopolamine, a muscarinic cholinergic antagonist drug. Methylscopolamine, a muscarinic cholinergic antagonist with only peripheral activity, failed to affect the analgesic response to prolonged footshock. Additionally, we and others have shown that oxotremorine, a potent muscarinic agonist drug, causes analgesia sensitive to opiate antagonist blockade (e.g., Lewis *et al.*, 1983a, Pedigo & Dewey, 1981), suggesting that acetylcholine may stimulate the release of opioid peptides involved in pain inhibition. From these findings, we conclude that a muscarinic cholinergic synapse exists in the central opioid pathway mediating stress analgesia.

Very little is known of the neurochemistry of nonopioid analgesia. Understanding these systems may prove to be clinically relevant. If these systems can be harnessed and utilized therapeutically, perhaps problems associated with opioid analgesia (e.g., tolerance and dependence) can be avoided. We have found that nonopioid stress analgesia is reduced by reserpine (Lewis *et al.*, 1982c; Terman, Lewis, & Liebeskind, 1981). Because reserpine is a relatively nonspecific drug affecting all monoaminergic neurons, attempts were made to define more precisely which monoamine is critical. Nonopioid stress analgesia was unaffected by specific dopamine, norepinephrine, or serotonin receptor antagonists or depletors, although monoaminergic agonists potentiated this analgesia (Terman, Lewis, & Liebeskind, 1982a; cf., however, Tricklebank, Hutson, & Curzon, 1982). This form of stress analgesia, however, does appear to depend on the monoamine, histamine, in that it is reduced by diphenhydramine, an H_1 receptor blocker, but not by cimetidine, an H_2 antagonist (Terman, Lewis, & Liebeskind, 1982b). Furthermore, it appears that histamine of neuronal origin is critical. Nonopioid stress analgesia is reduced by depletion of both neuronal and mast cell histamine stores with α-fluoromethylhistidine, an inhibitor of the synthetic enzyme, histidine decarboxylase. On the other hand, it is not altered by administration of Compound 48/80, a drug depleting histamine of mast cell origin only (Terman et al., 1982b). That histamine is involved in central mechanisms of antinociception is supported by the demonstration of histamine in brain regions thought to be involved in pain inhibition (see Schwartz et al., 1981) and by the fact that analgesia follows microinjections of histamine into these areas (Glick & Crane, 1978).

VII. The Neuroanatomy of Stress Analgesia

The neuroanatomical substrates of stress analgesia appear to overlap considerably with those involved in opiate analgesia and SPA. For example, we and others have reported that both opioid and nonopioid stress analgesia rely to some extent on the integrity of spinal pathways (Chance, 1980; Hayes et al., 1978b), particularly the dorsolateral funiculus (DLF) (Lewis et al., 1983c; Watkins, Cobelli, & Mayer, 1982b). Thus, both forms of stress analgesia share a common substrate and rely on activation of centrifugal paths.

The nucleus raphe magnus (NRM), a cell group whose axons project to the spinal cord through the DLF (see Fields & Basbaum, 1979), also appears to be involved in stress analgesia as well as opiate analgesia and SPA (Azami, Llewelyn, & Roberts, 1982; Chance, 1980; Prieto, Cannon, & Liebeskind, 1983; Zorman, Hentall, Adams, & Fields, 1981). This nucleus has been implicated in endogenous mechanisms of antinociception (Fields, 1984) and has been associated with opioid (Prieto et al., 1983; Zorman et al., 1981) and nonopioid (Satoh, Akaike, Nakazawa, & Takagi, 1980) systems. In our work, NRM lesions reduced nonopioid stress analgesia but did not affect the opioid form (Cannon et al., 1983; cf., however, Watkins et al., 1982b). These same lesions attenuated morphine analgesia (see also Azami et al., 1982), indicating that, although morphine and opioid stress analgesia are similar in many respects, their anatomical substrates are not entirely coextensive.

Yet another indication that stress can activate central nervous system pain-inhibitory pathways derives from the finding that cross-tolerance develops between opioid stress analgesia and opioid mediated SPA (Penner, Terman, & Liebeskind, 1982). Animals made tolerant to the opioid form of stress were seen to be cross-tolerant to opioid SPA, although nonopioid SPA was unaffected. Repeated exposure to nonopioid stress affected neither opioid nor nonopioid SPA.

VIII. Evidence for Two Independent Opioid Forms of Stress Analgesia

We have recently found (Terman et al., 1984) that 3 minutes of continuous footshock (2.5 mA), parameters previously seen to elicit a nonopioid form of stress analgesia according to several criteria (e.g., Lewis et al., 1980a, 1980b, 1981c), can provoke naloxone- or naltrexone-sensitive analgesia in some animals. By systematically varying duration of exposure while holding other footshock parameters constant, we have now established that 3 minutes is an intermediate duration between those values eliciting clearly opioid and those eliciting clearly nonopioid forms of stress analgesia. Thus, robust naltrexone antagonism of continuous footshock stress analgesia was observed at 1 and 2 minute footshock durations, whereas an equipotent analgesia elicited by the same footshock applied continuously for 4 or 5 minutes was completely insensitive to this drug (Terman et al., 1983b). Further characterization of these forms of stress analgesia revealed that the analgesic response to 1 minute of continuous footshock develops tolerance after 14 exposures and cross-tolerance both with morphine and with the opioid form of stress analgesia elicited by prolonged, intermittent footshock described previously. The analgesic response to 4 minutes of continuous footshock, by contrast, does not develop tolerance, is unaffected by morphine tolerance, and is not cross-tolerant with either the 1 minute continuous or 20 minute intermittent forms of opioid stress analgesia. Thus, this form of stress analgesia is mediated by nonopioid mechanisms (Terman et al., 1984).

Several studies have investigated the similarities and differences between the two opioid forms of stress analgesia elicited by 1 minute continuous and 20 minute intermittent footshock. We find that both develop tolerance, and each manifests cross-tolerance with the other, with morphine, and with the naloxone-sensitive form of SPA (Penner et al., 1982; Terman et al., 1984). On the other hand, whereas analgesia to the 20 minute intermittent footshock is reduced by hypophysectomy (Lewis *et al.*, 1981b), is dependent upon adrenal medullary enkephalin-like peptides (Lewis *et al.*, 1982c), and relies on central muscarinic cholinergic mechanisms (Lewis *et al.*, 1983a), analgesia to the 1 minute continuous footshock is independent of these hormonal and cholinergic systems. Presumably this form of stress analgesia is dependent on opioids of central, not peripheral, origin (see Tricklebank *et al.*, 1982).

We also find that the opioid or nonopioid nature of continuous footshock analgesia depends on current intensity (Terman *et al.*, 1984). Three minutes of continuous footshock at 1.5 or 2.0 mA elicits naltrexone-sensitive analgesia, whereas a more intense shock (3.0 or 3.5 mA) delivered for the same time causes analgesia insensitive to this drug. Therefore, considering either the intensity or duration of continuous footshock, it appears that the values used in our earlier work (2.5 mA for 3 minutes) are slightly higher than optimal for eliciting opioid stress analgesia and slightly lower than optimal for eliciting stress analgesia of the nonopioid sort. It is important to add, however, that, whereas small increments in intensity or duration of continuous footshock cause a sudden shift from an opioid to a nonopioid mechanism, applying exactly the same total amount of footshock as that yielding nonopioid analgesia (4 minutes continuously), but applying it intermittently for 20 minutes, once again evokes an opioid form (although a different opioid form) of stress analgesia. Thus, no one parameter (footshock intensity, duration, or temporal pattern) uniquely determines the neurochemical basis of stress analgesia, although each can be made the critical variable by holding the other two constant.

Of special interest to the topic of this volume, we have recently found that consciousness and higher brain structures are importantly involved in some, but not all, forms of stress analgesia. Continuous footshock (2.5 mA for 1 or 4 minutes) can elicit analgesia in decerebrate rats or rats given a surgical level of pentobarbital anesthesia (Klein, Lovaas, Terman, & Liebeskind, 1983; Klein, Terman, & Liebeskind, 1984; Terman *et al.*, 1984). Stress analgesia in these animals, measured by the tail-flick test, is indistinguishable in magnitude, duration, or sensitivity to naltrexone antagonism from that displayed by sham-operated or unanesthetized controls. On the other hand, the analgesic response to 20 minutes of intermittent footshock is completely abolished by anesthesia or decerebration (Klein *et al.*, 1983, 1984; Terman *et al.*, 1984; see also Jensen & Smith, 1981). This finding serves once again to dissociate the two opioid forms of stress analgesia elicited by continuous versus intermittent footshock. It is also evident that if some forms of stress analgesia can be studied under conditions of surgical anesthesia to certain practical or ethical advantage, other forms, unfortunately, cannot.

IX. Early Experience Influences Stress Analgesia: The Effects of Prenatal Alcohol Exposure

An ample literature suggests that perinatal administration of handling stress or adrenal corticosteroids can profoundly influence the adult's behavioral and endocrinological response to stress (for review see Ader, 1975). Exposure to alcohol *in utero* also appears to affect the adult's sensitivity to stress (Taylor, Branch, Liu, & Kokka, 1982). How these perinatal manipulations may specifically affect the analgesic response to stress has not been thoroughly researched. That stress analgesia may be affected, however, is suggested by findings that neonatally administered stress can alter brain enkephalin levels (Torda, 1978) and affect analgesic responsiveness to morphine (Bardo, Bhatnagar, & Gebhart, 1981). We have been investigating the long-term effects of prenatal alcohol exposure and have found that such exposure augments the analgesic response to stress in the adult rat. Specifically, an opioid, rather than a nonopioid, mediated form of stress analgesia is enhanced (Nelson *et al.*, 1982). Adult, female rats, prenatally exposed to alcohol, were tested for analgesia following two forms of footshock: intermittent (2.5 mA, 1 sec on per 5 sec for 10 min) and continuous (2.5 mA, on for 2 min). These footshock parameters elicit naloxone-sensitive (opioid) and naloxone-insensitive (nonopioid) forms of stress analgesia, respectively. Compared to controls, rats prenatally exposed to alcohol showed a markedly potentiated opioid stress analgesia (Nelson *et al.*, 1982). Nonopioid stress analgesia was unaffected by the early exposure to alcohol. These results suggest that fetal exposure to alcohol produces long-term effects on the functioning of endogenous opioid analgesia systems. Interestingly, repeated daily exposure of adult rats to the opioid form of footshock stress causes those prenatally exposed to alcohol, but not controls, to increase their voluntary consumption of ethanol (Nelson *et al.*, 1983a).

On the basis of the preceding results, it appears that prenatal exposure to alcohol causes pronounced alterations in endogenous opioid systems. To test this hypothesis further, we recently carried out several experiments using morphine as a pharmacological probe to assess the status of opioid systems in rats prenatally exposed to alcohol. We found that these rats exhibited markedly enhanced responsiveness to the analgesic, hypothermic, and pituitary-adrenal activating effects of morphine (Nelson *et al.*, 1983b). Since these behaviors occur at varying doses of the drug and are presumed to be mediated by different brain loci, it appears that the perturbations due to prenatal alcohol exposure are widespread. One possible explanation of these findings may be that prenatal alcohol exposure causes changes in brain opiate receptors leading to increased sensitivity to morphine. However, this simple explanation may not suffice. Our opiate receptor binding studies reveal no differences in opiate receptor number (of either the mu or delta subtype) between prenatal alcohol-exposed and normal or pair-fed controls in frontal cortex, midbrain, striatum, thalamus, medulla, or hippocampus (Nelson *et al.*, 1984). The only differences we found were in hypothalamus, but in this region both prenatal alcohol-exposed and offspring of pair-fed dams were receptor deficient compared to offspring of normally fed dams.

X. IMMUNOSUPPRESSIVE AND TUMOR-ENHANCING EFFECTS OF STRESS

One lesson to be learned from our investigations of the phenomenon of stress analgesia is that variations in stress parameters (e.g., intermittent versus continuous footshock of the same intensity and total duration) can elicit neurochemically very different responses (opioid versus nonopioid analgesia). An extensive but often contradictory literature relates stress to changes in tumor development and immune function in human beings and laboratory animals (Ader, 1981; Levy, 1982; Peters & Mason, 1979). We have recently begun to investigate this problem in rats, hypothesizing that our dissection of stress parameters into those causing opioid and nonopioid forms of analgesia would help account for some of the variability encountered by previous workers in this field. Our earliest results suggest that this approach is proving fruitful.

We now find that footshock stress that releases opioids (indicated by the naltrexone sensitivity of the resultant analgesia) is immunosuppressive and facilitates the development of a mammary tumor in rats. In female Fischer 344 rats, the activity of natural killer (NK) cells (lymphocytes thought to be important in cancer surveillance) is markedly suppressed following 4 daily exposures to intermittent (opioid), but not continuous (nonopioid), footshock. This suppression is attenuated in rats treated with naltrexone prior to each stress session (Shavit *et al.*, 1983a). Moreover, the same stress regimen that results in suppression of NK activity also causes a decrease in survival time and percentage of survival of Fischer rats implanted with a mammary ascites tumor (MAT 13762 B). These effects are blocked in animals implanted with slow-release naltrexone pellets (Lewis *et al.*, 1983b). Continuous (nonopioid) footshock stress affects neither NK activity nor tumor development.

The mechanisms by which opioid peptides interact with these systems are no doubt complex and remain to be elucidated. In further work

INTRINSIC CONTROL MECHANISMS OF PAIN PERCEPTION

on this subject we have attempted to determine whether the tumor-enhancing effects of stress could be mimicked by morphine and whether the adverse effects of stress would tolerate upon repeated exposure. The results of this study gave mixed support for the hypothesized role of opioid peptides in these phenomena. The tumor-enhancing and immunosuppressive effects of stress were mimicked by administration of morphine (albeit in very high doses) (Lewis *et al.*, 1984; Shavit *et al.*, 1984a, 1984b). However, in the case of tumor enhancement, no evidence of tolerance was obtained, nor were the effects of stress reduced in morphine-tolerant rats (cross-tolerance) (Lewis *et al.*, 1984). Nevertheless, taken together, these results suggest a significant role for opioids in the interactions between stress, the immune system, and cancer.

XI. SUMMARY AND CONCLUSIONS

These studies provide clear evidence that exposure to stress is an adequate stimulus for activation of intrinsic pain-suppressive systems. Our initial results (Lewis *et al.*, 1980a) demonstrated that a single stressor, inescapable footshock, can selectively activate either an opioid or a nonopioid mechanism of analgesia; thus, stress analgesia is not a unitary phenomenon. Neurochemically, neuroanatomically, and hormonally different analgesia substrates appear to exist; and which of these is called into play appears to depend on variations in the temporal parameters and intensity of the footshock stress stimulus.

Certainly, there is much we need to learn about when endogenous pain-inhibitory systems are active and what natural stimuli or environmental circumstances occasion their use. One important factor appears to be ability of the organism to exert control over the stressful stimulus. In the work of Maier and colleagues, inescapable (i.e., uncontrollable), but not escapable, stress appears to activate an opioid analgesia system (Maier *et al.*, 1980). Although both the 20 minute intermittent and the 3 minute continuous footshock procedures employed in our studies are inescapable, only the former activates an opioid system. It may be that only the 20 minute paradigm is perceived as "inescapable" by the rats. This notion is supported by our finding, in collaboration with Maier, that exposure to 20 minute intermittent, but not 3 minute continuous, footshock causes behavioral deficits termed "learned helplessness," previously shown to result from experience with uncontrollable stress (Maier *et al.*, 1983). The importance of controllability in determining the ultimate effects of stress is also apparent in studies of stress-induced immunosuppression and tumor enhancement. Others have previously shown that exposure to inescapable, but not escapable, stress facilitates tumor development (Visintainer, Volpicelli, & Seligman, 1982; Sklar & Anisman, 1979) and suppresses T-cell function (Laudenslager *et al.*, 1983). We have recently obtained parallel results measuring NK activity (Shavit *et al.*, 1983b).

Although inescapable footshock at best merely models natural stress conditions, it is proving useful as a highly precise, reliable, and controllable probe for elucidating anatomical substrates and neurochemical mechanisms of antinociception. More naturalistic work by others suggesting that sexual behavior (Crowley, Rodriguez-Sierra, & Komisaruk, 1977), fighting (Miczek, Thompson, & Shuster, 1982), and food deprivation (Bodnar *et al.*, 1978b; McGivern *et al.*, 1979) can be adequate stimuli for triggering opioid or nonopioid analgesia systems apparently similar to those we are studying encourages the belief that a rapprochement between these more mechanistic and naturalistic kinds of studies can ultimately be made. Finally, the experience we have gained in these studies about the neurochemically and hormonally diverse mechanisms activated by different stress parameters is beginning to provide some measure of predictive control in our attempts to establish reliable relationships between stress and both tumor development and immune function.

REFERENCES

ADER, R. (1975). Early experience and hormones: Emotional behavior and adrenocortical function. In B. E. ELEFTHERIOU & R. SPROTT (Eds.), *Hormonal correlates of behavior*. New York: Plenum Press, pp. 7–33.

ADER, R. (1981). *Psychoneuroimmunology*. New York: Academic Press.

AKIL, H., MAYER, D. J., & LIEBESKIND, J. C. (1972). Comparaison chez le rat entre l'analgésie induite par stimulation de la substance grise péri-aqueducale et l'analgésie morphinique. *Comptes Rendus de l'Académie des Sciences (Paris)*, 274, 3603–3605.

AKIL, H., MADDEN, J., PATRICK, R. L., & BARCHAS, J. D. (1976a). Stress-induced increase in endogenous opiate peptides; concurrent analgesia and its partial reversal by naloxone. In H. W. KOSTERLITZ (Ed.), *Opiates and endogenous opioid peptides*. Amsterdam: Elsevier, pp. 63–70.

AKIL, H., MAYER, D. J., & LIEBESKIND, J. C. (1976b). Antagonism of stimulation-produced analgesia by naloxone, a narcotic antagonist. *Science*, 191 961–962.

AKIL, H., WATSON, S. J., YOUNG, E., LEWIS, M. E., KHACHTURIAN, H., & WALKER, J. M. (1984). Endogenous opioids: Biology and function. *Annual Review of Neuroscience*, 7, 223–255.

AMIR, S., & AMIT, Z. (1978). Endogenous opioid ligands may mediate stress-induced changes in the affective properties of pain related behavior in rats. *Life Sciences*, 23, 1143–1152.

AMIR, S., AMIT, Z. (1979). The pituitary gland mediates acute and chronic pain responsiveness in stressed and non-stressed rats. *Life Sciences*, 24, 439–448.

AZAMI, J., LLEWELYN, M. B., & ROBERTS, H. H. T. (1982). The contribution of nucleus reticularis paragigantocellularis and nucleus raphe magnus to the analgesia produced by systemically administered morphine, investigated with the microinjection technique. *Pain, 12,* 229–246.

BARDO, M. T., BHATNAGAR, R. K., & GEBHART, G. F. (1981). Opiate receptor ontogeny and morphine-induced effects: Influence of chronic footshock stress in preweanling rats. *Developmental Brain Research, 1,* 487–495.

BASBAUM, A. I., MARLEY, N. J., O'KEEFE, J., & CLANTON, C. H. (1977). Reversal of morphine and stimulus produced analgesia by subtotal spinal cord lesions. *Pain, 3,* 43–56.

BODNAR, R. J., GLUSMAN, M., BRUTUS, M., SPIAGGIA, A., & KELLY, D. D. (1979). Analgesia induced by cold-water stress: Attenuation following hypophysectomy. *Physiology and Behavior, 23,* 53–62.

BODNAR, R. J., KELLY, D. D., SPIAGGIA, A., EHRENBERG, C., & GLUSMAN, M. (1978a). Dose-dependent reductions by naloxone of analgesia induced by cold-water stress. *Pharmacology, Biochemistry, and Behavior, 8,* 667–672.

BODNAR, R. J., KELLY, D. D., SPIAGGIA, A., & GLUSMAN, M. (1978b). Biphasic alterations of nociceptive thresholds induced by food deprivation. *Physiological Psychology, 6,* 391–395.

BODNAR, R. J., KELLY, D. D., STEINER, S. S., & GLUSMAN, M. (1978c). Stress-produced analgesia and morphine-produced analgesia: Lack of cross-tolerance. *Pharmacology, Biochemistry, and Behavior, 8,* 661–666.

CANNON, J. T., LEWIS, J. W., WEINBERG, V. E., & LIEBESKIND, J. C. (1983). Evidence for the independence of brain stem mechanisms mediating analgesia induced by morphine and two forms of stress. *Brain Research, 269,* 231–236.

CANNON, J. T., PRIETO, G. J., LEE, A., & LIEBESKIND, J. C. (1982). Evidence for opioid and nonopioid forms of stimulation-produced analgesia in the rat. *Brain Research, 243,* 315–321.

CHANCE, W. T. (1980). Autoanalgesia: Opiate and non-opiate mechanisms. *Neuroscience and Biobehavior Review, 4,* 55–67.

CHANCE, W. T., & ROSECRANS, J. A. (1979a). Lack of cross-tolerance between morphine and autoanalgesia. *Pharmacology, Biochemistry, and Behavior, 11,* 639–642.

CHANCE, W. T., & ROSECRANS, J. A. (1979b). Lack of effect of naloxone on autoanalgesia. *Pharmacology, Biochemistry, and Behavior, 11,* 643–646.

CHANCE, W. T., WHITE, A. C., KRYNOCK, G. M., & ROSECRANS, J. A. (1977). Autoanalgesia: Behaviorally activated antinociception. *European Journal of Pharmacology, 44,* 283–284.

CHANCE, W. T., WHITE, A. C., KRYNOCK, G. M., & ROSECRANS, J. A. (1978). Conditional fear-induced decreases in the binding of (^{3}H)-N-Leu-enkephalin to rat brain. *Brain Research, 141,* 371–374.

CHESHER, G. B., & CHAN, B. (1977). Footshock induced analgesia in mice: Its reversal by naloxone and cross-tolerance with morphine. *Life Sciences, 21,* 1569–1574.

CROWLEY, W. R., RODRIGUEZ-SIERRA, J. F., & KOMISARUK, B. R. (1977). Analgesia induced by vaginal stimulation in rats is apparently independent of a morphine-sensitive process. *Psychopharmacology, 54,* 223–225.

D'AMOUR, F. E., & SMITH, D. L. (1941). A method for determining loss of pain sensation. *Journal of Pharmacology and Experimental Therapeutics, 72,* 74–79.

DENNIS, S. G., CHOINIERE, M., & MELZACK, R. (1980). Stimulation-produced analgesia in rats: Assessment by two pain tests and correlation with self-stimulation. *Experimental Neurology, 68,* 295–309.

DENNIS, S. G., & MELZACK, R. (1980). Pain modulation by 5-hydroxytryptaminergic agents and morphine as measured by three pain tests. *Experimental Neurology, 69,* 260–270.

FIELDS, H. L. (1984). Brainstem mechanisms of pain modulation. In L. KRUGER & J. C. LIEBESKIND (Eds.), *Neural mechanisms of pain. Advances in Pain Research and Therapy, Vol. 6.* New York: Raven Press, pp. 252.

FIELDS, H. L., & BASBAUM, A. I. (1979). Anatomy and physiology of a descending pain control system. In J. J. BONICA, J. C. LIEBESKIND, & D. G. ALBE-FESSARD (Eds.), *Advances in pain research and therapy, Vol. 3.* New York: Raven Press, pp. 427–440.

GEISLER, G. J., & LIEBESKIND, J. C. (1976). Inhibition of visceral pain by electrical stimulation of the periaqueductal gray matter. *Pain, 2,* 43–48.

GLICK, S., & CRANE, L. A. (1978). Opiate-like and abstinence-like effects of intracerebral histamine administration in rats. *Nature, 273,* 547–549.

GUILLEMIN, R., VARGO, T., ROSSIER, J., MINICK, S., LING, N., RIVIER, C., VALE, W., & BLOOM, F. (1977). β-endorphin and adrenocorticotropin are secreted concomitantly by the pituitary gland. *Science, 197,* 1367–1369.

HAYES, R. L., BENNETT, G. J., NEWLON, P. G., & MAYER, D. J. (1976). Analgesic effects of certain noxious and stressful manipulations in the rat. *Society for Neuroscience Abstracts, 2,* 939.

HAYES, R. L., BENNETT, G. J., NEWLON, P. G., & MAYER, D. J. (1978). Behavioral and physiological studies of non-narcotic analgesia in the rat elicited by certain environmental stimuli. *Brain Research, 155,* 69–90.

HAYES, R. L., PRICE, D. D., BENNETT, G. J., WILCOX, G. L., & MAYER, D. J. (1978b). Differential effects of spinal cord lesions on narcotic and non-narcotic suppression of nociceptive reflexes: Further evidence for the physiological multiplicity of pain modulation. *Brain Research, 155,* 91–102.

HÖKFELT, T., LJUNGDAHL, A., TERENIUS, L., ELDE, R., & NILSON, G. (1977). Immunohistochemical analysis of peptide pathways possibly related to pain and analgesia: Enkephalin and substance P. *Proceedings of the National Academy of Sciences, 74,* 3081–3085.

HOSOBUCHI, Y., ADAMS, J. E., & LINCHITZ, R. (1977). Pain relief by electrical stimulation of the central gray matter in humans and its reversal by naloxone. *Science, 197,* 183–186.

HUGHES, J., SMITH, T. W., KOSTERLITZ, H. W., FOTHERGILL, L. A., MORGAN, B. A., & MORRIS, H. R. (1976). Identification of two related pentapeptides from the brain with potent opiate agonist activity. *Nature, 258,* 577–579.

JACKSON, R. L., MAIER, S. F., & COON, D. J. (1979). Long-term analgesic effects of inescapable shock and learned helplessness. *Science, 206,* 91–93.

JENSEN, T. S. & SMITH, D. F. (1981). The role of consciousness in stress-induced analgesia. *Journal of Neural Transmission, 52,* 55–60.

KLEIN, M. V., LOVAAS, K. M., TERMAN, G. W., & LIEBESKIND, J. C. (1983). The effects of decerebration and spinal transection on three discrete forms of stress-induced analgesia. *Society for Neuroscience Abstracts, 9,* 795.

KLEIN, M. V., TERMAN, G. W., & LIEBESKIND, J. C. (1984). Effects of pentobarbital on three forms of stress-induced analgesia. *Society for Neuroscience Abstracts, 10,* 1105.

LAUDENSLAGER, M. L., RYAN, S. M., DRUGAN, R. C., HYSON, R. L., & MAIER, S. F. (1982). Coping and immunosuppression: Inescapable but not escapable shock suppresses lymphocyte proliferation. *Science, 221,* 568–570.

LEVY, S. M. *Biological mediators of behavior and disease: Neoplasia.* New York: Elsevier Biomedical.

LEWIS, J. W., CANNON, J. T., & LIEBESKIND, J. C. (1980a). Opioid and nonopoid mechanisms of stress analgesia. *Science, 208,* 623–625.

LEWIS, J. W., CANNON, J. T., & LIEBESKIND, J. C. (1983a). Involvement of central muscarinic cholinergic mechanisms in opioid stress analgesia. *Brain Research, 270,* 289–293.

LEWIS, J. W., CANNON, J. T., STAPLETON, J. M., & LIEBESKIND, J. C. (1980b). Stress activates endogenous pain-inhibitory systems: Opioid and nonopioid mechanisms. *Proceedings of the Western Pharmacology Society, 23,* 85–88.

LEWIS, J. W., CANNON, J. T., LIEBESKIND, J. C., & AKIL, H. (1981a). Alterations in brain β-endorphin immunoreactivity following acute and chronic stress. *Pain, Supplement 1,* S263.

LEWIS, J. W., CHUDLER, E. H., CANNON, J. T., & LIEBESKIND, J. C. (1981b). Hypophysectomy differentially affects morphine and stress analgesia. *Proceedings of the Western Pharmacology Society, 24*, 323–326.

LEWIS, J. W., SHAVIT, Y., TERMAN, G. W., GALE, R. P., & LIEBESKIND, J. C. (1983–84). Stress and morphine affect survival of rats challenged with a mammary ascites tumor (MAT 13762B.) *Natural Immunity and Cell Growth Regulation, 3*, 43–50.

LEWIS, J. W., SHAVIT, Y., TERMAN, G. W., NELSON, L. R., GALE, R. P., & LIEBESKIND, J. C. (1983b). Apparent involvement of opioid peptides in stress-induced enhancement of tumor growth. *Peptides, 4*, 635–638.

LEWIS, J. W., SHERMAN, J. E., & LIEBESKIND, J. C. (1981c). Opioid and nonopioid stress analgesia: Assessment of tolerance and cross-tolerance with morphine. *Journal of Neuroscience, 1*, 358–363.

LEWIS, J. W., STAPLETON, J. M., CASTIGLIONI, A. J., & LIEBESKIND, J. C. (1982a). Stimulation-produced analgesia and intrinsic mechanisms of pain suppression. In G. FINK & L. J. WHALLEY (Eds.), *Neuropeptides—Basic and clinical aspects.* Edinburgh: Churchill Livingstone, pp. 41–49.

LEWIS, J. W., TERMAN, G. W., WATKINS, L. R., MAYER, D. J., & LIEBESKIND, J. C. (1983c). Opioid and nonopioid mechanisms of footshock-induced analgesia: Role of the spinal dorsolateral funiculus. *Brain Research, 269*, 231–236.

LEWIS, J. W., TORDOFF, M. G., LIEBESKIND, J. C., & VIVEROS, O. H. (1982b). Evidence for adrenal medullary opioid involvement in stress analgesia. *Society for Neuroscience Abstracts, 8*, 778.

LEWIS, J. W., TORDOFF, M. G., SHERMAN, J. E., & LIEBESKIND, J. C. (1982c). Adrenal medullary enkephalin-like peptides may mediate opioid stress analgesia. *Science, 217*, 557–559.

LIEBESKIND, J. C., GIESLER, G. J., JR., & URCA, G. (1976). Evidence pertaining to an endogenous mechanism of pain inhibition in the central nervous system. In Y. ZOTTERMAN (Ed.), *Sensory functions of the skin in primates.* Oxford: Pergamon Press, pp. 561–573.

LIVINGSTON, R. B. (1959). Central control of receptors and sensory transmission systems. In J. FIELD (Ed.), *Handbook of physiology, Section 1: Neurophysiology,* Vol. 1. Washington, DC: American Physiological Society, pp. 741–760.

MACLENNAN, A. J., DRUGAN, R. C., HYSON, R. L., MAIER, S. F., MADDEN, J., & BARCHAS, J. D. (1982). Corticosterone: A critical factor in an opioid form of stress-induced analgesia. *Science, 215*, 1530–1532.

MADDEN, J., AKIL, H., PATRICK, R. L., & BARCHAS, J. D. (1977). Stress-induced parallel changes in central opioid levels and pain responsiveness in the rat. *Nature, 265*, 358–360.

MAIER, S. F., DAVIES, S., GRAU, J. W., JACKSON, R. L., MORRISON, D. H., MOYE, T., MADDEN, J., & BARCHAS, J. D. (1980). Opiate antagonists and the long-term analgesic reaction induced by inescapable shock in rats. *Journal of Comparative and Physiological Psychology, 94*, 1172–1183.

MAIER, S. F., SHERMAN, J. E., LEWIS, J. W., TERMAN, G. W., & LIEBESKIND, J. C. (1983). The opioid/nonopioid nature of stress-induced analgesia and learned helplessness. *Journal of Experimental Psychology: Animal Behavior Processes, 9*, 80–90.

MAIXNER, W., & RANDICH, A. (1984). Role of the right vagal nerve trunk in antinociception. *Brain Research, 298*, 374–377.

MAYER, D. J., & HAYES, R. L. (1975). Stimulation-produced analgesia: Development of tolerance and cross-tolerance to morphine. *Science, 188*, 941–943.

MAYER, D. J., WOLFLE, T. L., AKIL, H., CARDER, B., & LIEBESKIND, J. C. (1971). Analgesia from electrical stimulation in the brainstem of the rat. *Science, 174*, 1351–1354.

McGIVERN, R. F., BERKA, C., BERNTSON, G. G., WALKER, J. M., & SANDMAN, C. A. (1979). Effect of naloxone on analgesia induced by food deprivation. *Life Sciences, 25*, 885–888.

MICZEK, K. A., THOMPSON, M. L., & SHUSTER, L. (1982). Opioid-like analgesia in defeated mice. *Science, 215,* 1520–1522.

MILLAN, M. J., PRZEWLOCKI, R., & HERZ, A. (1980). A non-β-endorphinergic adenohypophyseal mechanism is essential for an analgetic response to stress. *Pain, 8,* 343–353.

MILLAN, M. J. TSANG, Y. F., PRZEWLOCKI, R., HOLLT, V., & HERZ, A. (1981). The influence of foot-shock stress upon brain, pituitary, and spinal cord pools of immunoreactive dynorphin in rats. *Neuroscience Letters, 24,* 75–79.

NELSON, L. R., LEWIS, J. W., LIEBESKIND, J. C., BRANCH, B. J., & TAYLOR, A. N. (1982). Fetal exposure to ethanol potentiates opioid stress analgesia in adult rats. *Society for Neuroscience Abstracts, 8,* 596.

NELSON, L. R., LEWIS, J. W., LIEBESKIND, J. C., BRANCH, B. J., & TAYLOR, A. N. (1983a). Stress-induced changes in ethanol consumption in adult rats exposed to ethanol *in utero. Proceedings of the Western Pharmacology Society, 26,* 205–209.

NELSON, L. R., LEWIS, J.W., LIEBESKIND, J. C., KOKKA, N., RANDOLPH, D., BRANCH, B. J., & TAYLOR, A. N. (1983b). Enhanced responsiveness to morphine in adult rats following fetal ethanol exposure. *Society for Neuroscience Abstracts, 9,* 1242.

NELSON, L. R., TAYLOR, A. N., BRANCH, B. J., LIEBESKIND, J. C., & LEWIS, J. W. (1984). Fetal exposure to ethanol affects sensitivity to morphine but not brain opiate receptor binding in rats. *Society for Neuroscience Abstracts, 10,* 964.

OLESON, T. D., TWOMBLY, D. A., & LIEBESKIND, J. C. (1978). Effects of pain-attenuating brain stimulation and morphine on electrical activity in the raphe nuclei of the awake rat. *Pain, 4,* 211–230.

OLIVERAS, J. L., BESSON, J. M., & LIEBESKIND, J. C. (1974). Behavioral and electrophysiological evidence of pain inhibition from midbrain stimulation in the cat. *Experimental Brain Research, 20,* 32–44.

PEDIGO, N. W., & DEWEY, W. L. (1981). Acetylcholine induced antinociception; comparisons to opiate analgesia. In G. PEPEU & H. LADINSKY (Eds.), *Cholinergic mechanisms: Phylogenetic aspects, central and peripheral synapses, and clinical significance. Advances in Behavioral Biology, Vol. 25.* New York: Plenum Press, pp. 795–807.

PENNER, E. R., TERMAN, G. W., & LIEBESKIND, J. C. (1982). Cross-tolerance between opioid mediated stimulation-produced and stress-induced analgesia. *Society for Neuroscience Abstracts, 8,* 619.

PERT, A., & WALTER, M. (1976). Comparison between naloxone reversal of morphine and electrical stimulation induced analgesia in the rat mesencephalon. *Life Sciences, 19,* 1023–1032.

PETERS, L. J., & MASON, K. A. (1979). Influence of stress on experimental cancer. In B. A. STOLL (Ed.), *Mind and cancer prognosis.* New York: Wiley, pp. 103–124.

PRIETO, G. J., CANNON, J. T., & LIEBESKIND, J. C. (1983). N raphe magnus lesions disrupt stimulation-produced analgesia from ventral but not dorsal midbrain areas in the rat. *Brain Research, 261,* 53–57.

REYNOLDS, D. V. (1969). Surgery in the rat during electrical analgesia induced by focal brain stimulation. *Science, 164,* 444–445.

RICHARDSON, D. D., & AKIL, H. (1977). Pain reduction by electrical brain stimulation in man. Part 2: Chronic self-administration in the periventricular gray matter. *Journal of Neurosurgery, 47,* 184–194.

ROSSIER, J., FRENCH, E. D., RIVIER, C., LING, N., GUILLEMIN, R., & BLOOM, F. E. (1977). Foot-shock induced stress increases β-endorphin levels in blood but not brain. *Nature, 270,* 618–620.

ROSSIER, J., GUILLEMIN, R., & BLOOM, F. E. (1978). Foot-shock induced stress decreases leu[5]-enkephalin immunoreactivity in rat hypothalamus. *European Journal of Pharmacology, 48,* 465–466.

SATOH, M., AKAIKE, A., NAKAZAWA, T., & TAKAGI, H. (1980). Evidence for involvement of separate mechanisms in the production of analgesia by electrical stimulation of the nucleus reticularis paragigantocellularis and nucleus raphe magnus in the rat. *Brain Research, 194*, 525–529.

SCHWARTZ, J. C., BARBIN, G., DUCHEMIN, A. M., GARBARG, M., POLLARD, H., & QUACH, T. T. (1981). Functional role of histamine in the brain. In G. C. PALMER (Ed.), *Neuropharmacology of central nervous system and behavioral disorders*. New York: Academic Press, pp. 539–570.

SELYE, H. (1956). *The stress of life*. New York: McGraw-Hill.

SHAVIT, Y., LEWIS, J. W., TERMAN, G. W., GALE, R. P., & LIEBESKIND, J. C. (1983a). Endogenous opioids may mediate the effects of stress on tumor growth and immune function. *Proceedings of the Western Pharmacology Society, 26*, 53–56.

SHAVIT, Y., LEWIS, J. W., TERMAN, G. W., GALE, R. P., & LIEBESKIND, J. C. (1984a). Opioid peptides mediate the suppressive effect of stress on natural killer cell cytotoxicity. *Science, 223*, 188–190.

SHAVIT, Y., RYAN, S. M., LEWIS, J. C., LAUDENSLAGER, M. L., TERMAN, G. W., MAIER, S. F., GALE, R. P., & LIEBESKIND, J. C. (1983b). Inescapable but not escapable stress alters immune function. *Physiologist, 26*, A–64.

SHAVIT, Y., TERMAN, G. W., MARTIN, F. C., GALE, R. P., & LIEBESKIND, J. C. (1984b). Naltrexone-sensitive suppression of the immune system's natural killer cells by morphine. *Society for Neuroscience Abstracts, 10*, 726.

SKLAR, L. S., & ANISMAN, H. (1979). Stress and coping factors influence tumor growth. *Science, 205*, 513–515.

TAYLOR, A. N., BRANCH, B. J., LIU, S. H., & KOKKA, N. (1982). Long-term effects of fetal ethanol exposure on pituitary-adrenal response to stress. *Pharmacology, Biochemistry, and Behavior, 16*, 585–589.

TERMAN, G. W., LEWIS, J. W., & LIEBESKIND, J. C. (1981). Monoaminergic mechanisms of stress analgesia. *Society for Neuroscience Abstracts, 7*, 879.

TERMAN, G. W., LEWIS, J. W., & LIEBESKIND, J. C. (1982a). Role of the biogenic amines in stress analgesia. *Proceedings of the Western Pharmacology Society, 25*, 7–10.

TERMAN, G. W., LEWIS, J. W., & LIEBESKIND, J. C. (1982b). Evidence for the involvement of histamine in stress analgesia. *Society for Neuroscience Abstracts, 8*, 619.

TERMAN, G. W., LEWIS, J. W., & LIEBESKIND, J. C. (1983a). Opioid and nonopioid mechanisms of stress analgesia: Lack of cross-tolerance between stressors. *Brain Research, 206*, 147–150.

TERMAN, G. W., LEWIS, J. W., & LIEBESKIND, J. C. (1983b). The sensitivity of opioid-mediated stress analgesia to narcotic antagonists. *Proceedings of the Western Pharmacology Society, 26*, 49–52.

TERMAN, G. W., SHAVIT, Y., LEWIS, J. W., CANNON, J. T., & LIEBESKIND, J. C. (1984). Intrinsic mechanisms of pain inhibition and their activation by stress. *Science, 226*, 1270–1277.

TORDA, C. (1978). Effects of recurrent postnatal pain-related stressful events on opiate receptor-endogenous ligand system. *Psychoneuroendocrinology, 3*, 85–91.

TRICKLEBANK, M. D., HUTSON, P. H., & CURZON, G. (1982). Analgesia induced by brief footshock is inhibited by 5-hydroxytryptamine but unaffected by antagonists of 5-hydroxytryptamine or by naloxone. *Neuropharmacology, 21*, 51–56.

URCA, G., & LIEBESKIND, J. C. (1979). Electrophysiological indices of opiate action in awake and anesthetized rats. *Brain Research, 161*, 162–166.

VISINTAINER, M. A., VOLPICELLI, J. R., & SELIGMAN, E. P. (1982). Tumor rejection in rats after inescapable or escapable shock. *Science, 216*, 437–439.

VIVEROS, O. H., DILIBERTO, E. J., JR., HAZUM, E., & CHANG, K.-J. (1980). Enkephalins as possible adrenomedullary hormones: Storage, secretion, and regulation of synthesis.

In E. Costa & M. Trabucchi (Eds.), *Neural peptides and neuronal communication*. New York: Raven Press, pp. 191–201.

Viveros, O. H., & Wilson, S. P. (1983). The adrenal chromaffin cell as a model to study the co-secretion of enkephalins and catecholamines. *Journal of the Autonomous Nervous System, 7*, 41–58.

Watkins, L. R., Cobelli, D. A., & Mayer, D. J. (1982b). Opiate vs. non-opiate footshock analgesia (FSIA): Descending and intraspinal components. *Brain Research, 245*, 97–106.

Watkins, L. R., Cobelli, D. A., Newsome, H. H., & Mayer, D. J. (1982c). Footshock induced analgesia is dependent neither on pituitary nor sympathetic activation. *Brain Research, 245*, 81–96.

Watkins, L. R., & Mayer, D. J. (1982). The organization of endogenous opiate and non-opiate pain control systems. *Science, 216*, 1185–1192.

Watson, S. J., Akil, H., & Barchas, J. D. (1979). Immunohistochemical and biochemical studies of the enkephalins, β-endorphin and related peptides. In E. Usdin, W. E. Bunney, & N. S. Kline (Eds.), *Endorphins in mental health research*. New York: Oxford University Press, pp. 30–44.

Yaksh, T. L, & Rudy, T. A. (1978). Narcotic analgetics: CNS sites and mechanisms of action as revealed by intracerebral injection techniques. *Pain, 4*, 299–359.

Yaksh, T. L., Yeung, J. C., & Rudy, T. A. (1976). An inability to antagonize with naloxone the elevated thresholds resulting from electrical stimulation of the mesencephalic central gray. *Life Sciences, 18*, 1193–1198.

Young, R. F., Feldman, R. A., Kroening, R., Fulton, W., & Morris, J. (1984). Electrical stimulation of the brain in the treatment of chronic pain in man. In L. Kruger & J. C. Liebeskind (Eds.), *Neural mechanisms of pain. Advances in Pain Research and Therapy, Vol. 6.* New York: Raven Press, pp. 289–303.

Zorman, G., Hentall, I. D., Adams, J. E., & Fields, H. L. (1981). Naloxone-reversible analgesia produced by microstimulation in the rat medulla. *Brain Research, 219*, 137–148.

5 Inhibition and Cognition

Toward an Understanding of Trauma and Disease

JAMES W. PENNEBAKER AND CLAUDIA W. HOOVER

I. INTRODUCTION

When we are upset or confused about an event, it often helps to write or to talk about it with someone. The mere act of organizing and categorizing the event makes us feel better and allows us to devote our attention to other things. Certain events, such as getting a parking ticket or having an airline lose our bags, can be assimilated and explained relatively easily. Others, however, such as being assaulted or being rejected by one's spouse, require far more cognitive work in order to organize, understand, and ultimately to forget. One problem that occasionally occurs is that we are sometimes unable to discuss certain personally traumatic events for fear of embarrassment or punishment. In such cases, we must actively inhibit the confiding process. As will be seen, the inhibition process is itself stressful. Hence, the combined physiological effects of experiencing the trauma, attempting to assimilate the trauma, and inhibition can sum to produce long-term stress and susceptibility to disease. The model that we propose has evolved from rather diverse literatures and serendipitous observations. Because our research in this area is in a nascent stage, our model should be viewed as a tentative conceptual framework that will undoubtedly be revised over the next few years.

Our interest in traumatic events was piqued by a series of results that we uncovered while examining the nature of the reporting of physical symptoms. As part of a large survey administered to over 400 college

---

A version of this paper was presented at the annual meeting for the Society for Psychophysiological Research, Pacific Grove, CA, 1983.

JAMES W. PENNEBAKER ● Department of Psychology, Southern Methodist University, Dallas, Texas 75275. CLAUDIA W. HOOVER ● Center for Behavioral Medicine, Du Pont Associates, Rockville, Maryland 20852.

students, we had included an item asking, "Prior to the age of 17, did you have a traumatic sexual experience (e.g., rape, being molested)?" Among high-symptom reporters, 14.4% responded affirmatively whereas only 2.5% of the low-symptom reporters did so (Pennebaker, 1982). Later surveys revealed that reports of a sexual trauma were highly correlated with physician visits, drug use, and increased incidence of cardiovascular, digestive, kidney, lung, skin, and other disorders. Finally, as will be discussed in greater detail below, those reporting sexual traumas claimed that the traumatic event had occurred several years earlier and that, by and large, they had not confided in others about the event.

A second issue that has long puzzled us (as well as many psychotherapists) is why psychotherapy, self-disclosure, or even writing a diary makes people feel better and makes them less prone to illness? A particularly intriguing example comes from the seminal work of Harold G. Wolff (Wolf & Goodell, 1968) wherein Wolff and his colleagues perform a number of stress tests on patients with psychosomatic diseases in order to isolate specific psychological precursors to physiological change. Wolff often presents clinical data indicating that once the patient understands the psychological causes of his or her health problems, the symptoms gradually or, on occasion, abruptly subside.

A third enigma concerns the nature of physiological responses to deception and inhibition in laboratory or real-world polygraph settings. There is little doubt that inducing a subject to lie in the guilty knowledge test (GKT) produces an impressive physiological response. Further, if the subject must respond *no* to a series of words (one of which he is lying about), after the lie word, further *no* responses produce much smaller physiological responses than *no* responses preceding the lie word. By the same token, when we lie in the real world, we often can feel our own body changing in response to the lie. Perhaps most significant is that our interviews with professional polygraphers suggest a dramatic change in physiological responses after a confession. For example, if a suspect is initially polygraphed on a set of standardized questions, he or she is judged to be deceptive based on exaggerated physiological responses to key questions. However, if, after the first series of tests, the suspect confesses to the crime, later physiological responses to the same questions (to which he or she is now telling the truth) disappear or are greatly reduced. Not only are the phasic responses to the key questions lower, but the person's overall autonomic activity is reduced (despite the fact that the person may now face severe punishment because of his or her confession).

The common thread linking all of these phenomena is that linguistically organizing and, perhaps, communicating aspects of personal traumas reduce the psychological and physiological aftereffects of traumas. Conversely, if an individual is inhibited or prohibited from organizing trauma-relevant information, individuals may become more susceptible to disease processes. As will be seen, these cognitive and inhibitory processes extend beyond the traditional views of the effects of major life events (e.g., Holmes & Rahe, 1967) or the buffering effects of social support (Cobb, 1976).

In the first section of the chapter, we will present evidence indicating that the effects of major life crises—specifically sexual trauma, divorce of parents, and death of a parent—persist over several years in the forms of illnesses and physical symptom reporting. The results from several survey studies will indicate that the fundamental difference in these traumas is the degree to which individuals confide in others. Further, failure to confide or discuss the trauma with others can exacerbate the physiological effects of traumas. The second major section of the chapter deals with the general problem of inhibition. Starting from a molecular level, evidence will be presented that indicates that the inhibition of ongoing behavior results in heightened physiological activity. Further, personality research suggests that chronic inhibitors evidence generally higher autonomic activity. We will then provide preliminary evidence that indicates that certain types of traumas require that the person actively inhibit disclosing his or her experiences. Hence, the combined effects of inhibition and failure to assimilate traumatic experience cognitively produce maximal long-term physiological effects. In the final section, we will discuss the relationship of our framework to the psychotherapy, coping, and psychoanalytic literatures.

II. Personal Traumas and Health

The results of the studies to follow concern the impact of major traumatic events several years after the events occurred. It is tempting to claim that we had clear hypotheses and a conceptual framework from the beginning. In fact, our earlier surveys were designed to study bulimia and related eating disorders (see Barrios & Pennebaker, 1983). However, as our initially serendipitous findings were uncovered, the present framework gradually emerged. Nevertheless, in order to give the false impression of foresight, we will present the following studies as though they represented carefully planned programmatic research.

On the basis of the overwhelming number of confirmatory studies, there is little doubt that major life events can adversely affect health (e.g., Kobasa, 1982). Most work within the life change literature indicates that the risk of serious illness increases significantly as a function of the number and severity of the life changes. Of particular relevance to the present investigation, virtually all of the studies using standardized life event scales, such as the Schedule of Recent Experience (Holmes & Rahe, 1967), have focused on changes in health for six months to two years following major life events. With the exception of a small number of retrospective studies (e.g., LeShan, 1966; Schmale & Iker, 1971), few investigators have examined the long-term effects of a selected group of major life changes on health patterns.

From a preliminary study of symptom reporting (Pennebaker, 1982), we suspected that traumatic sexual experiences, divorce of parents, or the death of a parent could have adverse health consequences over several years. Common sense (as well as survey results to be discussed below) dictates that each of these events would be viewed as maximally traumatic (and therefore roughly equivalent) by the child or adolescent. When we first started our research, we were simply interested in the similarities and differences among these events in their relationship to health indicators.

The results of three surveys are discussed briefly below. The first, which was completed by 716 female undergraduates from the University of Virginia and the University of Mississippi, was part of a 400-item questionnaire that assessed symptom and emotion reports, family history, eating habits, dating patterns, and the like. The second survey was based on readership response to a questionnaire published in *Psychology Today* magazine dealing with health issues in general (Rubenstein, 1982). Although over 24,000 individuals mailed their surveys to the magazine, only the data from a random sample of 2,020 respondents were analyzed. The third questionnaire survey was, in fact, a series of surveys given to one class (Medical Psychology) of 80 students at the University of Virginia over the course of the semester. Sampling problems and related issues will be discussed in greater detail after the results are presented.

A. Initial Survey

All 716 subjects in the first survey were contacted in various psychology classes and asked to complete the questionnaire without receiving credit. Although the response rate was only 67%, a random sample of nonrespondents was contacted by phone to learn if they differed in major respects from the respondents. No differences were found for demographic, health, or other variables between the respondent and nonrespondent samples. The major reasons for not completing the survey were "not enough time" and "I forgot."

INHIBITION AND COGNITION 111

Subjects were divided into 4 groups: Control, Death of parent, Divorce of parents, and Sex Trauma (hereafter designated as Control, Death, Divorce, and Sex Trauma). Students were assigned to the Death group if either or both of their parents had died by the time the respondent was 17. The Divorce subjects had to have natural parents who had been divorced or legally separated by the time they were 17. Subjects were assigned to the Sex Trauma group based on their responding affirmatively to the question: "Prior to the age of 17, did you have a traumatic sexual experience (e.g., rape, being molested)?" There are two immediate problems with defining the Sex Trauma group. The first concerns whether or not the person honestly revealed that she had had a traumatic sexual experience and, if so, what had been the nature of this experience. Fortunately, we were able to conduct intensive interviews with a subsample of 17 respondents. Of the three who had answered the sexual trauma question in the affirmative, one had been raped and two had been molested. We of course have no idea how many of the Control subjects had had sexual traumas. Nevertheless, we feel that the size of our Sex Trauma group is probably conservative.

The second problem is that some of the subjects had experienced both a divorce and a sexual trauma, a divorce and a death, or all three. In order to maximize cell frequencies, assignment to condition was prioritized in the order of sexual trauma, death, divorce. It should be noted that subjects who had experienced a sexual trauma and a divorce and/ or death did not differ statistically from the sexual trauma only subjects on any of the major health-dependent measures.

The primary dependent measures included the degree to which subjects experienced selected physical symptoms and emotions on "the average day," with 1 = never and 7 = almost always. Subjects were also asked whether or not they had been to a physician or student health center within the past eight months for illness. Additional questions were included asking how many *very* close male and female friends they had and, if they were in trouble or very emotionally upset, how likely it would be that they would confide in no one (where 7 = extremely likely).

Each of the dependent measures was subjected to a one-way analysis of variance. As can be seen in Table 1, those who claimed to have had a traumatic sexual experience were far more likely to report a variety of physical symptoms and negative emotions than any of the other groups. Although the Death and Divorce groups tended to have higher means on these items than the Control group, simple contrasts (using the mean-square error term) did not yield significant differences. Although the physician visit item did not attain significance, this may have been due to a ceiling effect since a relatively high proportion of all sub-

TABLE 1

Self-Reports of Selected Variables by Type of Trauma for the Initial Study[a]

Variable	Control	Divorce of parents	Death of parent	Sexual trauma	Significance
Physical symptoms					
Headache	2.6	2.8	2.6	3.3	.01
Upset stomach	2.3	2.3	2.3	2.8	.05
Tense muscles	3.0	3.0	2.3	3.8	.01
Racing heart	2.4	2.5	2.3	3.2	.01
Light headed	2.2	2.6	2.0	3.0	.01
Negative emotions					
Stress	4.0	4.0	3.5	4.5	.04
Depressed	3.2	3.4	3.0	3.5	ns
Guilty	2.8	2.8	2.8	3.1	ns
Angry	2.9	2.9	2.7	3.2	ns
Isolated	3.2	3.0	2.9	3.7	.09
Fatigue	4.4	4.9	3.7	4.6	.01
Other data					
Number of close friends	8.1	7.4	9.0	8.0	ns
Confided in no one	2.6	2.5	2.4	3.6	.01
Visited health center or physician (percent)	51.4	58.0	46.3	60.3	ns
Age	19.4	19.6	19.3	19.8	ns
N	536	81	41	58	

[a] Symptoms and emotions were coded along 7-point scale with 1 = never experience on the average day and 7 = always experience on the average day. Probability levels are based on overall F from a one-way analysis of variance.

jects responded affirmatively. Finally, although the Sex Trauma group did not differ from the others in respect to the total number of friends, it is noteworthy that they were most likely not to confide in anyone if they were in trouble.

B. Psychology Today Sample

In the May, 1982, issue of *Psychology Today*, a four-page questionnaire dealing with health was printed asking the readers to complete it and mail it to the magazine's main office. Fortunately, the editor in charge of the survey, Carin Rubenstein, allowed us to include several questions and to reanalyze the data. Within two months, over 24,000 individuals returned the completed survey (about 1.2% of the magazine's circulation). Of the surveys, a random sample of 2,020 was analyzed. The data indicated that the respondents mirrored the general readership of the magazine (mean age = 35.1, 68% female, median income around $25,000). At the outset, it should be noted that a survey of this nature is not truly random nor does it represent a clearly defined population. Individuals who completed the questionnaire may well have been far more health-conscious than nonrespondents.

On the basis of the survey responses, four groups (Control, Death, Divorce, and Sex Trauma) were defined in the same manner as in the initial survey described above. Overall, 22% of the women and 10% of the men reported having experienced a sexual trauma prior to the age of 17. Of the 367 in the Sex Trauma group, 21% had also experienced a divorce of parents and 11% had had a parent die prior to the age of 17. Separate analyses comparing those with a sexual trauma only with those with a sexual trauma and divorce and/or death yielded virtually no significant differences for any of the health-dependent measures.

Unlike the initial study, subjects' reports of illnesses, physical symptoms, and emotions were based on binary yes–no responses to the question, "Which of the following bothered you in the past year?" These data are expressed as percentages of respondents answering affirmatively in Table 2. Finally, 10 life change items adapted from the Schedule of Recent Experience asking whether or not the subjects had experienced each item within the past year (e.g., death of spouse or loved one, loss of job). These items were summed to make a total life change score.

As can be seen in Table 2, most illnesses, symptoms, and negative emotions occurred with greater frequency among all three trauma groups. As in the first study, these effects were most pronounced for the Sex Trauma group. It is of interest that the groups did not differ in the number of close friends nor in their having someone to confide in. Finally, inspection of the total life change scores indicates that the trauma groups had experienced more life events than the Controls. Although statistically significant, the magnitude of differences between groups is relatively small. It should be noted that the group differences for the health effects remain significant when the life change score is controlled for.

These data raise a number of important issues. First, the magnitude of differences in the various health indicators as a function of group is large considering that these traumatic events took place close to 20 years earlier. Second, there are undoubtedly a number of important mediating factors. For example, the health differences could reflect poor health practices (e.g., the Sex Trauma group was more likely to smoke and not eat a balanced diet), more negative emotions (which could directly cause health problems), or simply greater attentiveness to bodily sensations. We cannot, however, explain the results simply in terms of differences

TABLE 2

Self-Reports of Selected Variables by Type of Trauma for the *Psychology Today* Sample[a]

Variable	Control	Divorce of parents	Death of parent	Sexual trauma	p
Illness and symptoms (percentage reporting in last year)					
Ulcers	9.0	10.9	7.9	14.4	.01
Indigestion or upset stomach	39.9	50.7	36.3	50.1	.01
Chronic constipation	6.9	7.9	9.6	12.8	.01
Diarrhea	8.7	12.4	7.3	14.1	.01
Frequent headaches	24.2	30.3	28.4	32.7	.01
High blood pressure	8.3	6.4	10.8	11.1	.12
Heart or chest pain	8.5	8.9	7.9	13.9	.01
Dizzy spells	10.2	12.4	7.9	14.4	.06
Kidney or bladder infection	16.7	20.9	20.4	25.6	.01
Chronic lung disease or bronchitis	4.7	8.4	6.2	8.1	.03
Influenza, throat or lung infections	49.7	57.2	48.3	52.8	.17
Trouble getting breath	6.2	9.9	7.3	11.7	.01
Pain or numbness in muscles or joints	11.1	14.9	14.2	16.8	.02
Menstrual problems	19.3	27.3	19.8	26.4	.01
Cognitive and emotional reports (percentage reporting):					
Difficulty concentrating	25.0	28.8	24.4	31.8	.05
Tire easily	28.6	30.3	27.2	38.2	.01
Restlessness	20.3	28.8	23.3	26.7	.01
Fatigue	28.6	30.3	27.2	38.1	.01
Nightmares	10.2	15.9	14.7	20.7	.01
Depressed or blue	49.3	62.1	55.1	60.0	.01
Guilty	17.1	22.3	21.0	30.7	.01
Lonely	32.4	38.3	39.2	41.1	.01
Angry or irritable	47.2	53.7	50.5	54.5	.01
Irrational fears	11.2	9.4	14.7	18.8	.01
Loss of interest in sex	18.9	18.4	26.7	27.5	.01
Other data:					
Number of close friends	6.1	5.3	5.4	5.6	.08
Do you now confide in close friends (1 = yes 5 = no)	1.4	1.4	1.5	1.5	.22
Number of days sick in last year	4.3	6.3	5.6	5.0	.07
Number of physician visits last year	3.1	3.9	3.3	3.8	.15
Number of days hospitalized last year	0.8	1.0	1.8	1.7	.03
Age in years	36.1	31.7	38.4	35.0	.01
N (males)	530	81	56	73	
N (females)	746	120	120	294	
Total N	1,276	201	176	367	

[a] Probability levels (p values) are based on overall one-way analyses of variance for each of the dependent measures by condition.

in present measures of social support or recent life crises. As will be discussed below, these results may reflect the coping strategies that the trauma (especially sexual traumas) subjects employed during and following their earlier trauma.

On the original questionnaire, respondents were asked to include their name and telephone number for possible future telephone interviews. Rubenstein called 15 subjects who had claimed to have had a sexual trauma. In her article, Rubenstein (1982) notes:

> One woman was raped at 16; another was a victim of incest at 8; yet another had been fondled at the age of 5 by a man selling ponies. A 51-year-old woman from Los Angeles told me that she had been raped, at 5, by her neighbor, who was a friend of the family. . . . "I never told anyone about it. You're the first," she said. Later on, not making the connection, she remarked, "I've always had health problems with organs in that area . . . since I was 5." (page 34)

Rubenstein (personal communication) notes that every person that she talked with related an experience that would objectively be defined as sexually traumatic. Further, she found that the majority had not discussed this traumatic event with anyone at the time and, if they eventually did, several months or years had elapsed in the interim. The failure of conveying and, perhaps, organizing or assimilating such a traumatic event may have long-term health implications. Before discussing this issue in detail, however, we must first present results from a third survey study that bears directly on the confiding issue.

C. Medical Psychology Class Survey

Each year, the first author teaches an upper-division undergraduate course entitled Medical Psychology that is restricted to 80 students. Although the course has a higher percentage of pre-med students (38%) than most higher level courses in psychology, their mean grade point average, health center visits, and scores on standardized individual difference measures (e.g., I–E locus of control, Jenkins Activity Survey, Self-consciousness Scale) are virtually identical with those of students enrolled in Introductory Psychology and Social Psychology classes. The course was comprised of 55 women and 20 men, with a mean age of 20.5. During the semester, students complete a number of questionnaires that are pertinent to the course. The data to be presented below are based on the responses of 75 students enrolled in the class during the Spring of 1983. Two of the questionnaires are particularly relevant. The first assessed the types of traumas the students had had prior to the age of 17, how upsetting each was, and the degree to which they confided in others about the trauma (all along 7-point scales with $1 =$ not at all and $7 =$ a great deal). Separate questionnaires completed later in the semester required students to report if they had had each of 20 serious health problems (e.g., asthma, pneumonia, diabetes). Finally, students completed a number of individual difference measures that assess: the general proclivity to report physical symptoms (i.e., PILL from Pennebaker, 1982), self-consciousness (including Private Self-consciousness, Public Self-consciousness, and Social Anxiety from Fenigstein, Scheier, & Buss, 1975), Type A behavior (the student version of the Jenkins Activity Survey from Krantz, Glass, & Snyder, 1974), cognitive and social anxiety (the CSAQ from Schwartz, Davidson, & Goleman, 1978), and social desirability (Marlowe-Crowne Social Desirability Scale from Crowne & Marlowe, 1964). These data are included for comparison purposes with other samples and will not be discussed in detail.

Unlike the previous studies, the death of parent question was expanded to include death of family member or very close personal friend. The divorce question included either divorce or separation of parents. Overall, 10 subjects reported having had a traumatic sexual experience, 17 had experienced the death of a family member or close personal friend, and 12 had had parents who had been divorced or separated. The mean ages at which these traumas occurred were 12.9 for sexual trauma, 9.3 for death, and 12.0 for divorce. The mean ratings for how upsetting the various traumas were (with $7 =$ extremely upsetting) were 5.1 for sexual trauma, 5.3 for death, and 5.8 for divorce. In response to the question, "To what degree did you confide in others about this event" with $7 =$ confided a great deal, the means for the various groups were 2.1 for sexual trauma, 3.3 for death, and 3.8 for divorce ($p < .01$).

Initial analyses of variance using the four groups (Control, Death, Divorce, and Sex Trauma) as independent variables and self-reported disease, symptom reporting, health center usage, and social factors as dependent measures yielded results similar to the previous studies. As before, the Sex Trauma group reported experiencing the most number of major diseases (3.1 versus 1.8 for Divorce, 1.1 for Death and 1.1 for Controls, $p < .01$), and the most visits to the student health center in the past year (3.6 versus 1.8, 1.1, and 1.3 for Sex Trauma, Divorce, Death, and Control groups respectively, $p < .01$). In addition, all trauma groups reported higher overall frequency and severity of symptom reporting relative to controls (means for the groups: 23.0, 22.1, 20.1, and 14.4 for Sex Trauma, Divorce, Death, and Controls respectively, $p < .01$). Finally, the four groups did not differ in the total number of close friends that they had (8.2, 6.8, 6.8, 8.3, $p = .65$).

A striking aspect of the response patterns for these data was the marked variability in the degree to which people either did or did not confide about each of the traumas. Even though the sexual trauma groups in each of the above studies have evidenced the greatest health problems, we assume that this is due, in part, to their not discussing and subsequently organizing the event. We would predict that *any* traumatic event that was not talked about would have deleterious effects. In order to test this idea, we divided our subjects in the present experiment into three groups: No Trauma, Trauma and Confided, and Trauma and Not Confided. That is, on the basis of their responses to the three different traumas (whether sex, death, or divorce), if any trauma was reported they were assigned to either the Confided or Not Confided group by their self-reported degree of confiding of the relevant trauma. In short, no distinction was made among types of trauma. (Subjects were assigned to the No Confide condition if, on their confiding question, they responded with a 1, 2, or 3 along the 7-point scale).

One-way analyses of variance were performed on the disease, symptom reporting, and related variables. *A priori* contrasts using the mean-square error term (one-tailed tests) were also computed for each dependent measure. As can be seen in Table 3, having experienced a traumatic event and not having confided in others about it was associated with the highest disease incidence, most number of visits to the student health center for illness or injury, and overall symptom reporting. In terms of specific diseases, this trend was significant for the following: severe acne ($p = .03$), tumor ($p = .05$), migraine headache ($p = .035$), severe injury ($p = .12$), ulcer ($p = .06$), severe depression ($p = .02$), and appendectomy ($p = .05$). No differences were found for asthma, high blood pressure, anorexia nervosa, cancer, mononucleosis, diabetes, severe allergy, severe obesity, or other disorder (due in part to the extremely low frequency of these disorders among the sample).

The results of this study are comparable with the previous ones that we have reported. First, those who have had a sexual trauma report the most health problems. Second, there are no differences among the groups in terms of the number of close friends that they have. Third, the primary factor that separates the groups is an event that happened, on the average, 7 years earlier.

The distinguishing characteristic of the present survey is that not confiding in others about a traumatic experience, irrespective of the nature of the experience, appears to underlie the differences in health status among the trauma groups. Further, our results indicate that sexual traumas are far less likely to be confided than are other types of major uncontrollable events such as death or divorce of parents. We must now stand back and address what it could be about confiding or not confiding that could affect disease processes.

TABLE 3

Self-reports of Selected Variables by Trauma and Confiding for Medical Psychology Class Sample

Variable	No trauma	Trauma and confide	Trauma and not confide	Significance
Number of Diseases	1.1	1.6	2.2	.03
Number of health center visits	0.7	1.2	2.1	.05
Number of close friends	8.3	7.9	6.1	ns
Individual difference measures:				
Symptom reporting (PILL)	14.4	21.9	20.6	.01
Self-consciousness scale:				
Private	23.6	25.5	25.1	ns
Public	26.1	29.9	27.1	.04
Social anxiety	12.5	13.5	14.8	ns
CSAQ:				
Cognitive anxiety	17.0	19.4	20.1	.07
Somatic anxiety	15.2	18.6	18.7	.01
Jenkins Activity Survey: (Student version)	7.8	8.8	9.1	ns
Marlowe-Crowne social desirability scale:	13.7	12.3	11.3	.07
Total N	36	23	16	

III. The Failure to Confide: The Role of Inhibition

There are two important aspects of the confiding issue. The first has been addressed indirectly by the social support and social comparison literatures. For example, the act of confiding assumes that the person has access to intimate others. Interacting closely with others can serve to buffer the effects of life crises (e.g., Cobb, 1976). The person receives feedback that he or she is loved and important. In addition, the act of confiding serves as a way of obtaining the information that the person's thoughts and actions are normal. That is, the person can compare his or her feelings about the traumatic event with similar others. Such a social comparison process should be anxiety-reducing in that the individual learns that he or she is not as "abnormal" or unique as he or she may have feared (Festinger, 1954; Valins & Nisbett, 1972). Note that these approaches assume that the traumatic event is, in and of itself, physiologically damaging in the long run but that social factors can reduce the effects of this process.

An alternative way by which to view the confiding results is that actively inhibiting or suppressing knowledge of the event to others is in itself physiologically stressful. Although the traumatic event undoubtedly does produce major physiological upheavals in the short run (Selye, 1976) and, to a lesser degree, in the long run, the act of inhibiting by *not* confiding in others may require additional physiological work. In short, the inhibitory processes of actively not confiding together with the normal physiological upheavals of the trauma itself sum to produce maximal long-term stress which should ultimately be manifested in disease.

If such a process occurs, we must first demonstrate that behavioral inhibition is associated with heightened physiological activity. Second, it must be established that the physiological correlates of inhibition persist over long periods of time. Finally, if such an explanation accounts for the higher illness rates among those who have had traumatic experiences but have not confided these events, we must demonstrate that failure to confide reflects an inhibitory process. In this section, we will present evidence to support each of these necessary links. We will then discuss some of the possible physiological mechanisms that may account for the disease processes themselves. We must first, however, briefly discuss the general nature of inhibition.

A. The Nature of Inhibition

Few concepts in all of psychology have had a more sordid history than inhibition. Among its difficulties are its different meanings and the responses to which it has been applied across the various subdisciplines of psychology. For example, on a neuronal level, the firing of one nerve may decrease the probability of other neurons' firing. Similarly, reciprocal inhibition allows one group of muscles to contract while antagonistic muscles must not contract (e.g., when extending one's arm). In visual and auditory perception, the firing of one group of cells may block the firing of adjacent cells in order to enhance contrast, as in lateral inhibition (Bekesy, 1967). In addition, certain afferent fibers can be blocked by the cortex to aid in orienting (Hernandez-Peon, 1960) or in reducing transmission of pain signals (Melzack, 1973). Pavlov (1927) developed an entire taxonomy of inhibitory processes to explain phenomena such as extinction of a conditioned response over time and spontaneous recovery (internal inhibition) and the failure of a conditioned stimulus to elicit a conditioned response due to the presence of a novel stimulus (external inhibition). Spence (1936) and Hull (1950) viewed conditioned inhibition as the main factor responsible for the weakening of a conditioned response. One of the major criticisms of the use of the term *inhibition* was leveled by Skinner (1938), who argued that the reduction in the intensity of a response could more parsimoniously be explained by a reduction in excitation. Later evidence that strongly supported the existence of active inhibitory processes has been put forward by a number of animal researchers, including Rescorla (1967), Konorski (1967), and Terrace (1972). Inhibition constructs have also been used among verbal learning experts to explain differential encoding and recall of word lists (Melton, 1963). Freud (1926/1959) viewed inhibition as a restriction of the ego which has been either imposed as a measure of precaution or brought about as a result of an impoverishment of energy.

Although each of the above uses of the inhibition concept has been applied to vastly different phenomena, the concept's usefulness is in describing a general process wherein a given event does not occur due to the action of another event. Within the present context, we infer that inhibition is occurring when a person is unable or unwilling to behave in a given manner (e.g., disclosing, confiding) for fear of perceived negative sanctions (humiliation, punishment, etc.). Further, if these negative sanctions were not perceived to be present, the specific behavior would occur. In short, inhibition in this context is an active process (cf. Terrace, 1972).

Some supplementary remarks about this definition in regard to cognitive processes are in order. In line with current thinking about perceptual, cognitive, and attribution processes (Gibson, 1979; Kelley, 1972; Neisser, 1976), we assume that individuals seek to understand their environments and, in the case of humans, themselves. When an unexpected and potentially self-relevant event occurs, it behooves the individual to understand and cognitively assimilate the event in order to maintain some degree of predictability and control over the environment. Talking, writing, or even thinking about an important and complex event is required in order to understand it (e.g., Jourard, 1971). Confiding in others about a traumatic event should hasten this process. Further, it allows them to receive information about potential coping strategies (Lazarus, 1966). If the individual must actively inhibit this assimiliation, both the work of inhibition and the assimilation process should sum to produce long-term physiological stress. We will return to these cognitive issues in the final section of the paper.

B. *Inhibition and Physiological Activity*

If our model is to be viable, we must first demonstrate that inhibition is associated with physiological activity. For several years, Jeffrey Gray has been examining the physiological substrates of inhibitory and excitatory processes in animals. In an impressive integration of the literature, Gray (1975) has shown that in passive avoidance paradigms (wherein the animal must not perform a learned behavior in order to avoid punishment) or in temporal inhibition (wherein the organism must not respond for a certain amount of time in order to be reinforced, as in DRL procedures), there is an increase in activity of the septal and hippocampal regions of the brain, which is referred to as the Behavioral Inhibition System (BIS). When the activity of these brain systems is blocked by drugs or destroyed, the rats exhibit a marked decline in the ability to inhibit behaviors. Interestingly, certain drugs such as amphetamines or caffeine appear to increase the activity of the BIS.

In a compelling extension of Gray's work, Fowles (1980) proposed that activity of the BIS was associated with heightened electrodermal activity in humans. The counterpart of the BIS, the behavioral activation system (BAS), was posited to correlate with cardiovascular activity. Fowles bases his argument on a number of human psychophysiological investigations. For example, passive avoidance paradigms with humans result in changes in electrodermal activity (EDA) but not in heart rate. Active avoidance, on the other hand, is associated with increased heart rate and blood pressure but not with EDA. Although we will return to this issue in dealing with chronic inhibitors and noninhibitors later, it is important to emphasize the link between behavioral inhibition and specific physiological activity.

Particularly relevant to the present argument is the expanding literature related to the psychophysiological correlates of deception (see Waid & Orne, 1981, 1982). One paradigm that has been employed extensively is the guilty knowledge test (GKT) wherein a subject is induced to lie while various autonomic measures are monitored. One variation of this procedure requires the subject to write down a number between 1 and 10. The experimenter then asks, "Is the number 1?" "Is the number 2?" and so on. The subject is instructed to answer no to each of the questions, including the number that was actually written down (the lie word). Researchers are able to detect the lie word at rates far above chance. In addition, of all autonomic channels, EDA appears to be the most reliable indicator of deception (Waid & Orne, 1981). Drugs that Gray (1975) posits should decrease inhibitory tendencies, such as tranquilizers, tend to lower EDA responses to deception (Waid & Orne, 1981). We can tentatively infer, then, that phasic inhibitory responses are associated with autonomic activity, especially EDA.

At this point, we must be able to demonstrate that deception is associated with inhibition of behavior and at the same time with a corresponding increase in physiological activity, such as EDA. In a recent experiment, Carol Chew and the first author (Pennebaker & Chew, in press) directly tested this link. In the experiment, 25 women and 5 men participated in a variant of the GKT on two occasions. All subjects selected one of five words printed on separate index cards. They then denied holding each of the five words while skin resistance was continuously monitored. Throughout the procedure, the experimenter (who was blind to the lie word) called out the possible words from an adjacent room. Following the initial test, which was identical for all subjects, 20 subjects were randomly assigned to the Observe condition and 10 to the No Observe. In both conditions, subjects were given a second group of five words to choose from. For the Observe subjects, a second experimenter sat directly in front of them and explained that he was attempting to guess which word they had chosen by watching their behavior. For the No Observe subjects, the second experimenter merely said that the general procedure would be the same as before and then left the room.

For the Observe subjects, the experimenter closely watched the subject's face throughout the second GKT. He pressed one button whenever there was a change in eye gaze and a second one whenever there was a change in facial expression (inter-rater reliability of this procedure using videotapes is high, $r = .87$). The observer's button-press responses were recorded simultaneously with the subject's skin resistance on a polygraph in the adjacent room. As in the initial session, the first experimenter called out the words from the adjacent room, 14 seconds apart.

Skin resistance level and button presses corresponding to eye movement (EM) and change in facial expression (FE) were coded every two seconds for all words across both sessions. The skin resistance measures were converted to skin conductance and then standardized on a within-subject basis to allow simple comparison with EM and FE. The various measures were tabulated separately for the lie word and the mean of the four truth words.

Between-within analyses of variance on the skin conductance scores indicated that the overall skin conductance level (SCL) increased from the first session to the second for the Observe and decreased for the No Observe subjects ($p < .001$). As can be seen in Figure 1, SCL was significantly higher for the lie word than for the truth words ($p < .001$), especially during the 0–4 seconds after their lie or truth response. More revealing, however, was the relationship between the overt behaviors and SCL for the Observe subjects (behavioral measures were, of course, not obtained in the No Observe conditions).

As depicted in Figure 2, there was a significant reduction in behaviors for the lie word relative to the truth words ($p < .02$). Closer examination of the behavioral data reveals that subjects were least likely

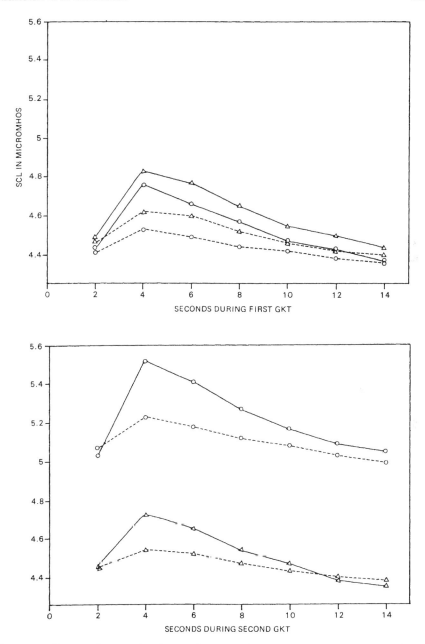

FIGURE 1. Skin conductance levels at each 2-second interval for the first and second guilty knowledge tests. Subjects' "no" responses occurred at the 2-second point. △—△ No observe—Lie word; △---△ No observe—truth words; O—O Observe—Lie word; O---O Observe—Truth words.

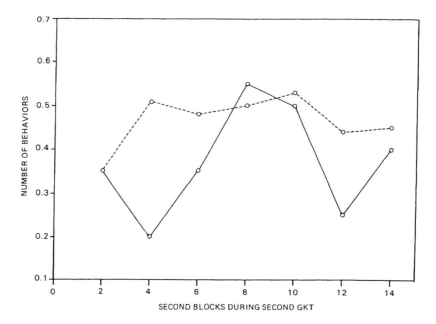

FIGURE 2. Mean number of behaviors (changes in eye movement and facial expression) during each 2-second time block during the second guilty knowledge test (Observe subjects only). O—O Lie word; O- - -O Truth words.

to change eye gaze or facial expression during the 0–4 seconds following their verbal response on the lie word relative to the truth word ($p <$ .05). This behavioral inhibition coincided with the greatest increase in SCL. Although one might be tempted to speculate that the reduction in behavior caused the increase in SCL in a hydraulic manner, we prefer to think that the concomitant changes in these measures reflect a centrally mediated inhibitory process. That is, whenever one must inhibit ongoing activity, there is a corresponding physiological change mediated, perhaps, by the septal-hippocampal brain regions. A final aspect of these data must be mentioned. It is significant that the behavioral responses did not increase in intensity above baseline levels following the lie. This suggests that behavioral tendencies are not like a boiling caldron that, when suppressed, build up steam and explode once the lid is removed. Unlike a Freudian view of energy conservation and leakage, behavioral inhibition is an active process involving work that is itself measureable on a physiological level.

C. Long-term Inhibition: Personality Considerations

The research reviewed above indicates that short-term behavioral inhibition is correlated with phasic increases in autonomic activity. What

INHIBITION AND COGNITION

evidence do we have to suggest that individuals who chronically inhibit their behaviors manifest higher overall physiological levels? The research evidence to support this idea derives from three areas: levels of socialization (including sociopathy), repressive coping styles, and emotional expression. Each will be discussed separately.

1. Level of Socialization

Many researchers have explicitly or implicitly assumed that individuals can be categorized along a dimension of socialization level (e.g., Gough, 1960; Trasler, 1978; Waid & Orne, 1981). On the lower extreme would be the sociopath, an individual who is impulsive, selfish and irresponsible, with a low tolerance of frustration (cf., Hare, 1978). At the other extreme is the individual who adheres to social norms and, in general, lacks sociopathic tendencies. For a number of reasons, far more research has focused on those who are poorly socialized than on those who are highly socialized. One hallmark of the sociopath is his or her general behavior patterns suggesting a deficit in inhibition. The sociopath typically performs poorly on passive avoidance and delayed reinforcement tasks (see Hare, 1978, and Fowles, 1980, for reviews). In addition, the sociopaths appear to have a low tolerance for alcohol (Cleckley, 1976). Of particular import is the fact that sociopaths have generally been found to have lower tonic SCLs and, during noxious stimulation, reduced phasic EDA (Hare, 1978).

Complementing this work, Waid and Orne (e.g., 1981, 1982) have examined subjects who are classified either as highly or poorly socialized as measured by the Socialization scale of the CPI developed by Gough (1960). Across a number of studies, these researchers find that poorly socialized college students consistently yield smaller skin conductance responses to deception than highly socialized subjects. If we make the inferential leap that those individuals who are highly socialized tend to inhibit behaviors in general, we can see how chronic inhibition is correlated with greater physiological activity (at least that related to the BIS) in general.

2. Repressive Coping Styles

Within the humanistic and psychoanalytic literatures, an individual who is defined as a repressor is one who excludes from consciousness both cognitive and emotional factors that are potentially threatening to the ego (Ross & Abrams, 1965). Such an individual may deny that he or she is anxious or upset even though behavioral and physiological measures would indicate otherwise. Early work on repressors found that they had higher recognition thresholds for anxiety-producing stimuli (e.g., Eriksen, 1966). One problem that has impeded empirical research on this personality measure has been the lack of ways of assessing whether or not a person is, in fact, repressing.

An intriguing approach to this problem was proposed by Crowne and Marlowe (1964), who developed the Social Desirability Scale. Individuals who score high on this scale publicly adhere to social norms to an extreme degree. Further, these authors indicate that such individuals are affectively inhibited and defensive. A recent important study by Weinberger, Schwartz, and Davidson (1979) sought to define repressors as those who score high on the Social Desirability Scale and low on the Taylor (1953) Manifest Anxiety Scale (MAS). These individuals were separated from those who were defined as high anxious (from the MAS—irrespective of social desirability) and truly low anxious (low MAS and low social desirability). During the actual experiment, subjects participated in a phrase association task wherein they had to respond to aggressive, sexual, or neutral sentences with a phrase that completed the thought expressed in each stimulus sentence. In addition to reaction time, heart rate, skin resistance, and forehead muscle tension were recorded during the task. Overall, repressors exhibited significantly higher forehead muscle tension and skin resistance responses than either the high or low anxious group throughout the task. Both the repressors and high anxious subjects evidenced elevated heart rate relative to the low anxious subjects.

These results are important for two reasons. First, they suggest that a repressive coping style as measured by the Social Desirability Scale (which could be viewed as analogous to a high level of socialization) is associated with increased physiological responding. Second, measures of repression have been associated with cancer (Kissen, 1966), high blood pressure (Davies, 1970), and physical disease in general (Blackburn, 1965). We will return to the relationship between repression and inhibition in a later section.

3. Emotional Expression

The relationship between the expression of emotion and the autonomic correlates of the emotion has been an area of intensive investigation. Beginning with the pioneering work of Jones (1960), it was found that the more emotionally expressive a child was, the smaller his or her electrodermal responses. According to Jones, the act of socialization forced the child to inhibit emotional expression, outwardly causing the efferent discharge to occur along "hidden" physiological channels. Jones further notes that the socialization process encourages the inhibition of overt responding.

One aspect of the emotional expression research concerns the relationship between "sending accuracy" along nonverbal channels and autonomic activity (EDA and heart rate). Sending accuracy is measured by the ability of observers to detect a person's emotional state by viewing facial expression. In an intriguing series of studies, Buck (1979) reports large and consistent negative correlations between sending accuracy of the sender and the sender's EDA and heart rate. Similarly, Notarius and Levenson (1979) found that subjects who were classified as natural inhibitors (on the basis of facial expressiveness) were more physiologically reactive in terms of heart rate, skin conductance, and respiration rate when exposed to threat of a shock than were subjects classified as natural expressers. These data are in line with Jones's findings that the more expressive, the lower the physiological response.

It should be noted that a number of investigators have found significant positive rather than negative relationships between facial expressiveness and various autonomic indices on a within-subject (as opposed to a between-subject) basis (e.g., Laird, 1974; Lanzetta, Cartwright-Smith & Kleck, 1976). Whether these inconsistencies reflect methodological differences is beyond the scope of this paper.

4. Summary

Each of the lines of research discussed above is relevant to the general inhibition concept. Individuals who are highly socialized, high in social desirability, and lacking in emotional expressivity evidence higher tonic and phasic EDA and, for some studies, heart rate and muscle tension. Unfortunately, none of the studies cited above have examined illness rates or disease processes. Although there is some evidence that repressors are more prone to hypertension, cancer, and disease states in general, we would expect that traumatic experiences would interact with each of these individual difference measures to increase the overall probability of illness.

It must be emphasized that the link between each of these individual difference measures and inhibition processes is not firmly established. Whether or not the individual who is characterized as exhibiting a repressive coping style, lacking in emotional expressiveness, and/or behaving in a highly socialized way would be less likely to confide following a traumatic experience is an empirical question worthy of future research. Common sense would argue that each of these personality types would be more hesitant to confide simply because of fears of social sanctions.

D. Failure to Confide as Inhibition

To this point, we have demonstrated that short-term behavioral inhibition is associated with increased physiological activity. We have presented data from a number of studies indirectly suggesting that long-term inhibition, as measured by specific individual difference variables, is associated with overall higher autonomic activity. Together, these two lines of research indicate that we can view inhibition as physiological work or, in Selye's (1976) terms, as a type of stressor. What evidence do we have to indicate that not confiding about a traumatic event represents an inhibitory process? Unfortunately, our research into this question is merely in the planning stage. A small number of in-depth interviews that we have conducted together with sporadic case studies in the literature strongly indicate that not confiding does, in fact, require considerable inhibitory effort.

Three recent in-depth interviews of adult women who had had sexually traumatic experiences and did not confide these events to anyone offer interesting insights. Person A was molested by her stepfather between the ages of 11 and 14. She noted that she simply could not tell her mother because "it would break her heart." She wanted to tell her friends, but she knew they would never understand. Another reason for not telling anyone was that she felt that it was her fault that she was being molested. Person B witnessed her mother in a sexual liason with a friend of the family at age 13. She noted that she desperately wanted to tell her father and often thought and even dreamed of doing so. In fact, she said that she had "to actively restrain from telling Dad on those (frequent) days when there was a family fight." Person C was sexually assaulted by a cousin at age 9. After the event, she became shy and withdrawn. Although she wanted to tell somebody about the event, she assumed that she would be punished for provoking it. In each of these cases, the victim constantly thought about the event for years, wanted to tell others, but did not feel that she could.

The literature on rape and sexual assault confirms these anecdotal reports. Binder (1981) conducted a survey of adult women dealing with sexual assault. Although her response rate was only 33%, of those reporting having been sexually assaulted, only about 15% reported the assault to the police. Unfortunately, the author does not report how many of these women did not tell anyone. Nevertheless, the case quotations within the article suggest that many did not confide in anyone because of embarrassment, guilt, fear of the offender, or a feeling that it was the victim's own fault. Burgess and Holmstrom (1974) studied the reactions of 92 adult women rape victims and identified a general rape trauma syndrome which includes increased somatization, phobic reactions, self-blame, and nightmares (see also Kilpatrick, Resick, & Veronen, 1981, for discussion of long-term somatic and emotional disturbances of rape victims). In their article, the authors point out that a significant proportion of rape victims do not report the event to anyone. Hence, clinicians should be especially attentive to rape trauma symptoms.

We readily admit that case reports are the last refuge of scientific scoundrels. We feel, however, that the overall picture suggests that failure to confide a traumatic event represents a significant risk to one's health.

IV. Summary and Final Considerations

People seek to understand their world. To do this, they must often organize and assimilate complex and personally traumatic events. One of the most efficient and natural ways of accomplishing this is by translating thoughts and feelings into language. The traumatic event and the assimilation process themselves can be viewed as direct stressors on the body. On occasion, individuals may not be able to accomplish this organization process for fear of punishment, humiliation, or embarrassment. Actively to inhibit behavior requires additional work which is manifested in physiological activity. The longer one must inhibit this cognitive organization process and the greater the magnitude of the trauma, the more the inhibitory processes are engaged. Over time, the combined physiological stresses of the organization process and the inhibitory process produce increased wear and tear on the body, thus increasing the probability of disease.

Although a great deal of evidence has been put forward in support of this general conceptual framework, there are a number of empirical issues that remain to be resolved. At this point, we are not able to specify the precise physiological mechanisms that underlie the inhibitory process. Gray's (1975) hypotheses concerning relevant brain structures associated with inhibition offer a promising beginning. Undoubtedly, other central nervous system structures are involved. We must also await research linking these inhibitory processes to immune, hormonal, and autonomic nervous system functions. At this point, it is premature for us to "physiologize" too much. We can, however, speculate about the relationship of our framework to a number of related research endeavors relevant to psychotherapy, self-disclosure, and coping processes in general.

A. Inhibition and Psychotherapy

There is little doubt that psychotherapy is an effective way by which to reduce anxiety and even the incidence of psychosomatic disease. Jerome Frank (1974) and a number of recent researchers (e.g., Nicholson & Berman, 1983; Smith, Glass, & Miller, 1980) indicate that virtually all forms of psychotherapy (whether cognitive, behavioral, or psychodynamic) yield significant improvements in patients' self-reports and behaviors by the end of treatment which continue to persist several months or years after treatment. We suggest that one of the benefits of psychotherapy is that it promotes the cognitive reorganization and assimilation of important and, on occasion, traumatic events. In accomplishing this goal, the person no longer *needs* to inhibit his or her urge to assimilate the event by talking with others (e.g., Pennebaker & O'Heeron, 1984). Much of psychotherapy, then, reduces stress directly by allowing the cognitive reorganization process to occur and, indirectly, by nullifying the need to inhibit (see also excellent discussions of similar processes by Horowitz, 1976, and Silver, Boon, & Stones, 1983). One can readily see how this process could also be accomplished through confession, talking to a stranger on a plane, or confiding in a close friend.

Note that we are in no way denying other benefits of psychotherapy, such as the acquisition of new coping skills, stress management techniques, and the like. Many problems that psychotherapists must deal with *have* been previously disclosed and assimilated but continue to persist, for example, snake phobias. In short, the processes on which we have focussed represent only a portion of the variables that are at play within the psychotherapeutic mileu.

B. Cognitive Organization and Self-disclosure

In his book, *The Transparent Self*, Jourard (1971) argues that the act of self-disclosure allows for one's feelings and thoughts to become more concrete. Self-disclosure, then, helps the person to know himself better. Interestingly, Jourard posited that self-disclosure had motivational properties, and if this motive was blocked adverse physiological problems would result (see also Archer, 1980, for an excellent review).

Neither Jourard nor we think that public self-disclosure is the only method by which to organize and assimilate self-relevant information. For example, expressing one's experiences on paper may be almost as effective in allowing for the assimilation and subsequent reduction in inhibition processes to occur. We base this idea on both personal experiences and a recent pilot study.

In the experiment (conducted by Melissa Conrad and the first author), subjects wrote two essays while heart rate was continuously monitored. Half of the 16 subjects were required to write their first essay about an intensely personal experience that they had never told anyone. We assured the subjects that they could keep the essays and that we would not read them. The remaining subjects wrote about what had happened to them the day before the experiment. For the second essay, all subjects were to describe how their bedroom was decorated. Those writing a personal essay evidenced an increase in heart rate during the initial essay but a significant heart rate decrease (below initial baseline) during the second essay. The control subjects' heart rates did not deviate from basal heart rate levels throughout the experiment. Finally, self-reports of physical symptoms dropped significantly from the beginning of the study to the end for the personal essay subjects but were unchanged for the control group.

There are a number of alternative explanations for these findings other than increased assimilation and decreased inhibition (e.g., opponent process, contrast effects). Nevertheless, from a theoretical perspective, such a treatment approach involving the use of personal diaries or journals may have merit.

C. Links to Other Theories

Many aspects of our approach have been suggested by others in one form or another. In this final section, we will focus on the similarities and differences between the present perspective and those within the psychodynamic and coping literatures.

a. Psychodynamic Views of Inhibition. Within the psychodynamic literature, a number of terms are used that bear a certain degree of similarity to our use of *inhibition*. For example, the defense mechanism of suppression is invoked to define the active process of putting certain disturbing thoughts out of one's mind. Freud's use of the inhibition construct is similar to ours in that it requires work or energy (Freud, 1926/1959). At this point, the psychodynamic perspective of inhibition and our own diverge. Inhibition and suppression, according to a Freudian analysis, represent work in that they oppose some intrapsychic process. They act to allow the ego to repress forbidden desires. Note that in Freud's discussion of symptoms and Alexander's (1950) analyses of illness problems develop when these defense mechanisms fail. Hence, disease processes are not the result of effectively used psychological processes such as inhibition or suppression. Our model posits that the inhibitory process itself is stressful.

As we use the term, an active process must be engaged in order not to do or say something. This is the central feature in the connection between life traumas and illness. For Freud, the life trauma itself may be reminiscent of an earlier conflict which has been repressed, thus bringing the long-since buried ideational content to the psychic surface, which itself is damaging. Once it surfaces, either the ego must again perform the energy-consumptive task of repressing the ideational content or, if this process is incomplete, neurotic symptoms should develop. In short, Freud focuses on inhibition (or suppression) in the service of avoiding potentially greater intrapsychic conflict, whereas we have pointed to the process of inhibition itself as a potential stressor.

b. Coping and Appraisal. An important issue in the link between life traumas and disease is the role that cognitive style takes in mediating the effects of stress. Lazarus and his colleagues (e.g., Lazarus, 1966; Folkman & Lazarus, 1982) have developed a broad theory of stress and coping which posits a person's cognitive appraisal of threats as a critical determinant of the coping process. The theory posits that coping is determined by three appraisal processes. The primary appraisal concerns the evaluation of the consequences of a situation for the individual's immediate well-being. The secondary appraisal process entails an evaluation of what can be done about the situation, that is, a mental "taking stock" of available resources that may ameliorate the effects of the stressor(s). After these appraisal processes have initially occurred, a third process—reappraisal—is initiated that allows for the assessment of how accurately the first two processes reflect the situation. At this point, a person may reassess and change his or her earlier assumptions and decisions.

Following the appraisal process, a coping strategy is adopted. Folkman and Lazarus (1982) posit that coping strategies will be directed either to the problem itself or to the emotional reaction to the problem. The four general modes of coping include direct action, information seeking, inhibition of behavior, and cognitive changes that could include restructuring, rationalization, and so forth. Although the bulk of research on these coping processes has been concerned with the relatively short-term behavioral and physiological responses to both major and minor life experiences (e.g., death of a child, reactions to surgery), our work suggests that we should begin focusing on coping with personal traumas that may take place for years after the event. Clearly, after several months or years following a trauma, the only coping strategies that would most likely be employed would include inhibition of behavior and, to a lesser extent, continued cognitive changes.

D. Summary

In this chapter, we have argued that individuals seek to understand and organize personally traumatic events. Certain events, such as rape, death of a parent, or divorce of parents, require considerable effort to understand and assimilate. Some major events cannot easily be discussed with others because of perceived negative social sanctions, embarrassment, or fear. Not being able to confide about such events requires the person actively to inhibit his or her behavior. As we have indicated, behavioral inhibition is associated with physiological activity. Much of our earlier work suggests that victims of sexual assault are often loathe to discuss the event with anyone. These individuals—who, we are hypothesizing, must actively inhibit their urge to tell others of their experience—are far more likely to report a number of physical symptoms, illnesses, and use of medical facilities. Although life stressors such as these are themselves physiologically damaging, the act of inhibition compounds the wear and tear on the body.

The research that we have presented is just beginning. Many of the unifying links in our model are based on speculation or case studies. Although we are certain that a number of revisions will be necessary in the future, we are optimistic about the theoretical and clinical implications of our initial findings.

REFERENCES

ALEXANDER, F. (1950). *Psychosomatic medicine: Its principles and applications.* New York: Norton.

ARCHER, R. L. (1980). Self-disclosure. In D. M. WEGNER & R. R. VALLACHER (Eds.), *The self in social psychology.* New York: Oxford, pp. 183–205.

BARRIOS, B. A., & PENNEBAKER, J. W. (1983). A note on the early detection of bulimia nervosa. *The Behavior Therapist, 6,* 10–19.

BEKESY, G. V. (1967). *Sensory inhibition.* Princeton, NJ: Princeton University Press.

BINDER, R. (1981). Why women don't report sexual assault *Journal of Clinical Psychiatry, 42,* 437–438.

BLACKBURN, R. (1965). Emotionality, repression-sensitization, and maladjustment. *British Journal of Psychiatry, 111,* 399–400.

BUCK, R. W. (1979). Individual differences in nonverbal sending accuracy and electrodermal responding: The externalizing-internalizing dimension. In R. ROSENTHAL (Ed.), *Skill in nonverbal communication.* Cambridge: Oelgeschlager, Gunn & Hain, pp. 44–67.

BURGESS, A. W., & HOLMSTROM, L. L. (1974). Rape trauma syndrome. *American Journal of Psychiatry, 131,* 981–986.

CLECKLEY, H. (1976). *The mask of sanity.* St. Louis: Mosby.

COBB, S. (1976). Social support as a moderator of life stress. *Psychosomatic Medicine, 38,* 300–314.

CROWNE, D. P., & MARLOWE, D. (1964). *The approval motive: Studies in evaluative dependence.* New York: Wiley.

DAVIES, M. (1970). Blood pressure and personality. *Journal of Psychosomatic Research, 14,* 89–104.

ERIKSEN, C. W. (1966). Cognitive responses to internally cued anxiety. In C. D. SPIELBERGER (Ed.), *Anxiety and behavior.* New York: Academic Press, pp. 317–360.

FENIGSTEIN, A., SCHEIER, M. & BUSS, A. (1975). Public and private self-consciousness: Assessment and theory. *Journal of Consulting and Clinical Psychology, 43,* 522–527.

FESTINGER, L. (1954). A theory of social comparison processes. *Human Relations, 7,* 117–140.

FOLKMAN, S., & LAZARUS, R. S. (1982). Stress and coping theory applied to the investigation of mass industrial psychogenic illness. In M. J. COLLIGAN, J. W. PENNEBAKER, & L. MURPHY (Eds.), *Mass psychogenic illness: A social psychological perspective.* Hillsdale, NJ: Erlbaum, pp. 237–255.

FOWLES, D. C. (1980). The three arousal model: Implications of Gray's two-factor theory for heart rates, electrodermal activity, and psychopathy. *Psychophysiology, 17,* 87–104.

FRANK, J. (1974). *Persuasion and healing.* New York: Schocken Books.

FREUD, S. (1926/1959). Inhibitions, symptoms, and anxiety. In J. Strachey (Ed.), *Complete psychological works of Sigmund Freud* (Vol 20). London: Hogarth, pp. 77–174.

GIBSON, J. J. (1979). *The ecological approach to visual perception.* Boston: Houghton-Mifflin.

GOUGH, H. G. (1960). Theory and measurement of socialization. *Journal of Consulting Psychology, 24,* 23–30.

GRAY, J. A. (1975). *Elements of a two-process theory of learning.* New York: Academic Press.

HARE, R. D. (1978). Electrodermal and cardiovascular correlates of psychopathy. In R. D. HARE & D. SCHALLING (Eds.), *Psychopathic behavior: Approaches to research.* New York: Wiley.

HERNANDEZ-PEON, R. (1960). Neurophysiological correlates of habituation and other manifestations of plastic inhibition (internal inhibition). In H. Jasper & G. Smirnov (Eds.), *The Moscow colloquium on electroencephalography of nervous activity. EEG Clinical Neurophysiology, Supplement 13,* 101–112.

HOLMES, T. & RAHE, R. (1967). The social readjustment rating scale. *Journal of Psychosomatic Research, 4,* 213–218.

HOROWITZ, M. J. (1976). *Stress response syndromes.* New York: Jacob Aronson.

HULL, C. L. (1950). Simple qualitative discrimination learning. *Psychological Review, 57,* 303–313.

JONES, H. E. (1960). The longitudinal method in the study of personality. In I. ISCOE & H. W. STEVENSON (Eds.), *Personality development in children.* Chicago: University of Chicago Press.

JOURARD, S. M. (1971). *Self-disclosure: An experimental analysis of the transparent self.* New York: Wiley.

KELLEY, H. H. (1972). *Attribution in social interaction.* New York: General Learning Press.

KILPATRICK, D. G., RESICK, P. A., & VERONEN, L. J. (1981). Effects of rape experience: A longitudinal study. *Journal of Social Issues, 37,* 105–122.

KISSEN, D. M. (1966). The significance of personality in lung cancer in men. *Annals of the New York Academy of Science, 125,* 820–826.

KOBASA, S. (1982). The hardy personality: Toward a social psychology of stress and health. In G. S. SANDERS & J. SUIS (Eds.), *Social psychology of health and illness.* Hillsdale, NJ: Erlbaum, pp. 3–32.

KONORSKI, J. (1967). *Integrative activity in the brain.* Chicago: University of Chicago Press.

KRANTZ, D., GLASS, D. & SNYDER, M. (1974). Helplessness, stress level and the coronary-prone behavior pattern. *Journal of Experimental Social Psychology, 10,* 284–300.

LAIRD, J. D. (1974). Self-attribution of emotion: The effects of expressive behavior on the quality of emotional experience. *Journal of Personality and Social Psychology, 20,* 475–486.

LANZETTA, J. T., CARTWRIGHT-SMITH, J., & KLECK, R. E. (1976). Effects of nonverbal dissimulation on emotional experience and autonomic arousal. *Journal of Personality and Social Psychology, 33,* 354–370.

LAZARUS, R. (1966). *Psychological stress and the coping process.* New York: McGraw-Hill.

LESHAN, L. L. (1966). An emotional life-history pattern associated with neoplastic disease. *Annals of the New York Academy of Sciences, 125,* 780–793.

MELTON, A. W. (1963). Implications of short-term memory for a general theory of memory. *Journal of Verbal Learning and Verbal Behavior, 2,* 1–21.

MELZACK, R. (1973). *The puzzle of pain.* New York: Basic.

NEISSER, U. (1976). *Cognition and reality.* San Francisco: Freeman, 1976.

NICHOLSON, R. A., & BERMAN, J. S. (1983). Is follow-up necessary in evaluating psychotherapy? *Psychological Bulletin, 93,* 261–278.

NOTARIUS, C. I., & LEVENSON, R. W. (1979). Expressive tendencies and physiological response to stress. *Journal of Personality and Social Psychology, 37,* 1204–1210.

PAVLOV, I. (1927). *Conditioned reflexes.* New York: Oxford.

PENNEBAKER, J. W. (1982). *The psychology of physical symptoms.* New York: Springer-Verlag.

PENNEBAKER, J. W., & CHEW, C. H. (in press). Deception, electrodermal activity, and inhibition of behavior. *Journal of Personality and Social Psychology.*

PENNEBAKER, J. W., & O'HEERON, R. C. (1984). confiding in others and illness rates among spouses of suicide and accidental death victims. *Journal of Abnormal Psychology, 93,* 473–476.

RESCORLA, R. A. (1969). Pavlovian conditioned inhibition. *Psychological Bulletin, 72,* 77–94.

ROSS, N., & ABRAMS, S. (1965). Fundamentals of psychoanalytic theory. In B. Wolman (Ed.), *Handbook of clinical psychology.* New York: McGraw-Hill, pp. 303–339.

RUBENSTEIN, C. (1982). Wellness is all: A report on *Psychology Today's* survey of beliefs about health. *Psychology Today, 16,* 28–37.

SACKHEIM, H. A., & GUR, R. C. (1978). Self-deception, self-confrontation, and consciousness. In G. E. SCHWARTZ & D. SHAPIRO (Eds.), *Consciousness and self-regulation* (Vol. 2). New York: Plenum Press.

SCHMALE, A. H. & IKER, H. (1971). Hopelessness as a predictor of cervical cancer. *Social Science and Medicine, 5,* 95–100.

SCHWARTZ, G., DAVIDSON, R. & GOLEMAN, D. (1978). Patterning of cognitive and somatic processes in the self-generation of anxiety: Effects of meditation versus exercise. *Psychosomatic Medicine, 40,* 321–328

SELYE, H. (1976). *The stress of life.* New York: McGraw-Hill.

SILVER, R. L., BOON, C., & STONES, M. H. (1983). Searching for meaning in misfortune: Making sense of incest. *Journal of Social Issues, 39,* 81–102.

SKINNER, B. F. (1938). *The behavior of organisms.* New York: Appleton-Century-Crofts.

SMITH, M. L., GLASS, G. V., & MILLER, T. I. (1980). *The benefits of psychotherapy.* Baltimore: Johns Hopkins University Press.

SPENCE, K. W. (1936). The nature of discrimination learning in animals. *Psychological Review, 43,* 427–449.

TAYLOR, J. (1953). A personality scale of manifest anxiety. *Journal of Abnormal and Social Psychology, 48,* 285–290.

TERRACE, H. S. (1972). Conditioned inhibition. In R. A. BOAKES & M. S. HALLIDAY (Eds.), *Inhibition and learning.* London: Academic Press, pp. 99–119.

TRASLER, G. (1978). Relations between psychopathy and persistent criminality: Methdological and theoretical issues. In R. D. HARE & D. SCHALLING (Eds.), *Psychopathic behavior: Approaches to research.* New York: Wiley, pp. 273–298.

Valins, S., & Nisbett, R. E. (1972). Attribution processes in the development and treatment of emotional disorder. In E. E. Jones et al. (Eds.), *Attribution: Perceiving the causes of behavior*. Morristown, NJ: General Learning Press, pp. 137–150.

Waid, W. M., & Orne, M. T. (1981). Cognitive, social and personality processes in the physiological detection of deception. In L. Berkowitz (Ed.), *Advances in experiment social psychology* (Vol. 14). New York: Academic Press, pp. 61–106.

Waid, W. M., & Orne, M. T. (1982). Reduced electrodermal response to conflict, failure to inhibit dominant behaviors, and delinquent proneness. *Journal of Personality and Social Psychology, 43*, 769–774.

Weinberger, D. A., Schwartz, G. E., & Davidson, R. J. (1979). Low-anxious, high-anxious, and repressive coping styles: Psychometric patterns and behavioral and physiological responses to stress. *Journal of Abnormal Psychology, 88*, 369–380.

Wolf, S., & Goodell, J. (1968). *Harold G. Wolff's stress and disease*. Springfield, IL: Thomas.

6   *Mechanisms of Biofeedback Control*

On the Importance of Verbal (Conscious) Processing

J. MICHAEL LACROIX

I. INTRODUCTION

> A young woman sitting alone in a small room watches a television screen which provides her with an analog on-line display of her heart rate, and, presumably using the information provided on the screen, attempts to raise and lower her heart rate appropriately when cued to do so by the letter R or the letter L shown in the upper left-hand corner of the screen.

This is the paradigmatic procedure for biofeedback training. The typical outcome of practice with this paradigm is that after some training the subject comes to produce larger changes of the appropriate nature in the target physiological system in response to instructions than he or she did at the outset of training. This acquisition in response control is usually attributed to learning (but see Riley & Furedy, 1981, for a contrasting view).

There are at least two general questions arising from the use of this paradigm and the response control to which it leads that should be, and indeed have been, of interest to psychologists. The first pertains to potential applications of the biofeedback paradigm to the treatment of psychosomatic disorders. The second concerns the learning mechanisms that underlie the acquisiton of response control in the biofeedback paradigm, and, reciprocally, whether what takes place in the context of the biofeedback paradigm can tell us anything about the learning process generally. It is to this second question that this chapter is addressed. It is important to point out, in the context of conflicting claims about the value of biofeedback, that these two issues are orthogonal to one an-

---

J. MICHAEL LACROIX ● Department of Psychology, Glendon College, York University, Toronto M4N 3M6.

other: biofeedback may well be useful in the treatment of a variety of disorders and yet prove to be theoretically uninteresting.

I will begin by providing a brief historical review of work on the question of whether the biofeedback *paradigm* fosters a unique or at least distinctive kind of learning, which I will refer to as the biofeedback *phenomenon*. The outcome of that review will be essentially negative. I will then call upon a number of cognate literatures suggesting that certain features of the biofeedback paradigm as it is used presently make it singularly inappropriate for promoting exactly the kind of biofeedback learning phenomenon that many had thought to be characteristic of the paradigm. Finally, I will develop a two-process theory of learning in biofeedback that takes into account what is going on in the paradigmatic case and that also makes predictions as to manipulations that should foster the distinctive biofeedback phenomenon.

II. A PROMISE UNFULFILLED

One of the attractions of the biofeedback paradigm has been the promise that it might tell us something important about the learning process. Indeed, historically, the interest in what was then known as operant autonomic conditioning stemmed primarily from the fact that researchers thought the paradigm potentially critical for two-process learning theories (Katkin & Murray, 1968). This particular line of interest soon faded, not because of any problems with the paradigm, but primarily because of a loss of interest in two-process learning theories and in traditional learning theories generally, which came under heavy attack from a number of directions in the late 1960s and early 1970s. With the waning of interest in two-process theories, the bulk of research in biofeedback began to focus on applications. However, the promise of the biofeedback paradigm for Learning Psychology was not forgotten, and I think it is accurate to say that most biofeedback researchers and practitioners maintained a belief throughout this period that there was something different about the kind of learning fostered by the paradigm, but they were unable to specify what it was because the theoretical structures of Learning Psychology were shifting too rapidly.

In a series of papers beginning at a conference in Chapel Hill in 1972, Jasper Brener sought to move our conceptualizations of the learning process in biofeedback away from those of Learning Psychology and to bring them closer to those of neurophysiology (Brener, 1974a, b; 1977a, b; Brener, Ross, Baker, & Clemens, 1979). Brener also transformed the promise of biofeedback from shimmering glimmer to testable proposition. Before describing his initial conceptualization of learning in the biofeedback paradigm (it has since changed significantly), it is important to draw attention to a distinction which is implicit in Brener's earlier writings and has been made explicit in his latest work (Brener, 1984), and to which I will return at greater length later in the chapter. This is the notion that learning can proceed in one of two basic ways. First, it can involve simply a reshuffling of existing behavioral/cognitive elements at a central level, as when a subject learns to associate two words already known to him or her in a paired-associates learning task, or when a new driver learns to associate a previously known stimulus (a red traffic light) with a variant of a behavior previously used in a number of other contexts (lifting the right foot and moving it over slightly). Second, learning can involve the acquisition of skills not previously within the subject's behavioral repertoire and thus may require an extensive recalibration of sensorimotor systems in order to construct an appropriate motor program. It is presumably this second type of learning that operates when a person learns to speak a foreign language or a baby learns to walk. In Brener's initial theoretical formulation, learning in the biofeedback paradigm was considered an instance of this second type of learning.

In this context, Brener envisaged the process of acquiring control of the target response in the biofeedback paradigm as primarily one of learned discrimination: the subject had to learn to discriminate and to identify interoceptive afferentation related to the target response, in order to exhibit control of the response. The feedback stimulus used in biofeedback was viewed as serving simply to identify the relevant afferentation. This was accomplished by a process of association or calibration, through repeated pairings of the exteroceptive feedback stimulus, which is by its very nature discriminable by the subject and some feature of which is directly related to appropriate changes in the target response, and the interoceptive afferentation which is also generated as a consequence of changes in that response. Thus, as biofeedback training progressed, the subject was expected to become gradually more proficient at discriminating changes in the target response. The set of interoceptive stimuli which the subject comes to identify with the production of the target response was referred to in Brener's terminology as the *response image*. Once the subject had formulated an appropriate response image, activation of this response (e.g., by appropriate instructions to produce the response) was envisaged to lead automatically to control of the response. The theory also predicated that the response image underwent refinement as a function of practice in the biofeedback paradigm. As variability occurred in the response complex produced during repeated attempts to control the response, the exteroceptive feedback was expected to become a reliable predictor of a progressively smaller set of interoceptive stimuli, eventually to become a reliable predictor only of those interoceptive stimuli arising from changes in the target response itself—provided sufficient training was given and subject to operating biological constraints. Thus, over the course of biofeedback training, both control and discrimination of the target response were expected to become gradually more specific to the target response.

In sum, Brener viewed learning in the biofeedback paradigm as resting upon the development of new, discriminative skills, which were necessary and sufficient for the development of an appropriate motor program for controlling the target response. It is important to emphasize that this view is and continues to be shared by many, if not most biofeedback investigators. A few examples should suffice. Thus, in answering the question, What is biofeedback? Turk, Meichenbaum, and Berman (1979) wrote: "By trial and error the subject learns to *recognize* the subjective state and subtle internal changes associated with an alteration in physiological activity" (p. 1322; italics added). Similarly, Surwit and Keefe (1983) stated that biofeedback is "based on the notion that increasing *awareness* of the physiological response will lead to improved voluntary control of those responses" (p. 2; italics added). Or again, in discussing how biofeedback works in reducing frontalis EMG and tension headaches, Cox and Hobbs (1982) suggested that it served "to increase the patients' *awareness* of physiological dysregulation" (p. 387; italics in original).

Does practice in the biofeedback *paradigm* lead to a biofeedback *phenomenon*, a form of learning characterized by a recalibration of sensorimotor systems essential to the development of an appropriate motor program? Such a phenomenon, if we take Brener's formulations as its testable expression, should be evidenced by the following observations. First, subjects who have undergone training to control a given target response in the biofeedback paradigm should perform well on tests of their ability to discriminate changes in that response. Second, if the presence of an appropriate response image is indeed a sufficient condition for control of the response, subjects who can successfully discriminate changes in a given autonomic or other "internal" response should perform well on tests of their ability to control that response. Third, practice in the biofeedback paradigm, if it results in a gradual refinement of the response image, should lead to the gradual elimination of components of the response complex that are not strongly correlated with the target response; thus, control (and discrimination) should become more specific to the target response as a function of practice in the biofeedback paradigm.

Four years ago I carried out an exhaustive review of the literature with respect to those predictions from Brener's theory (Lacroix, 1981).

I will not duplicate that review here. Suffice it to say that the conclusion from that review was essentially negative. Moreover, because of the methodological diversity which characterized the literature, Anne Gowen and I (Lacroix & Gowen, 1981) carried out an extensive experiment which tested simultaneously the three major theoretical predictions outlined above. These were tested in a comparative design (Roberts, 1974) that contrasted the evolution of control and discrimination with respect to two target responses, heart rate and skin conductance, under homologous conditions. Again, the results were essentially negative. Moreover, I have seen nothing in the literature in the past four years to convince me that the biofeedback paradigm as it is typically used leads to the development of a biofeedback phenomenon. Training in the biofeedback paradigm does not necessarily enhance subjects' ability to discriminate changes in the target physiological response. Performance on tests of response discrimination are not usually correlated with performance on tests of response control. And training in the biofeedback paradigm does not usually lead to greater response specificity as a function of practice. There are a few notable exceptions to these generalizations, and I will deal with them shortly.

Before dealing with these exceptions, however, and with the larger question of the nature of the learning process in the biofeedback paradigm, I would like to consider two challenges to these general conclusions. First, there has been mounting criticism of the various methods used to measure subjects' ability to discriminate autonomic and other internal responses. These have been voiced particularly strongly by Roberts on theoretical grounds (Roberts, 1977; Roberts, Williams, Marlin, Farrell, & Imiolo, 1984) and by Katkin, (Katkin, Morell, Goldband, Bernstein, & Wise, 1982) and Ross and Brener (1981) on empirical grounds. The thrust of those criticisms is on the one hand that inability to perform on a discrimination task often simply reflects inadequacies in the task. On the other hand, and conversely, successful performance on a discrimination task often reflects a lack of control over potentially confounded variables, suggesting that subjects can discriminate internal responses that they cannot in fact discriminate and leading to a spurious relationship between discrimination and control. The upshot of those criticisms is that the first two predictions from Brener's theory (that subjects who can control a response should also be able to discriminate that response and that subjects who can discriminate a response should also be able to control it) simply cannot be evaluated cleanly, leading some investigators (Roberts & Marlin, 1979; Roberts et al.; 1984) to seek alternative ways of assessing awareness of the response in biofeedback. I do not think that the criticisms that have been offered are necessarily fatal to the use of any response discrimination measure, and I think that our own work which shows no relationship between response control and response discrimination deals adequately with both lines of criticism (Lacroix & Gowen, 1981). Nevertheless, even if it is granted that the first two predictions from Brener's theory cannot be assessed unambiguously, the third prediction from the theory (that biofeedback training should lead to greater response specificity as a function of practice) remains unconfirmed.

The second challenge to my conclusion that use of a biofeedback paradigm does not foster a biofeedback learning phenomenon is the argument that training in the paradigm is seldom carried out extensively enough to allow a biofeedback phenomenon to become manifest. Miller (1981) made this point rather colorfully when he suggested that much of the literature on learning in the biofeedback paradigm could be likened to a literature concerned with skating behavior in which all the studies would focus on people putting on their skates and tying their laces, and in which the general conclusion would be that skating is very much like walking. The desirability of using longer training regimens in biofeedback studies is a point well taken and has also been made by others (e.g., Steiner & Dince, 1981). However, it surely cannot be assumed that the form of the learning process will invariably be altered by adding X number of additional sessions of training to any experimental regimen, particularly as the literature varies widely with respect to the amount of training variable. Moreover, the requisite number of sessions for finally looking at "skating behavior" remains undefined.

These points notwithstanding, I would like to present some empirical evidence relevant to the insufficient training argument. This evidence comes from a recent experiment which focused on biofeedback training of *frontalis* EMG in muscle-contraction headache patients (Lacroix, Clarke, Bock, & Doxey, 1984). Training was extensive and I presume that it was sufficient to allow a putative biofeedback phenomenon to become apparent, as the patients obtained significant clinical benefits from the training, and these were maintained for at least six months after training. Figure 1 presents the response profiles obtained in these patients. The figure depicts the mean resting levels in four physiological functions during two sessions prior to any training (left-hand side) and two post-training baseline sessions (right-hand side). Training was provided over sixteen sessions, each of which included some programmed generalization (i.e., some practice without feedback or relaxation tapes, depending on the groups). It should be emphasized that the patients were instructed to practice the skills developed over the course of training during the final baseline sessions. Subjects in the biofeedback group received training to lower frontalis EMG (EMG 2 in the figure), subjects in the relaxation group received a fixed series of relaxation tapes, sub-

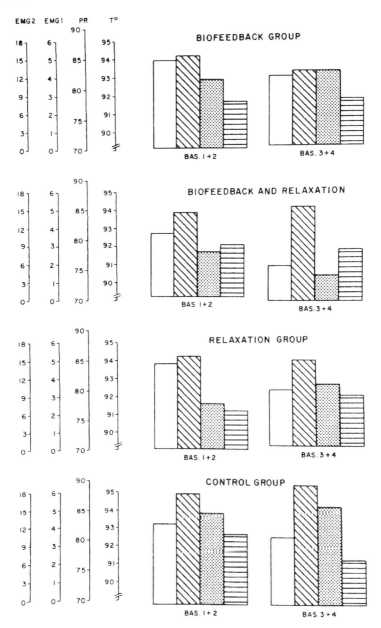

FIGURE 1. Mean resting levels in frontalis EMG (EMG-2), longissimus or posterior neck EMG (EMG-1), pulse rate (PR) and peripheral digit temperature (T° in degrees Fahrenheit) during two baseline sessions prior to, and two baseline sessions following an experimental treatment. The treatments were, respectively, biofeedback for decreases in EMG-2, biofeedback for EMG-2 and relaxation training, relaxation training only, and no treatment. The subjects were all muscle-contraction headache patients. (From Lacroix et al., 1984).

144 J. MICHAEL LACROIX

jects in the biofeedback and relaxation group received both frontalis EMG training and the relaxation tapes, and subjects in the control group received no training of any kind between the first two and the last two baseline sessions. The figure depicts, successively, the target EMG activity, EMG recorded from a different site (back or neck), pulse rate, and hand temperature.

What I find most interesting about these data is that the response profiles are so similar. Thus, a comparison of the profiles in the biofeedback and the relaxation groups reveals in both cases decreases in the two EMG measures and negligible increases in pulse rate and peripheral temperature. Indeed, analyses of variance carried out on these data yielded only two significant effects (a Time main effect for EMG 2, $F(1/51 = 16.56, p < .001$, and a Groups main effect for pulse rate, $F(3/51) = 2.9, p < .05$): none of the Groups $\times$ Time interactions approached statistical significance. It might be argued that differences in level of learning in different subjects might add so much noise to the data as to mask important differences between groups with respect to response specificity. We evaluated this possibility by carrying out an identical analysis, but using only the data from subjects who showed significant learning from the first two to the last two baseline sessions, as defined by the absence of overlap between the standard errors of the mean. The pattern of data was essentially the same: no group differences emerged with respect to response profiles. The message from these data, clearly, is that longer training regimens do not necessarily reveal a biofeedback phenomenon.

If it is not a biofeedback phenomenon that accounts for learning in the biofeedback paradigm, what does? I suggested earlier that although learning could entail an extensive recalibration of sensorimotor systems, it could also entail a simpler reshuffling of behavioral-cognitive elements at the central level. I have argued before (Lacroix, 1981) that this latter process is in fact the sort of process that is going on (usually) when subjects undergo training in the biofeedback paradigm. Briefly, what I think happens in the usual case is that the instructions given to the subject identify a set of existing behaviors within his or her behavioral repertoire. Insofar as this set is at all effective in producing appropriate changes in the feedback display, this set is then simply magnified over the course of training. This position will be developed at greater length later in the chapter, but to keep the skeptical reader at least open to the possibility I would like to introduce here one small bit of empirical evidence.

Figure 2 (from Lacroix, Clarke, Bock, Doxey, Wood, and Lavis, 1983) presents within-session changes in peripheral hand temperature in subjects suffering from migraine headaches trained to control peripheral

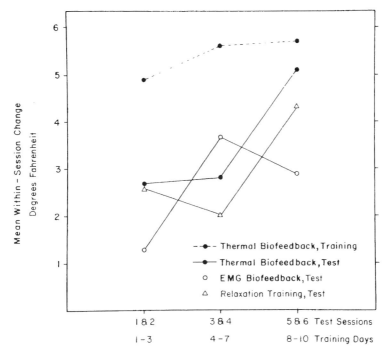

FIGURE 2. Mean within-session change in skin temperature in three groups of migraine headache patients who received biofeedback for increases in peripheral digit temperature, biofeedback for decreases in frontalis EMG, or relaxation training. Performance is displayed for the three groups on pairs of test (no feedback) sessions given before training, half-way through, and at the end of training, and in the thermal biofeedback group on training (feedback) sessions from the first, middle, and last third of training. (From Lacroix et al., 1983).

temperature or frontalis EMG or trained in progressive relaxation. The figure presents the hand temperature data from test (no feedback) sessions before training, half-way through an 18-session training regimen, and after the 18 training sessions, in the three groups, and also presents the comparable data from training (feedback) sessions in the early, middle, and late stages of training, in the skin temperature feedback group. What is particularly interesting here is that the temperature biofeedback group was able to produce substantial increases in skin temperature on training days from the outset of training: biofeedback training apparently resulted simply in generalization of this performance to no-feedback test conditions. Clearly, the temperature control task (which was accompanied by pronounced changes in migraine attacks in these patients, who had suffered from migraines for 20 years on average) was well within the subjects' behavioral repertoire.

Is the implication to be taken from these data and arguments that the biofeedback phenomenon is simply not to be found in the biofeedback paradigm, and that the paradigm is therefore of little interest to psychologists whose primary concern is with the learning process? Not quite. Although the biofeedback phenomenon appears to be rather like the Cheshire cat, there are some tantalizing suggestions of its presence in the literature. Two lines of evidence appear particularly promising. The first stems from a number of studies carried out before the biofeedback paradigm acquired the wide currency that it now holds, when scientists interested in the general area still referred to it as "operant autonomic conditioning." Although there are a number of procedural differences between biofeedback studies and operant autonomic conditioning studies, one that strikes me as particularly important pertains to the information given to the subjects. In the present biofeedback paradigm subjects are invariably given complete information about the response to be controlled and the direction (and sometimes the magnitude) of desired changes and are often (particularly in clinical studies) provided with specific suggestions as to response strategies that might be effective in controlling the target response. In contrast, in the earlier operant conditioning paradigm subjects were invariably kept ignorant of the response to be controlled, the contingency between the response and the reinforcer that was used, and often even of the very existence of any contingency on their behavior; in many studies, moreover, subjects who guessed correctly either the target response or the nature of the contingency were dropped from the analyses.

Yet it is precisely from those kinds of studies that the most encouraging evidence emerges for gradual acquisition functions (e.g. for heart rate: Ascough & Sipprelle, 1968; Levene, Engel, & Pearson, 1968; Shapiro, Tursky, & Schwartz, 1970; for electrodermal activity: Greene & Wirth, 1974; Kimmel & Baxter, 1964; Van Twyver & Kimmel, 1966; for blood pressure: Shapiro, Schwartz, & Tursky, 1972; Shapiro, Tursky & Schwartz, 1970; Shapiro, Tursky, Gershon, & Stern, 1969). Moreover, the most encouraging evidence for specificity of control also comes from some of these studies. For example, Ascough and Sipprelle (1968) reported an independence of target heart-rate changes from respiratory changes, and Cohen (1973) reported an independence between target heart-rate changes and EMG changes. Yet in the biofeedback paradigm our fine-grained analyses of the development of cardiac control indicate that instructions to control heart rate activate respiratory changes and that the acquisition of heart-rate control then takes place in the context of somatomotor activation (Kelly & Lacroix, 1983; Lacroix & Gowen, 1981), and this is in keeping with more molar analyses carried in other investigations (Clemens & Shattock, 1979; Lacroix & Roberts, 1978; Levenson & Ditto, 1981; Obrist *et al.*, 1975; Schober & Lacroix, 1985). Similarly, Van Twyver and Kimmel (1966) reported no relationship between target GSR changes and changes in forearm EMG or respiration frequency, whereas in the biofeedback paradigm we have invariably found target electrodermal changes to be embedded in a somatomotor-respiratory complex (Lacroix & Gowen, 1981; Lacroix & Roberts, 1978).

Not all operant autonomic conditioning experiments have yielded gradual acquisition functions or specificity of control, of course, and even those studies that have provided such evidence of a biofeedback learning phenomenon are far from entirely convincing. My point here is simply to draw attention to these studies, because they at least provide suggestive evidence of a learning process akin to the biofeedback phenomenon, whereas studies carried out in the biofeedback paradigm simply do not. One final point about the specificity of control which is (sometimes) evident in these earlier investigations: it is interesting to note that the specificity which is apparent in these studies does not develop in the sense that components of the response complex initially activated by the subject are eliminated as a function of training. Rather, control appears specific to the target response from the outset of training (e.g. Schwartz, 1972; Shapiro, Tursky, & Schwartz, 1970).

The operant autonomic conditioning studies constitute the first line of evidence which suggests that the biofeedback phenomenon might provide a description of the learning process in some cases. The second line of evidence stems from studies carried out within the current biofeedback paradigm, but with patients suffering from various physiological dysfunctions. Evidence of gradual acquisition functions and of control specific to the target response has been provided by Engel and Bleecker (1974), for example, on the control of cardiac arrhythmias and by Miller and Brucker (1979) on the control of diastolic blood pressure in a hypotensive patient. I would like to indicate here that the variable that distinguishes these studies from other studies with the biofeedback paradigm that have not yielded any evidence of a biofeedback phenomenon is not *simply* the clinical status of the subjects, since our work with clinical populations, referred to earlier, has not not provided any evidence of learning in terms of a biofeedback phenomenon in these patients. Presumably it is the specific nature of the disorder and not simply the presence of a psychophysiological disorder which is critical. I will return to this point and these studies in the last section of the chapter.

III. The Verbal (Consciousness?) Interface

In the last couple of years I have become intrigued with the implications of the differences in outcome pertaining to the biofeedback phenomenon between studies carried out with the biofeedback paradigm and (some) studies carried out in the paradigmatic context of operant autonomic conditioning. Could the mere presence of a verbal label designating a target response have such dramatic effects as to affect the very form of the learning process? In this section I would like to focus on this general question, by first drawing upon a number of literatures cognate to the biofeedback literature that point to the importance of verbal labels and of verbal processing generally. I will then offer some speculations on the role of the verbal labels in the biofeedback paradigm, and these speculations will then be formalized in the general theory of learning in the biofeedback paradigm which is outlined in the following section.

First, it should be acknowledged that the putative importance of the verbal information given to the subjects in the context of biofeedback–operant conditioning studies has not been completely ignored in the literature. There has been some attention to the effects of providing the target response with different labels. Thus, Blanchard, Scott, Young, and Edmundson (1974) observed larger heart-rate changes when heart rate was designated as target and subjects were given feedback for heart rate than when the target response was designated as skin conductance or as an unspecified internal response and feedback was nonetheless provided for heart-rate changes. Quy and Kubiak (1974) examined the issue of "awareness" of the response. Two groups of subjects were punished by an electrical pulse for spontaneous electrodermal responses, but one group was given information about the target response and about the response-reinforcer contingency whereas subjects in the other group were told simply that the study focused on their physiological reactions to the electrical stimuli. Although a careful look at their study reveals statistical problems that make the results uninterpretable, their conclusions are worth noting:

> A subject's awareness of the process of control could be a condition which impedes, rather the encourages learning. This implies that the straightforward instrumental learning procedures with "naive" subjects may in fact produce more rapid and enduring control over autonomic functions than "aware" conditions of learning. (p. 505)

There has also been some interest in the effects of providing subjects with suggestions as to response strategies for controlling the target response. In our own work on this issue (Lacroix & Roberts, 1978), we have found the provision of such strategies to be deleterious to control of both electrodermal and cardiac target responses, and others have reported similar evidence (e.g. White, Holmes, & Bennett, 1977). Although the above studies are indicative of a peripheral interest in the biofeedback literature with issues related to the importance of verbal labels and verbal processing, it is clear that their concern was with the effects of different verbal information on level of control of the target response, that is, on performance. My concern here goes deeper, however: can such information affect not only performance level but also the form of the learning process?

It is interesting to note that the effect of providing a subject with the information as to the response to be controlled and as to the response-feedback contingency is to make the subject *aware* of that response, or to make the response *conscious*. The last several years have seen increasing attention to the question of whether being aware of information is necessary in order to act on that information, and to the meaning and the nature of *consciousness*. I do not plan to review here what is now a voluminous literature with ramifications in all areas of psychology. I would like simply to highlight some aspects of that literature which I think can shed some light on the issue of learning in the biofeedback paradigm.

First, it is clear that the brain comprises a number of different information-processing systems. Moreover, it appears that information can be processed *independently* by the different systems (or, at least, some of the information, some of the time, with respect to some of the information-processing systems). Evidence for this generalization can be adduced from cognitive (Nisbett & Wilson, 1977), clinical (Beahrs, 1982; Hilgard, 1976), and neurophysiological data (LeDoux, Wilson, & Gazzaniga, 1979) and is sensible on phenomenological grounds (I can drive my car without running into trees while my conscious attention is focused on the news being read on the radio). Thus for example, in a series of clever experiments, Nisbett and Wilson manipulated apparently innocuous variables that had significant effects on subjects' behavior. Yet the subjects attributed their behavior to variables that were controlled by the experimenters and therefore could not have been the basis for the behavior. Nisbett and Wilson concluded that subjects do not have access to their cognitive processes. Pennebaker (1982) recently described the same sort of phenomenon with respect to subjects' perception of physical symptoms. Following certain manipulations subjects would report certain symptoms consciously, and would invariably attribute these to internal factors rather than to the experimenter-controlled variables.

Yet another and dramatic example of appropriate behavior being produced in the absence of conscious realization is given by the results of a study by Risse and Gazzaniga (cited in LeDoux *et al.*, 1979). In this study, patients scheduled to undergo brain surgery had their left hemisphere anaesthetized by sodium amytal and had objects placed in their left hand (which is governed by the right hemisphere). When the left hemisphere had recovered from the anaesthetic, the patients were unable to name the objects but could pick them out correctly, by pointing, from among a larger group of objects, all along insisting that they were only guessing.

This last experiment is important in that it not only reinforces the argument that learning can proceed in information-processing systems other than the verbal system without the knowledge of the latter, it also develops this argument one small step further by pointing out that the different information-processing systems do not necessarily have access to each other's memories. If we agree, then, that behavior is governed by a number of information-processing systems that overlap only partially, how does one come to present a coherent self to the world, and for that matter to oneself: what is consciousness within this apparently anarchic universe within the brain/mind? LeDoux *et al.* (1979) have recently provided an elegantly simple answer to these questions.

LeDoux *et al.* argue that, given the importance of language, over the course of ontogeny the activities in the various information-processing systems come to be monitored more and more by the information-processing system on which we come to rely more and more: the verbal system. Gradually a concept of self develops which is equivalent to what the verbal system knows about itself and the others. In their view, then, *consciousness is equivalent to the activation of the verbal information-processing system.* This conceptualization gives the verbal system a triple importance. It is important in its own right, in the processing of verbal information. It is important as an interface between the other information-processing systems in the brain/mind through its monitoring activities. And it is important as a major interface between the person and the outside world. Thus, most demands on the individual coming from the outside world, because of their verbal nature, are first "handled" by the verbal system. It is through the verbal system interface that the other information-processing systems learn of these demands. The demands of the outside world are then processed by the verbal system and presumably by others, but since it is again the verbal system that interprets the outputs of the other systems to the outside world, the verbal system will also put its "stamp" on behavior generated by the other systems in the brain/mind.

That the verbal system interprets in its own "language" the outputs of the other information-processing systems was demonstrated dramatically in a series of split-brain studies by Gazzaniga and LeDoux (1978). Thus, when the patient's left and right hemispheres were presented simultaneously with different demands, leading to behavior which could be predicted only in part by the left (verbal) hemisphere, the verbal hemisphere nonetheless provided an instantaneous interpretation of the patient's behavior in terms of its own referents. For example when the patient's right hemisphere was instructed to scratch, and did so, the left hemisphere simply indicated that he was itchy.

The domination of the various information-processing systems by the verbal system is never complete, as any good clinician can attest. However, it is usually sufficient to provide enough of a semblance of unity that we can appear as a coherent person both to the outside world and to the verbal-conscious self. However, the partial nature of verbal predominance is revealed easily under a variety of conditions that favor the temporary ascendancy of other systems, such as hypnosis or dissociative disorders, and in patients with a severed corpus callosum or an anesthetized left hemisphere. The partial nature of verbal predominance is also evident in more normal conditions, as when we can process complex information (e.g., driving) while consciously-verbally engaged in some other task, or when nonverbal information-processing systems find nonverbal (and sometimes verbal) means of expression, as in the patient with a conversion reaction who chuckles while describing her symptomatology (or in the case of Freudian slips).

What are the implications of this conceptualization for the learning process? At a general level, the major implication is that we can expect that demands placed on the individual by the outside world (including demands to learn some new behavior) will be conveyed to the network of information-processing systems in the brain/mind by the verbal system and will be processed by that system unless conditions make such processing impossible. Moreover, any processing of information by other systems will be interpreted by the verbal system and will generate some sort of verbal coding. In terms of the general distinction made earlier, learning in the typical case will involve a reshuffling of behavioral-cognitive elements that are verbally coded. However, there are two sorts of conditions under which we may expect a demand from the outside world not to involve the verbal system. The first is in the case of highly predictable, well-rehearsed tasks that have been repeated so frequently that their processing has become automatized. Cognitive psychologists have been understandably concerned with the differences between highly automatized tasks and tasks requiring conscious-verbal processing and have drawn distinctions between these on a number of bases (e.g., Hasher & Zacks, 1979; Schneider & Shiffrin, 1977). The second category of conditions under which the verbal system might be bypassed comprises those conditions wherein the verbal system is unable to deal with the demands of the task. This might occur in cases in which the verbal system lacks the "language" or information or the proper interfacing with other systems to deal with the demands. Alternatively, this might occur in cases in which the task demands are not phrased in such a way as to allow the verbal system to access the relevant information that it has. These conditions are most likely to be met when the task to be learned is some sort of "skill." In terms of the general distinction made earlier, learning under those conditions will involve an extensive recalibration of sensorimotor systems in order to construct an appropriate motor program.

We can now see the relevance of this conceptualization to learning in the biofeedback paradigm. In this context, we might profitably envisage the verbal system in terms of an analogy, as a central library through which information pertaining to behavior is normally accessed. Demands are placed on a subject, for example, to raise his heart rate. Unless the behavioral strategy for producing increases in heart rate has become automatized, the subject has to "look up" what the task entails. If relevant information is found in the verbal library, including appropriate interfacing with the relevant behavior-production systems, and if implementation of the behavior program thus identified is successful (the feedback arrow goes up), there is no incentive to continue the search outside the verbal library system. Indeed, there is an extensive literature that shows that organisms do not work for redundant information (e.g., Egger & Miller, 1963; Kamin, 1968). The fact that the changes produced in this way may not be maximal is seldom, if ever, indicated to the subject. Nor is the subject typically instructed to produce changes specific to the target response. Thus, it is only in those instances wherein the verbal library cannot access information relevant to the appropriate behavioral programs (the operant autonomic conditioning studies?) or wherein the verbal system lacks the language or the interfacing to inform the subject as to what to do (the clinical cases such as those of Miller & Brucker, 1979) that learning could be expected to proceed along the lines of a biofeedback phenomenon.

IV. A Two-Process Theory

In this section I would like to develop a theory of how human subjects learn to control autonomic or other "internal" responses when provided with information about the target response in the form of a biofeedback signal in the biofeedback paradigm, or a reinforcer for appropriate responding in an operant autonomic conditioning paradigm. In keeping with the thrust of the previous section, the theory places considerable emphasis on the role of the verbal system both as the interface with the outside world that sets the task requirements and as the interface with the other information-processing/behavior-generating systems of the brain/mind. The theory presented here is basically an elaboration of the theory that I introduced in outline form in 1981 (Lacroix, 1981). However, it also echoes suggestions made by a number of other biofeedback investigators. Thus, the emphasis that I will place on what are called here *feedforward* processes parallels a similar emphasis in the recent work of Brener (1982), Qualls and Sheehan (1981) and Stilson, Matus, and Ball (1980). Moreover, the relatively large importance given to the task instructions owes much to Roberts's conceptual analysis of the environment in which biofeedback training takes place (Roberts & Marlin, 1979; Roberts *et al.*, 1984), although my emphasis here is on how the task demands are represented in the subject's verbal system and on the verbally mediated associations thus generated.

The theory is presented in the form of a flow-diagram in Figure 3. The diagram is not meant to be exhaustive of the operations involved, but for the sake of clarity the more obvious operations have been assumed (e.g., monitoring the effect of "trying harder" on the feedback display—upper right-hand quadrant). The theory envisages that control of autonomic responses may be acquired through two different kinds of processes. These are labeled *feedforward* and *feedback* processes (above and below the dotted line) in keeping with Brener's recent analysis of the neurophysiology of learning of skeletal-motor responses (Brener, 1984). Feedforward and feedback processes correspond to what I had earlier (Lacroix, 1981) referred to as efferent and afferent processes, respectively; the earlier terminology generated some confusion and I am happy to homogenize my nomenclature with that of Brener. Feedforward and feedback processes also correspond to the two general strategies in which learning can proceed and to which I made reference earlier: a central reshuffling of existing behavioral-cognitive elements and a recalibration of sensorimotor systems. One advantage of the present conceptualization is that it provides for possible interactions between these two general strategies, that is, for subjects to change from one strategy to the other when their initial selection is no longer effective or optimal.

Briefly, control of autonomic responses is envisaged to be acquired as follows. The instructions given to the subject lead him to engage in a search of his verbal library to determine whether it contains behavioral programs which are potentially relevant for control of the target response and are appropriately interfaced with pertinent nonverbal information-processing/behavior-generating systems. The behavioral program judged likely to be the most effective is then implemented and its effectiveness is evaluated in terms of whether the feedback display changes as expected. If it does, the subject may decide to try to improve on his performance either by carrying out the various components of the selected behavioral program with greater intensity, or by directing his attention to constituent elements of the programs which are acces-

154 J. MICHAEL LACROIX

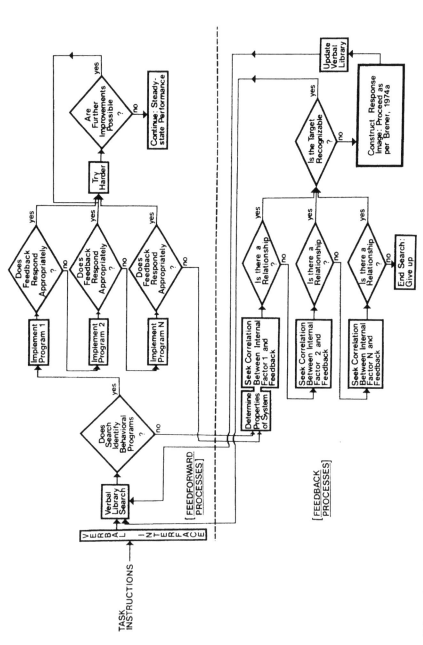

FIGURE 3. Schematic representation of the processes and operations involved in learning to control an "internal" response in biofeedback-like situations.

sible to (verbal) consciousness and, in as much as possible, identify a more effective subset. This may continue until the subject judges further improvements in performance to be unlikely or unworthy of the effort, and performance should remain at asymptote thereafter. If, however, the behavioral program initially activated is not effective in producing the desired change in the feedback display, the subject implements the next program in his hierarchy of potentially effective programs, more or less in keeping with Hull's notions of habit family hierarchies (Hull, 1952). The subject may thus implement a number of behavioral programs, successively, either until one is found to be effective or until all the programs identified from the verbal library have been exhausted and shown to be ineffective. At this point the subject's general strategy would switch from one that emphasizes feedforward processes to one that emphasizes feedback processes.

In sum, in most instances of autonomic learning the subject is believed to adopt a general learning strategy that emphasizes feedforward processes: he or she selects a previously constructed motor program and simply "plugs it in," with relatively little attention to feedback information from interoceptive afferentation related to the target effector. Instead, the "feedback" provided by the feedback display serves primarily to determine the appropriateness of the program which has been selected. Improvements in performance stem either from doing more of the same or from stressing components of the program that may be particularly effective. Even in the latter case, however, acquisition would *not* be expected to result in a gradual refinement in performance, as would be evidenced by the gradual elimination of responses not correlated with the target response. Instead, acquisition is conceptualized in terms of an additive model, with the smaller components of the behavioral program which have been identified by feedback training as particularly effective being superimposed on the other components, insofar as it is still the same program (albeit with minor modifications) which is activated.

Although feedforward processes would be expected to be employed in most instances of autonomic learning, they would not always be selected. There are a number of conditions that should lead subjects to emphasize feedback processes instead in learning to control the target response. First, all the programs identified from the verbal library may be ineffective. Second, the verbal library may fail to identify potentially relevant programs. Third, the library may identify relevant programs but these may be poorly interfaced with the nonverbal information-processing/behavior-generating systems such that the programs are judged to be impossible to carry out. In all these cases the subject would adopt a general learning strategy focusing on feedback processes; learning would then proceed along the lines of a biofeedback phenomenon.

For example, in the typical operant autonomic conditioning paradigm the subject would be unable to plug in an already existing centrally organized motor program to control the target response since the instructions may not provide enough information to implement a successful search; the subject would therefore have to go about constructing an appropriate program. Initially, this would involve monitoring of interoceptive afferentation from potentially relevant organ systems, with a view to determining which of the afferent processes monitored are correlated with variations in the feedback display. If a correlation can be established, the subject may then guess as to the nature of the target response and implement a new verbal library search on the basis of that new information, and this may then lead her to change to a strategy emphasizing feedforward processes (recall that I suggested earlier that subjects do not work for redundant information). However, should the target response not be recognizable or not readily map onto existing behavioral programs, acquisition of the response would then proceed in terms of the kinds of operations that Brener originally suggested (1974a) and that I summarized at the beginning of section II (construction of a response image; gradual development of specificity of control to the target response). In keeping with the emphasis that I have placed on the verbal system as the interface with the other information-processing systems, I surmise that successful construction of a new motor program on this basis would then result in some updating of the verbal library.

The theoretical framework presented here is empirically testable. Indeed, there are existing data that can be brought to bear on the theory and these have so far fitted rather nicely.

A first critical point at which the form of the acquisition process can be influenced is at the level of the task instructions. Presumably the more complete the verbal instructions the greater the likelihood that they will map onto existing behavioral programs, and the smaller the likelihood that acquisition will proceed in keeping with a biofeedback phenomenon (as operationalized by an ability to discriminate afferentation related to the occurrence of the target response, or by a developing specificity of control). In keeping with this analysis, I referred earlier to a report by Blanchard *et al.* that subjects performed differently in a heart-rate control task as a function of whether the target response was defined as heart rate, skin conductance, or an unspecified internal response. This is evidence of the importance of the verbal labels in determining performance, presumably as a function of the behavioral programs which the labels elicit from the verbal library. Also in keeping with this analysis are our findings (Lacroix & Roberts, 1978) that providing subjects with strategy suggestions led to a deterioration of performance on both heart-rate and skin conductance control tasks: again, this points to the importance of the verbal information provided to the subjects in determining which behavioral programs are selected from the verbal library. More generally, I think that the differences discussed earlier between the data obtained in the biofeedback paradigm and those obtained (sometimes) in the operant autonomic conditioning paradigm also are attributable to differences in the outcome of the verbal library search stemming from differences in the instructions given the subjects.

A second point at which the form of the acquisition process can be influenced is at the level of the verbal library search itself. More specifically, the outcome of that search is likely to be influenced by a number of variables in addition to the instructions. Among these variables are individual difference factors: some subjects may be likely to engage in more extensive library searches or may possess "better" libraries—perhaps in terms of their verbal cross-references. In keeping with this view, we have found (Offutt & Lacroix, 1983) as have others (Qualls & Sheehan, 1981) that subjects who score high on the Absorption scale exhibit very good control of their internal responses without need for feedback training and indeed are not helped by biofeedback training, whereas low absorbers exhibit little control of the target internal response without feedback and improve with biofeedback training. Absorption is a trait which correlates with hypnotic susceptibility and reflects subjects' ability to tune out the world and draw on their own inner resources (Tellegen & Atkinson, 1974). The clinical data to which I referred earlier (Engel & Bleecker, 1974; Miller & Brucker, 1979) point to another variable likely to affect the outcome of the verbal library search operation. The patients in these studies may represent cases in which, although potentially effective behavioral programs may be referenced in the verbal library, the nature of the patient's injury may have affected the interface between the verbal library and other nonverbal information-processing/behavior-generating programs such that the patient cannot implement the program selected.

A third point at which the present theoretical framework lends itself to empirical test is at the level of the feedback provided to the subject as to the effectiveness of the initial (and subsequent) behavioral programs selected. Appropriate manipulations of the feedback display should lead subjects either to maintain their initial program or to abandon it in favor of an alternative. Changes (or retention) of the behavioral programs selected should be evident both in terms of patterns of physiological activity during attempts to control the target response and in terms of the subjects' verbal reports of what they are doing.

Manipulations of the feedback display also allow a test of the theory to be carried out at another point. If a subject is following a learning strategy that emphasizes feedforward processes, once the subject has decided to stay with a particular behavioral programme, her next task is to determine whether further improvements in performance can be accomplished. At this point, manipulations of the feedback display that suggest that the subject is doing very well should lead to asymptotic performance early, whereas manipulations of the display that suggest that there is considerable room for improvement should lead the subject to "try harder." In keeping with this analysis, Williamson, Monguillot, Hutchinson, Jarrell, and Blouin (1981) reported that subjects produced larger heart-rate changes in a heart-rate control task with low sensitivity feedback displays than with high sensitivity displays. It is worth noting here that these results are opposite to predictions from traditional motor skills theories, although they fit nicely with the present theory.

One final testable proposition from the theory may be mentioned. Assume that a subject follows a learning strategy that emphasizes feedback processes and proceeds to recalibrate his sensorimotor systems so as to construct a new motor program, that is, the subject learns in terms of a biofeedback phenomenon. At some point the verbal (consciousness) system, which monitors the other information-processing systems, should seek to code the new behavior program in terms of its own referents. This is exactly what Roberts *et al.* (1984) have recently reported. Their subjects were trained either to control heart rate or to produce lateralized changes in skin conductance, but possible clues as to the nature of the task were specifically concealed. In terms of the present conceptualization, this should have fostered a learning strategy that emphasizes feedback processes. Under these conditions, the subjects who learned to control the target response (but not those who failed to learn) were able to provide a verbal description of what they were doing which, although not always well articulated, nonetheless mapped onto some of the properties of the target response system.

In closing, I would like simply to return to the general issue raised in the introduction. Does the biofeedback *paradigm* foster a unique kind of learning, a biofeedback *phenomenon* such that it should be of particular interest to psychologists interested in the learning process? My attempt to answer this question has led me far afield and has led me to engage in considerable theoretical speculation. At this point my answer is that biofeedback training can lead to a biofeedback phenomenon, but that this kind of learning is evident only under certain (now unusual) conditions. The theory presented in this section attempts to specify what those conditions are and also to provide a basis for understanding what and how subjects learn in biofeedback situations more generally.

References

Ascough, J. C., & Sipprelle, C. N. (1968). Operant verbal conditioning of autonomic responses. *Behavior Research and Therapy, 6*, 363–370.

Beahrs, J. O. (1982). *Unity and multiplicity: Multilevel consciousness of self in hypnosis, psychiatric disorder and mental health.* New York: Brunner/Mazel.

Blanchard, E., Scott, R. E., Young, L. D., & Edmundson, E. D. (1974). Effect of knowledge of response on the self-control of heart rate. *Psychophysiology, 11*, 251–264.

Brener, J. A. (1974a). A general model of voluntary control applied to the phenomena of learned cardiovascular change. In P. A. Obrist A. H. Black, J. Brener, & L. V. DiCara (Eds.), *Cardiovascular psychophysiology: Current issues in response mechanisms, biofeedback, and methodology.* Chicago: Aldine.

Brener, J. (1974b). Factors influencing the specificity of learned cardiovascular change. In L. V. DiCara (Ed.), *Limbic and autonomic nervous systems research.* New York: Plenum Press.

Brener, J. (1977a). Sensory and perceptual determinants of voluntary visceral control. In G. E. Schwartz & J. Beatty (Eds.), *Biofeedback: Theory and research.* New York: Academic Press.

Brener, J. (1977b). Visceral perception. In J. Beatty & H. Legewie (Eds.), *Biofeedback and behavior.* New York: Plenum Press.

Brener, J. (1982). Psychobiological mechanisms in biofeedback. In L. White & B. Tursky (Eds.), *Clinical biofeedback: Efficacy and mechanisms.* New York: Guilford.

Brener, J. (1984). Operant reinforcement, feedback and the efficiency of learned motor control. In M. Coles, E. Donchin, & S. Porges (Eds.), *Psychophysiology: Systems, processes and applications* (Vol. 2). New York: Guilford.

Brener, J., Ross, A., Baker, J., & Clemens, W. J. (1979). On the relationship between cardiac discrimination and control. In N. Birbaumer & H. D. Kimmel (Eds.), *Biofeedback and self-regulation.* Hillsdale, NJ: Erlbaum.

Clemens, W. J., & Shattock, R. J. (1979). Voluntary heart rate control during static muscular effort. *Psychophysiology, 16*, 327–332.

Cohen, M. J. (1973). The relation between heart rate and electromyographic activity in a discriminated escape-avoidance paradigm. *Psychophysiology, 10*, 8–20.

Cox, D. J., & Hobbs, W. (1982). Biofeedback as a treatment for tension headaches. In L. White & B. Tursky (Eds.), *Clinical biofeedback: Efficacy and mechanisms.* New York: Guilford.

Egger, M. D., & Miller, N. E. (1963). When is a reward reinforcing?. An experimental study of the information hypothesis. *Journal of Comparative and Physiological Psychology, 56*, 132–137.

Engel, B. T., & Bleecker, E. R. (1971). Application of operant conditioning techniques to the control of cardiac arrhythmias. In P. A. Obrist, A. H. Black, J. M. Brener, & L. V. DiCara (Eds.), *Cardiovascular psychophysiology: Current issues in response mechanisms, biofeedback, and methodology.* Chicago: Aldine.

Gazzaniga, M., & LeDoux, J. P. (1978). *The integrated mind.* New York: Plenum Press.

Greene, W. A., & Wirth, H. G. (1974). Operant conditioning of the skin resistance response with different intensities of light flashes. *Bulletin of the Psychonomic Society, 4*, 177–179.

Hasher, L., & Zacks, R. T. (1979). Automatic and effortful processes in memory. *Journal of Experimental Psychology: General, 108*, 356–388.

Hilgard, E. R. (1976). Neodissociation theory of multiple cognitive control systems. In G. E. Schwartz & D. Shapiro (Eds.), *Consciousness and self-regulation: Advances in research* (Vol. 1). New York: Plenum Press.

Hull, C. L. (1952). *A behavior system.* New York: Wiley.

KAMIN, L. J. (1968). "Attention-like" processes in classical conditioning. In M. R. JONES (Ed.) *Miami Symposium on the Prediction of Behavior, 1967: Aversive Stimulation*. Coral Gables, Fla: University of Florida Press.

KATKIN, E. S., & MURRAY, E. N. (1968). Instrumental conditioning of autonomically mediated behavior: Theoretical and methodological issues. *Psychological Bulletin, 70*, 52–68.

KATKIN, E. S., MORELL, M. A. GOLDBAND, S., BERNSTEIN, G. L. & WISE, J. A. (1982). Individual differences in heart beat discrimination. *Psychophysiology, 19*, 160–166.

KELLY, B., & LACROIX, J. M. (1983, June). *The acquisition of heart rate control through biofeedback: Further evidence against an afferent process*. Paper presented at the annual meetings of the Canadian Psychological Association, Winnipeg.

KIMMEL, H. D., & BAXTER, R. (1964). Avoidance conditioning of the GSR. *Journal of Experimental Psychology, 68*, 482–485.

LACROIX, J. M. (1981). The acquisition of autonomic control through biofeedback: The case against an afferent process and a two-process alternative. *Psychophysiology, 18*, 573–587.

LACROIX, J. M., & GOWEN, A. (1981). The acquisition of autonomic control through biofeedback: Some tests of discrimination theory. *Psychophysiology, 18*, 559–572.

LACROIX, J. M., & ROBERTS, L. E. (1978). A comparison of the mechanisms and some properties of instructed sudomotor and cardiac control. *Biofeedback and Self-Regulation, 3*, 105–132.

LACROIX, J. M., CLARKE, M. A., BOCK, J. C., DOXEY, N., WOOD, A., & LAVIS, S. (1983). Biofeedback and relaxation in the treatment of migraine headaches: Comparative effectiveness and physiological correlates. *Journal of Neurology, Neurosurgery, and Psychiatry, 46*, 525–532.

LACROIX, J. M. CLARKE, M. A., BOCK, J. C. & DOXEY, N. C. S. (1984). Biofeedback and relaxation in the treatment of muscle contraction headache: Effectiveness, predictors, and physiological correlates. *Pain, Suppl. 2*, 302.

LEDOUX, . E., WILSON, D. H., & GAZZANIGA, M. S. (1979). Beyond commissurotomy: Clues to consciousness. In M. S. GAZZANIGA (Ed.), *Handbook of behavioral neurobiology: Vol. 2. Neuropsychology*. New York: Plenum Press.

LEVENE, H. I., ENGEL, B. T., & PEARSON, J. A. (1968). Differential operant conditioning of heart rate. *Psychosomatic Medicine, 30*, 837–845.

LEVENSON, R. W., & DITTO, W. B. (1981). Individual differences in ability to control heart rate: Personality, strategy, physiological, and other variables. *Psychophysiology, 18*, 91–100.

MILLER, N. E. (1981, August). Invited discussion at a symposium entitled *New Perspectives on Biofeedback* (D. SHAPIRO, Chair), at the annual meetings of the American Psychological Association, Los Angeles.

MILLER, N. E., & BRUCKER, B. S. (1979). A learned visceral response apparently independent of skeletal ones in patients paralyzed by spinal lesions. In N. BIRBAUMER & H. D. KIMMEL (Eds.), *Biofeedback and self-regulation*. Hillside, NJ: Erlbaum.

NISBETT, R. E., & WILSON, D. T. (1977). Telling more than we can know: Verbal reports on mental processes. *Psychological Review, 84*, 231–259.

OBRIST, P. A., GALOSY, R. A., LAWLER, J. E., GAEBELEIN, C. J., HOWARD, J. L., & SHANKS, E. M., (1975). Operant conditioning of heart rate: Somatic correlates. *Psychophysiology, 12*, 445–455.

OFFUTT, C., & LACROIX, J. M. (1983). Absorption: A predictor of biofeedback learning. *Psychophysiology, 20*, 461.

PENNEBAKER, J. W. (1982). *The psychology of physical symptoms*. New York: Springer-Verlag.

QUALLS, P. J., & SHEEHAN, P. W. (1981). Role of the feedback in electromyograph feedback: The relevance of attention. *Journal of Experimental Psychology: General, 110*, 204–216.

QUY, R. J., & KUBIAK, E. W. (1974). A comparison between "aware" and "naive" conditions in the suppression of GSR activity. *Quarterly Journal of Experimental Psychology, 26*, 561–565.

RILEY, D. M., & FUREDY, J. J. (1981). Effects of instructions and contingency of reinforcement on the operant conditioning of human phasic heart rate change. *Psychophysiology, 18*, 75–81.

ROBERTS, L. E. (1974). Comparative psychophysiology of the electrodermal and cardiac control systems. In P. A. OBRIST, A. H. BLACK, J. BRENER, & L. V. DiCARA (Eds.), *Cardiovascular psychophysiology: Current issues in response mechanisms, biofeedback and methodology*. Chicago: Aldine.

ROBERTS, L. E. (1977). The role of exteroceptive feedback in learned electrodermal and cardiac control: Some attractions of and problems with discrimination theory. In J. BEATTY & H. LEGEWIE (Eds.), *Biofeedback and behavior*. New York: Plenum Press.

ROBERTS, L. E., & MARLIN, R. G. (1979). Some comments on the self-description and discrimination of visceral response states. In N. BIRBAUMER & H. D. KIMMEL (Eds.) *Biofeedback and self-regulation*. Hillsdale, NJ: Erlbaum.

ROBERTS, L. E., WILLIAMS, R. J., MARLIN, R. G., FARRELL, T., & IMIOLO, D. (1984). Awareness of the response after feedback training for change in heart rate and sudomotor laterality. *Journal of Experimental Psychology: General, 113*, 225–255.

SCHNEIDER, W., & SHIFFRIN, R. M. (1977) Controlled and automatic human information processing: I. Detection, search, and attention. *Psychological Review, 84*, 1–66.

SCHOBER, R., & LACROIX, J. M. (1985). Effects of task instructions and contingency on the development of phasic heart rate control and its correlates. *Canadian Journal of Psychology*, in press.

ROSS, A., & BRENER, J. (1981). Two procedures for training cardiac discrimination: A comparison of solution strategies and their relationship to heart rate control. *Psychophysiology, 18*, 62–70.

SCHWARTZ, G. E. (1972). Voluntary control of human cardiovascular integration and differentiation through feedback and reward. *Science, 175*, 90–93.

SHAPIRO, D., SCHWARTZ, G. E., & TURSKY, B. (1972). Control of diastolic and blood pressure in man by biofeedback and reinforcement. *Psychophysiology, 9*, 296–304.

SHAPIRO, D., TURSKY, B., GERSHON, E., & STERN, M. (1969). Effects of feedback and reinforcement on the control of human systolic blood pressure. *Science, 163*, 588–590.

SHAPIRO, D., TURSKY, B., & SCHWARTZ, G. E. (1970). Differentiation of heart rate and systolic blood pressure in man by operant conditioning. *Psychosomatic Medicine, 32*, 417–423.

STEINER, S. S., & DINCE, W. M. (1981). Biofeedback efficacy studies: A critique of critiques. *Biofeedback and Self-Regulation, 6*, 275–288.

STILSON, D. W., MATUS, I., & BALL, G. (1980). Relaxation and subjective estimates of muscle tension: Implications for a central efferent theory of muscle control. *Biofeedback and Self-Regulation, 5*, 19–36.

SURWIT, R. S., & KEEFE, F. J. (1983). The blind leading the blind: Problems with the "double-blind" design in clinical biofeedback research. *Biofeedback and Self-Regulation, 8*, 1–2.

TELLEGEN, A., & ATKINSON, G. (1974). Openness to absorbing and self-altering experiences ("absorption"), a trait related to hypnotic susceptibility. *Journal of Abnormal Psychology, 83*, 268–277.

TURK, D. C., MEICHENBAUM, D. H., & BERMAN, W. H. (1979). Application of biofeedback for the regulation of pain: A critical review. *Psychological Bulletin, 86*, 1322–1338.

VAN TWYVER, H. B., & KIMMEL, H. D. (1966). Operant conditioning of the GSR with concomitant measurement of two somatic variables. *Journal of Experimental Psychology, 72*, 841–846.

WHITE, T. W., HOLMES, D. S., & BENNETT, D. H. (1977). Effects of instructions, biofeedback, and cognitive activities on heart rate control. *Journal of Experimental Psychology: Human Learning and Memory, 3,* 477–484.

WILLIAMSON, D. A., MONGUILLOT, J. E., HUTCHINSON, P., JARRELL, M. P., & BLOUIN, D. (1981). Effect of feedback sensitivity upon learned heart rate acceleration. *Psychophysiology, 18,* 712–715.

7 Learning and Long-term Physiological Regulation

BARRY R. DWORKIN

A complex animal is composed of many different semiautonomous homeostatic mechanisms, and compromises must frequently be negotiated to achieve and maintain a stable overall physiological state optimal for survival. As evidenced by general skeletal behavior (McFarland, 1971), the brain has the integrative capacity required to resolve competing demands of these mechanisms. However, the conception of the brain as a process control computer—receiving data from an array of critically placed transducers, comparing the measurements to established set points, and dispatching instructions under a fixed program to a network of switches, valves, and pumps—is, although an appealing analogy, not tenable in the light of available data. Critical physiological variables are regulated to within narrow limits for periods of weeks or even years. Feedback-stabilized electromechanical regulators, such as thermostats, can maintain steady-state conditions indefinitely, but to do so they employ physical sensors or transducers which remain calibrated indefinitely. In contrast all interoceptors adapt (Chernigovsky, 1960; Mountcastle, 1980; Widdicomb, 1974), and analogous biological control schemes using interoceptors as sensors could not maintain regulation for extended periods of time.

Figure 1 shows the response of a typical "slowly adapting" interoceptor on the application of a constant stimulus to its receptive surface (Mifflin & Kunze, 1982). The decline of impulse firing rate with time is

Parts of this chapter were originally presented as the Hinkle Lecture at Pennsylvania State University and lectures given at the Max Planck Institut in Munich and in Budapest during spring and summer of 1984.

BARRY R. DWORKIN ● Pennsylvania State University College of Medicine, Milton S. Hershey Medical Center, Hershey, Pennsylvania 17033. Work on this chapter was supported by a special fund of the Chronic Pain Unit of the Department of Rehabilitation Medicine, New York University Medical Center, the Goldwater Memorial Hospital in New York, and by the Deutsche Forschungsgemeinschaft (DFG) while the author was Guest Professor in the Psychologisches Institut of Tübingen University.

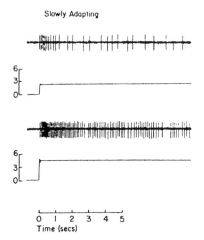

FIGURE 1. Record of slowly adapting venous low-pressure vagal receptors of the rat showing the fall-off in firing rate following application and maintenance of a stimulus. Adaptation occurs with both high- and low-strength stimuli. The classification as "slowly adapting" is made relative to other interoceptors, studied under similar conditions.

an established feature of all cells which have been studied. Receptors can only be considered "nonadapting" if observation is limited to minutes or at very most hours; extended observation with a carefully maintained constant stimulus intensity always reveals a monotonically declining output. Consequently, information about the absolute magnitude of the stimulus is progressively distorted by an interoceptor, and in fact the stimulus may, after a sufficient time, fail to register altogether; correlatively, a sufficiently gradual stimulus intensity change may entirely fail to activate the receptor. Nevertheless, in healthy animals, homeostatic variables do not slowly drift without correction.

Figure 2 is a schematic diagram of the negative feedback linear control model as it is applied to biological systems. The reference signal or set-point is the "target" value to which the output is regulated by the intervening mechanism. A linear systems analysis produces a description of the functional relationships among all of the nodes in the diagram, which can be used to predict the effect of a changed component characteristic or node condition on the output variable. In the general case, a component can transform the phase as well as amplitude between its input and output nodes. Thus, complete analysis requires a full characterization of the gain-frequency and phase-frequency functions for each component.

Although the linear systems model has become increasingly commonplace in the literature of visceral regulation, actual parametric analysis yielding unanticipated explanations of observed physiological phenomena has been rare. The baroreceptor regulation of blood pressure is an exception: frequency domain analysis has been used to describe the dynamic characteristics, predict impulse responses, and eval-

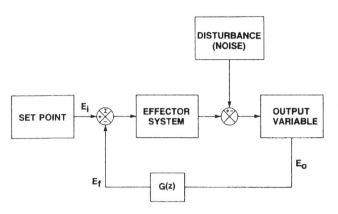

FIGURE 2. A general systems diagram of a conventional feedback-regulated physiological control system. $G(z)$ represents the characteristics of the feedback path which may include an interoceptor monitoring the status of the output variable. The output variable could be central, such as systemic arterial blood pressure, or local, such as the pH at some point in the splanchnic circulation. The disturbance or noise may include any load condition which would require a change in effector activity to maintain the output variable (E_o) constant. The crossed circles are nodes at which addition of the intersecting inputs occurs. All such models assume that the relationship between the effector output and the controlled variable is monotonic.

uate hypotheses about the mechanism of observed blood pressure oscillations (Sagawa, 1983). These studies reveal the potential power of the method. Respiration, thermoregulation (Satinoff, 1978), caloric balance, and several endocrine functions are among processes which have been subjected to analysis which possibly do more honor to the concepts than the exact methods of linear systems theory.

A general description of the system shown in Figure 2 requires either application of the La Place transformation technique or the development of a specific set of equations which are differential over time. However, the steady-state or static equilibrium condition at the nodes can be specified without reference to either time or frequency. Assuming that the open loop gain of the effector system is relatively high, that is, that for $G(z) = 0$ for all z, $\Delta E_o \gg \Delta E_i$, then with the loop closed at equilibrium:

(1) $$G(E_o) = -E_i$$

For a visceral regulatory mechanism in which the tissue condition is sensed or monitored by interoceptors, $G(z)$ describes the chain of neuronal components from the interoceptor to the transmitter release which modulates the activity of a visceral efferent. The point of interaction between the afferent and efferent limbs, that is, the node at which the transformed output or feedback is subtracted from the input, is indicated in Figure 2 by the summation symbol ($\sum$). In equation (1) G is considered to be a function of only the output variable, but G may also depend upon time, as would be true of an interoceptor which adapted to a constant stimulus. For example, suppose that the adaptation function is approximated by an exponential, similar to that shown for the intact Pacinian corpuscle (Lowenstein & Skalak, 1966):

$$(2) \qquad G(z) = -ze^{-\alpha t} + K$$

then, if $t = 0$, $G(z) = -z + K$, where z is the tissue condition being regulated. However, for $t \gg 0$, $G(z)$ approaches K for all z. In terms of Figure 2, $G(E_o) = K$ for any E_o. The implication is that after some specified time the activity of the effector output is not significantly influenced by the conditions at the output node, that is, negative feedback regulation of the effector is lost. Furthermore, if the adapting interoceptor is the only feedback component, for a very slowly changing (low frequency) input the gain of the overall system will increase to the open loop value. Thus, with an open loop gain sufficiently high to achieve accurate closed-loop regulation of relatively rapid transient disturbances, the sensitivity to low frequency input noise could be excessive.

Although equation (2) may not accurately represent any particular interoceptor, the general finding for all interoceptors is that the output gradually decays toward the baseline value some time after stabilization of the stimulus at the receptor surface. For some rapidly adapting interoceptors mechanical high-pass filtering is an important component of the adaptation mechanism (Lowenstein & Mendelson, 1965); however, even with the lamellae removed, the generator potential of the naked Pacinian corpuscle has a duration of less than 100 msec. (Lowenstein & Skalak, 1966) Other receptors, considered to be particularly slowly adapting, such as muscle spindle, bee hair-plate, or slow crustacean stretch receptors, can sustain generator potentials for only seconds or minutes. Table 1, taken from Chernigovsky's extensive monograph (1960), lists the approximate time of adaptation for a number of carefully studied interoceptors.[1]

If, given the strong evidence that adaptation is an inherent property of interoceptors, the linear systems model as ordinarily composed is not able to account for steady-state physiological regulation over epochs of

---

[1] Diamond (1955) reported that the output of isolated cat baroreceptors was invariant over periods of more than an hour; but one of the two curves, which he shows, actually has a slow but unambiguous negative slope during 80 minutes of observation. Moreover, the adaptation or resetting of the baroreceptor over hours or days has been extensively documented.

TABLE 1[a]
Time of Adaptation for Certain Interoceptors

Receptors	Numerical data characterizing the speed of adaptation of the receptor	Characteristics of the receptor's adaptation speed
	III. Interoceptors	
Mechanoreceptors of the carotid sinus (cat)	25% of the initial impulse frequency within 6 sec of stimulation; the initial rapid phase of adaptation is practically absent.	Very slow
Mechanoreceptors of the aortic arch (rabbit)	Complete adaptation within 5–10 min.	Very slow
Mechanoreceptors of the atrium (cat)	—	Very slow
Mechanoreceptors of the urinary bladder (dog)	1. Complete adaptation within several fractions of a second (only 10–30 impulses).	Rapid
	2. Incomplete adaptation within 15–25 min.	Very slow
Mechanoreceptors of the urinary bladder (cat)	Complete adaptation within fractions of a second.	Very rapid
Various types of stretch receptors of the lungs (cat)	Not more than 5% of the initial impulse frequency within 10 sec.	Very slow
	1. Decrease in impulse frequency by 10–55% during the 2nd sec of stimulation.	Slow
	2. Complete or almost complete adaptation by the end of the first sec of stimulation. These receptors are distinguished by a high threshold.	Very rapid

[a] From Chernigovsky, 1960.

weeks, months, or years, is there some plausible modification of the model which can? Certainly there are possibilities; for example, the inclusion of a peak-detecting memory element in the feedback loop would permit the storage of maximum and possibly also minimum values of interoceptor activity for very long periods of time. Unlike the sensory transduction process, long-term memory in particular appears to have almost unlimited temporal stability. However, the relationship between peak interoceptor activity and the effector output which would produce satisfactory regulation is not obvious; any peak detection or peak averaging scheme has the additional and probably more serious defect that very slow but consistent drift in the regulated variable could entirely fail to activate the interoceptor and eventually accumulate into a considerable regulatory error. Consequently, simple integration or summation of peak interoceptor activity within $G(z)$ could not completely compensate for the inherent low-frequency response limitations of interoceptors.

Another possibility is mechanical modulation of the stimulus on the interoceptor surface. This would be analogous to the electronic instrumentation technique used to measure very low frequency signals (<0.1 Hz.) with high-stability capacitor or transformer coupled amplifiers. A modulator or chopper converts the low-frequency signal into a high-frequency signal with an amplitude equal to the full difference between the instantaneous value of the low-frequency signal and some known reference. The modulated signal is amplified and another circuit eliminates the reference phase and filters or smooths the interrupted waveform to reconstruct the original signal. This arrangement achieves a high degree of amplification with minimal drift, using only circuits with short time constants. Because of the pulsitile nature of the cardiac cycle, certain central cardiovascular interoceptors are naturally exposed to regular mechanical "chopping" or modulation of the stimulus. This could prevent adaptation of those receptors; however, because in the biological system the modulation is incomplete, extraction of a steady-state variable, such as intravascular volume, would require an additional second type of receptor to measure the modulation independently. While such arrangements may exist,[2] this scheme would have a restricted domain because autonomic efferent control extends to anatomical regions in which pulse is almost absent or poorly correlated with measurable central contractile activity. In sum, the observed stability of many different physiological variables taken with the relatively rapid adaptation of all known interoceptors creates an internal contradiction for a linear systems model of long-term physiological regulation, which relies upon conventional sensory-neural transduction in the feedback loop.

---

[2] In principle, the atrial A and B receptors (Gilmore, 1983) have the respective characteristics and situations for measuring the modulation and peak-to-peak pressure amplitude. Thus, for certain central cardiovascular receptors receiving a mechanically modulated stimulus a relatively complicated scheme of independent modulation measurement and compensated demodulation of the signal could extend the low-frequency response of $G(z)$ sufficiently to transduce accurately a slowly changing variable, such as central volume.

LEARNING AND LONG-TERM PHYSIOLOGICAL REGULATION

One possible conclusion from these data and arguments is that sensory-neural transduction has no role in long-term regulation. This possibility was extensively developed by Granger and Guyton (1969), who proposed that the constancy and integration of central physiological variables is achieved by a kind of "whole body" autoregulation which does not involve nervous mechanisms. Their model is an assemblage of reasonably well documented humoral, physical, and reflex mechanisms organized into a linear systems framework, emphasizing the mutual interdependence of the components and the predominant role of intrinsic properties of the peripheral circulation in long-term regulation of central variables. In it regulation occurs at a local tissue level through a variety of autoregulatory mechanisms responsive to pO2, pCO2, and pH, as well as to specific metabolic products and vasoactive intermediaries; thus, each tissue's normal requirements are adjusted by intrinsic mechanisms not directly involving reflexes (Guyton, 1977). Central regulation is a net consequence of the local processes. As the vascular bed of a tissue dilates in response to metabolic requirements, its conductance increases, and the supplementary venous return to the heart enhances cardiac output enough to meet the additional requirements of the tissue. Guyton maintains that this mechanism alone has sufficient capacity to regulate cardiac output over a wide range of conditions short of strenuous exercise. The following quotations will provide some sense of the logic and assumptions of this theory:

> When local tissues vasodilate in an attempt to supply themselves with adequate blood flow, this instantly increases blood flow from the arteries into the veins. The increased venous pressure in turn causes increased venous return. And, finally, the heart responds to this increased venous return by increased pumping mainly because of the Frank-Starling mechanism. . . . Even a 1 to 2 mm Hg rise in right atrial pressure distends the heart sufficiently to double the cardiac output. In this way cardiac output automatically adjusts itself to the venous return. (Guyton, 1977, p. 763)

However, in the final analysis cardiac output is determined by the central or "background" control of blood volume by the kidney, which, as Guyton emphasizes, is the only significant long-term determinant of arterial pressure.

> In the minds of both physicians and physiologists, arterial pressure control is most often believed to be achieved either entirely or almost entirely through nervous mechanisms. However, as we shall see, this is far from true. (Guyton, 1977, p. 764)

And blood volume regulation by the kidney is primarily achieved through the pressure diuresis/natriuresis phenomena:

> Therefore, the overall mechanism of the blood volume system for pressure

regulation is the following: When arterial pressure rises too high, the kidneys automatically begin to excrete fluid. Furthermore, they will not stop excreting fluid until the arterial pressure returns to its original value. Conversely, when the arterial pressure falls below normal, the kidneys retain fluid, and again they will not stop retaining fluid until the pressure rises to its normal value. (Guyton, 1977, p. 766)

The complete Guyton-Granger model (1972) is complicated and although some isolated sections of the model have been experimentally verified, little evidence for its sufficiency or quantitative plausibility has been developed. It is particularly unclear whether parameters can be found for its numerous interacting regulatory loops, which will produce both dynamic stability and realistic response speed. In addition, the model does not acknowledge the hierarchical and redundant structure of most vertebrate regulatory mechanisms. *The fact that the renal output curve ultimately controls blood pressure is true but not very informative without a quantitative assessment of the role of different supervisory variables in establishing the parameters of the curve.* For example, Guyton emphasizes the importance of pressure diuresis and secondarily the renin-angiotensin system, but stimulation of the renal nerves can also significantly increase the pressure range of the kidney output curve. In fact, sufficiently strong sympathetic activation, as evoked by cerebral ischemia, can cause total shut-down. Chronic recordings in freely moving cats (Schad & Seller, 1975) reveal the presence of a continuous background activity in the renal nerves. This tonic efferent discharge is reduced by elevated blood pressure, proportionally increased by different levels of exercise, and almost completely eliminated by ganglionic blockade. Thus, in the unanesthetized freely moving animal the kidney output curve is almost certainly under some degree of tonic CNS control. And, although the fact that the baroreceptors adapt has been seen correctly by Guyton as a serious problem with regulatory theory based on reflexes:

> Earlier in this paper we stated that long-term control of arterial pressure is entirely different from acute control. There are 2 reasons for this. First, most of the nervous mechanisms adapt with time so that they have progressively less effect on the circulation after the 1st few minutes to the 1st few hours of activity. For instance, the baroreceptors gradually reset (adapt) to a new pressure level in less than 2 days. (Guyton, 1977, p. 766)

this observation does not justify the conclusion that nervous mechanisms do not affect long-term blood pressure regulation.

Measurement of the individual time constants and loop gains may eventually show that the entire regulatory jigsaw puzzle fits neatly together at a peripheral level without the necessary involvement of the brain in long-term regulation; however, the data to build that model have not been assembled and the fact that the system could in some manner function without the brain (Granger & Guyton, 1969) would not imply that it ordinarily did. Furthermore, there is now a significant body of evidence implicating tonic CNS efferent activity in steady-state regulation.

Experiments demonstrating shifts in long-term regulation following nerve section or pharmacological blockade of ganglionic transmission have provided the most direct evidence of the functional presence of tonic autonomic control of cardiovascular function.[3] The effect of total spinal anesthesia on blood pressure is a clear example. Loss of neurogenic vasomotor tone can reduce mean arterial pressure from 100 mmHg to 50 mmHg or less, and injection of very small doses of norepinephrine can immediately restore the original resting pressure (Guyton, 1982). This and similar experiments confirm the normal presence of vasomotor tone and its importance as a variable in long-term cardiovascular regulation.

Tonic sympathetic control of the resistance vessels has implications primarily for the regional distribution of the cardiac output; a similar control of venous tone is more important for central cardiovascular homeostasis. Since the veins have little if any myogenic tone, the sympathetic efferents are the major determinants of venous compliance. Thus, hexamethonium ganglionic blockade causes a decrease in the mean circulatory filling pressure requiring an infusion of 6–10 ml/Kg to restore the original level (Rothe, 1976). Several other studies report equal or greater estimates of neurogenic venous tone (Rothe, 1983). These results show that the total-body pressure–volume relationship, venous return, and, thus, the cardiac output are substantially regulated by tonic sympathetic nerve activity and, as with the sympathetic control of the kidney output curve, underline the obligatory role of autonomic efferents in long-term cardiovascular regulation. In addition to these "global" effects of autonomic activity there are other data on the independent distribution of sympathetic vasomotor tone to different tissues.

The vasculature of both the skin and adipose tissue are under independent tonic sympathetic control. Following therapeutic sympathectomy, blood flow in the adipose tissue of human limbs increases by approximately 100% (Henriken, 1977). The vasomotor control of the skin has been particularly well documented because of its role in thermo-

---

[3] Sympathetic and parasympathetic tonic control of a variety of functions in different organ systems has been demonstrated, and most of what is discussed in the remainder of this chapter is in principle equally applicable to noncardiovascular visceral regulation. However, only for cardiovascular and thermoregulatory control has long-term regulation been conceptualized in a sufficiently quantitative manner to permit a rigorous examination of the assumptions and logic; and thermoregulation involves specific brain receptors for which the primary adaptation characteristics are not yet established.

regulation. Since either vasoconstriction or vasodilatation can be induced by nerve block depending on whether the subject is being heated or cooled, and human forearm skin probably has tonically active vasodilator as well as constrictor mechanisms (Roddie, 1983), the steady-state sympathetic tone is difficult to estimate.[4] thus, although cutaneous nerve block under a thermoneutral condition produces little change in skin blood flow, the implications of that result for tonic control are not clear.

The tonic skeletal muscle vasoconstriction which occurs during REM sleep can be eliminated by regional sympathectomy, but nerve block in resting awake animals appears to have little net influence on muscle blood flow. However, in steady-state exercise sympathetic vasoconstriction significantly reduces local metabolic vasodilatation, and Shepherd (1983, p. 352) has noted, "The role of the sympathetic nerves may be to modulate the local dilator mechanisms to maintain the most economical ratio of blood flow to O_2 extraction."

Neurophysiological data concerning the characteristics of the sympathetic discharge verify the presence of a continuous background component in sympathetic nerve activity. These studies provide both detail about the characteristics and sources of variability of the sympathetic outflow and, along with other experiments demonstrating significant target-tissue effects of stimulating the same nerves, further evidence of the continuous presence of a functional sympathetic tone. Observations of continuous background discharges have been made from whole sympathetic nerves of freely moving unanesthetized cats (Schad & Seller, 1975) and humans (Delius, Hagbarth, Hongell, & Wallin, 1972), individual postganglionic neurons of cat cervical nerve (Mannard & Polosa, 1973; Polosa, Mannard, & Laskey, 1979), and intracellularly from cat and rabbit superior cervical ganglia (Mirgorodsky & Skok, 1969).

Detailed statistical analysis of the background firing, that is, continual discharge in the absence of experimental provocation, of individual sympathetic cervical preganglionic neurons (Mannard & Polosa, 1973) has revealed a complex pattern of activity containing burstlike rhythmic and continuous random components. The more regular activity is probably generated by oscillation in short-term reflex pathways, but the steady stochastic background is largely determined by supra-

---

[4] In general, nerve block or section experiments can lead to false negative conclusions regarding the presence of sympathetic tone if the outflow is distributed to antagonistic effectors, balanced within the field of observation; in contrast, finding that a block or lesion changes the resting state of a tissue is almost incontrovertible evidence of preexisting tonic influence of the nerve. The fact that reciprocal innervation may be balanced so that blocking both aspects is without net effect does not obviate the need for independent tonic control of each aspect.

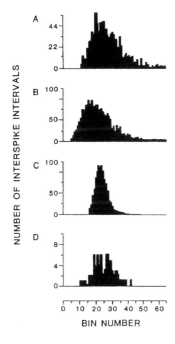

FIGURE 3. Interval histograms showing the statistical properties of sample neurons studied by Mannard and Polosa (1973) in the cat spinal cord near T_1. Cervical units were identified by supramaximal antidromic stimulation of the ipsilateral sympathetic nerve. A is a pentobarbital anesthetized preparation with an intact neuraxis, B is decerebrate, C transected at the cervical level, and D a decentralized isolated cord segment. The bin widths are 64, 16, 32, and 96 msec., respectively; *n.b.* in C and D the reduced number of spikes and restricted variability in interspike interval following the elimination of supraspinal influences. The rate, averaged over all units observed, was reduced to approximately 25% of that for intact and decerebrate preparations. This study compared the characteristics of the irregular background units shown in the figure to other rhythmical firing units in the same region; an approximately equal number of the two types were found.

spinal influences. Figure 3 shows distributions of interspike intervals observed in stochastic-type postganglionic neurons. The reduced variability and net activity observed after chord section or segmental isolation indicates the contribution of supraspinal inputs to the background activity. These changes are thought to reflect both modified firing patterns and reduced numbers of active units following decentralization. This result generally resembles that for alpha-motorneurons and underlines the similarity between the sympathetic efferent and skeletal motor outputs.

In sum, the notion that the nervous system participates only in short term-dynamic adjustments and not long-term or steady-state regulation has gradually become less tenable, and with it the idea of "whole-body" autoregulation. Nevertheless, Guyton, Coleman, and Granger's identification (1972) of the autoregulatory process as having the capability of providing a stable reference level—independent of neural adaptation—was an extremely valuable insight. Local autoregulatory systems which depend only on chemical or mechanical feedback can both respond rapidly to transient perturbations and have long-term stability. In normal tissue, constant pH is possibly the most important condition maintained by autoregulation. The local autoregulatory apparatus has many different components; fundamental among them are the chemical buffering systems of the intravascular, interstitial, and intracellular spaces. These molecular-level mechanisms vary in complexity from the hemoglobin binding of carbon dioxide to the bicarbonate/carbonic acid equilibrium system and the simple bulk affinity of protein for hydrogen ions. At a higher level of integration there are specific hemodynamic mechanisms which respond to elevations in metabolic product concentration with relaxation of sphincters and changes in vessel wall tension. Other mechanisms maintain a relatively constant regional blood flow independent of variations in central blood pressure through local humoral mechanisms and nonlinear mechanical compliance. There is, thus, a hierarchical structure in each tissue bed responsible for maintaining a constant local environment compatible with normal cell function (Johnson, 1964; Morff & Granger, 1982). This system responds rapidly and can maintain a nonadapting reference level indefinitely, as it is independent of sensory-neural transduction or in some instances even receptor–ligand interactions.

However, these local mechanisms by themselves can do little to assure the efficient allocation of resources among the various homeostatic mechanisms present in an organism. At times the cardiac output must be simultaneously divided among muscular, digestive, thermoregulatory, CNS, renal, and other requirements—with at least some structures necessarily receiving a less than adequate share. The importance of instrumental or Type II learning in controlling the distribution of the resources of skeletal behavior among competing homeostatic requirements is well established (Baum, 1974; Herrnstein, 1961; Sibby & McFarland, 1964; Weardon & Burgess, 1982). The learned regulation of eating and drinking has been studied for years by behavioral psychologists; an analogous role of learned visceral responses for autonomic function by regulation of the tonic sympathetic background would be phylogenetically parsimonious. But, assuming that Type II learning is applicable to visceral responses (Dworkin & Miller, 1977; Dworkin, 1980; 1984), how could it participate in physiological regulation given the rapid adaptation and limited specificity of interoceptors?

Ultimately the stabilization of pH through autoregulation depends upon adequate blood flow, and flow depends upon pressure. Autoregulatory sufficiency of a tissue exists when blood pressure is at a value that permits it a maximum range of deviation without affecting blood flow and blood flow can vary maximally without affecting pH. Under these conditions local pH is well stabilized against metabolic or central perturbations and an interoceptor sensitive to pH is infrequently or never activated; consequently, it will adapt and become silent. Thus, small regulatory wrinkles, for example, in blood pressure or local metabolic activity, will not be registered by the nervous system. For a pH receptor to be activated either individual blood pressure or metabolic

LEARNING AND LONG-TERM PHYSIOLOGICAL REGULATION

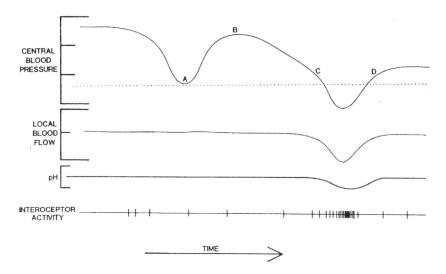

FIGURE 4. These hypothetical curves are constructed from well-established mechanisms (Johnson, 1964) and receptor characteristics (Mountcastle, 1980). They illustrate how receptor adaptation and autoregulation probably interact in a perfused metabolically active block of tissue. Because of autoregulation, the blood flow through the section remains constant despite a pressure transient at A. But from B to C there is a gradual drift in central pressure, and the limit of blood flow autoregulation is approached; subsequently, another pressure transient, beginning at C, exceeds the limit (dotted line) and local flow falls; a relatively rapid accumulation of metabolic waste (reflected in the pH) triggers the interoceptor, which is sensitive to falling pH.

transients must be imposing enough to swamp the autoregulatory apparatus, or a chronic state of imbalance must gradually evolve, which compromises the regulatory compliance by moving the operating point out of the autoregulatory and into the linear or high gain portion of the regulation–transfer function. With autoregulation thus strained, even a small perturbation could cause interoceptor activation. Figure 4 shows more specifically how this might work: an interoceptor is embedded in a block of tissue with a blood supply supporting local metabolic activity under steady-state conditions. This may be muscle in a state of mixed oxidative and anerobic metabolism—producing constant quantities of carbon dioxide and lactic acid, which are steadily transported out of the tissue by blood flowing through the capillary bed. The interoceptor is sensitive to the pH of the tissue; if the pH remains constant for an extended time, it will adapt and cease to fire. The dotted line represents the lowest systemic arterial pressure for which intrinsic tissue mechanisms can compensate. If blood pressure remains above this limit then the local autoregulatory apparatus is able to buffer fluctuations in pressure, and changes in pressure, such as at point A in the slide, will have no appreciable effect on either blood flow or pH. In contrast, when the pressure gradually drifts so that the local autoregulatory apparatus eventually becomes incompetent, although the drift may be so slow as not to be directly registerable by an interoceptor, occasional transient perturbations will periodically exceed the dynamic range of the regulator and cause fluctuations which stimulate the interoceptor. At point C the pressure has drifted down sufficiently for the dynamic limit of autoregulation to be approached, and the perturbation between C and D, which is no larger than at A, causes a decrease in flow. The temporary reduction in flow changes the metabolic balance in the tissue, reducing oxygen delivery and allowing for a rapid accumulation of acidic waste, which overwhelms the buffers and lowers the pH of the surface of the interoceptor. If the rate of change of pH exceeds the rate of adaptation of the interoceptor, it will fire. Given this analysis, the information transmitted to the brain by the local interoceptor is that the conditions in the tissue are getting close to the autoregulatory limit or "ragged edge." However, simply saying that information is transmitted to the brain is relatively meaningless without describing the mechanism that accommodates and uses the information. The remainder of this paper will attempt to explain how Type II visceral learning could be that mechanism.

The fundamental process of Type II learning is the association in time between a response and a subsequent reinforcing stimulus (Woody, 1982, p. 46 ff.). Similarly, the association between an autonomic response and interoceptor activity, signaling autoregulatory insufficiency, would be the crucial feature of Type II visceral learning. For visceral learning to modify the subsequent response probability and refine autonomic regulation it is necessary only that increased interoceptor firing closely follow the response, repeatedly, so that the nervous system can detect the correlation against the background of random events.

In Figure 5 each group of interoceptors is connected to only a single functionally related central efferent in an arrangement which resembles a conventional reflex regulator but works with adapting interoceptors. The tissue receives an autonomic efferent A from the CNS which either directly controls a specific local function, such as vasoconstriction, or sets the sensitivity of an autonomic reflex or intrinsic regulatory mechanism (Shepherd, 1983). The interoceptor I is sensitive to a specific condition of the tissue such as pH. Local autoregulation maintains the pH constant over a wide range of conditions, including considerable random variation in the firing rate of efferent nerve A. Thus, ordinarily the interoceptor is in a state of adaptation. However, some firing rates of A are incompatible with local requirements and cause the limit of auto-

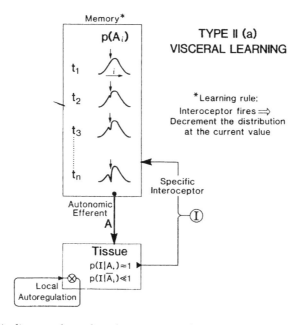

FIGURE 5. This diagram shows how long-term regulation can be achieved with adapting interoceptors and Type II visceral learning. The interoceptor (I) is specific in the sense that it can modify only a single structurally predetermined efferent system. Firing of the interoceptor causes the concurrently present efferent activity level (A_i) subsequently to have a reduced probability $p(A_i)$. As indicated by the conditional probabilities, interoceptor firing occurs when $A = A\downarrow$, but not at other values; consequently, repeated events, t_1–t_n, result in a cumulative reduction of the probability of additional occurrences of the particular activity level, A. In addition to involving a memory process, this scheme differs from a conventional negative feedback linear control model because monotonicity is not assumed for the relationship between the tissue condition and efferent activity level, A_i.

regulation to be exceeded, the pH to change, and the interoceptor to be activated. When this happens the Type II learning mechanism decrements or reduces the probability of the most recent value (A_i) of the activity of the efferent nerve. This is repeated with each firing of the interoceptor, and successive events of this kind eventually produce a cleft in the distribution of $p(A_i)$ which eliminates the incompatible value. Since the distributions are of probabilities, the total area remains constant even when a specific value is decremented and this feature can obliterate a cleft as well as form one: decrementing all except certain values is equivalent to incrementing those values. An anatomical substrate for this mechanism is not difficult to imagine and the analog for skeletal behavior is extinction of the learned response.

In this model the requirement of long-term stability is repositioned from the sensory receptor to the CNS, and the physiological reference level or set point is repositioned from the CNS to the autoregulated region surrounding the receptor. The result in both cases is consonant with contemporary physiological data and eliminates the paradox of receptor adaptation; however, there are some further implications of the involvement of learning in physiological regulation. In addition to storing information learning organizes behavior. The animal is a collection of regulatory mechanisms or feedback loops; each may have several inputs and outputs interacting with one another at spatially separated points. If the resources of the system are limited so that at least some of the variables must be chronically displaced from their optimal set point and if multiple criteria exist for overall system performance, an imposing problem of optimization emerges. Solving this problem is necessary to the survival of all complex animals. Earlier, I suggested that Type II learning had a well-established role in the matching of the homeostatic requirements and behavior of animals, through eating, drinking, and other skeletal responses. A mechanism for the optimization of multiple physiological variables through Type II visceral learning can be developed from a relatively direct extension of the model proposed for single-variable steady-state regulation. Figure 6 is identical to Figure 5 except that two more efferent systems, B and C, have been added. The probability distributions for these efferents are affected by recent interoceptor firing exactly as the distribution for A is; however, as the situation is depicted variation of activity in these efferents does not affect the status of the tissue sufficiently to disturb regulation and cause the interoceptor to fire. Consequently, interoceptor firing and the efferent activity on B or C are uncorrelated. Therefore, the value decremented in distributions $p(B_i)$ and $p(C_i)$ is different each time the interoceptor fires, and since the area under a probability distribution is constant, each operation cancels out the others without having a net effect. In contrast, since interoceptor firing is evoked by a certain activity level on efferent A, distribution $p(A_i)$ will be repeatedly decremented at that same value, eventually forming a cleft at the activity level incompatible with autoregulation.

If conditions changed so that fluctuations in C also began to strain the autoregulatory compliance of the tissue, a correlation would emerge between the interoceptor firing and the newly incompatible values of C. These new conditions could be due either to a change in local requirements in the tissue, so that previously satisfactory values of C became inadequate, or to a shift in the distribution of $p(C_i)$ produced by some central disturbance or input. Under the learning rule the distribution of $p(C_i)$ would now be decremented at the values associated with interoceptor firing. Thus, this arrangement is a mechanism for both iden-

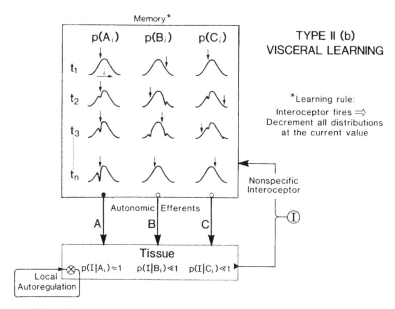

FIGURE 6. If the effect of interoceptor firing is not limited to a single efferent but distributes over several, under the Type II learning rule only the probability distributions of those efferents which significantly influence the tissue condition will be modified. The other distributions will be decremented as frequently (see Figure 5), but randomly, and the net effect will not alter their shape. With this arrangement, Type II learning could control the allocation of resources among different anatomical structures and also select the particular regulatory mechanisms which minimized net homeostatic imbalance. The behavioral foundations have been discussed in more detail elsewhere (Dworkin, 1980; Dworkin, 1984; McFarland, 1971).

tifying autonomic variables that assume inappropriate values and adjusting them.

Autonomic regulation based on visceral learning lends itself naturally to negotiation among the competing requirements of individual organ systems and tissues of a complex animal. For example, suppose that blood flow is required in both the mesenteric bed for digestion and in skeletal muscle for maintaining contraction, and that cardiac output is insufficient to satisfy both requirements completely. Optimal regional distribution, given the constraints, could be accomplished if the net activity of intestinal and skeletal muscle interoceptors were able, through Type II learning, to modify the autonomic efferents controlling shunts in both tissues. When regulatory compliance was exceeded in either tissue, its interoceptors would fire, reducing the probability of reoccurrence of the particular activity levels present on the mesenteric and skeletal vascular efferents at that moment. Interoceptor activity would be greatest when vasoconstriction was excessive in both circulations and least when both were autoregulating. If the mesenteric circulation was receiving more flow than necessary at the expense of skeletal muscle, the surplus would be wasted, because interoceptor activity cannot be reduced below that value present when flow is minimally sufficient for autoregulation. But the net interoceptor activity level would be higher than at an optimal adjustment because the skeletal bed, being deprived, would be in the linear portion of the regulation transfer function, and consequently the complementary deficit in flow would be reflected in proportionally increased metabolic imbalance and more frequent interoceptor firing. If interoceptor activity is additive, this process could regulate many different regions and kinds of tissue simultaneously without reliance on unrealistic and undemonstrated peripheral neuroanatomical specificity. Either greater density or heightened sensitivity of interoceptors in a critical tissue could establish differential priorities at a peripheral level.

Finally, it is a logical consequence of this scheme that the reference level or set point of a variable is not a centrally represented parameter but is partially preserved in each individual tissue by its requirement for maintaining an ability to compensate for perturbations through an autoregulatory response. If that ability is maintained, the interoceptors in the tissue will not be exposed to stimulus fluctuations of sufficient magnitude to cause impulse generation—they will remain silent and not signal the CNS. Functional demands in the tissue interact with central variables to determine the compliance limits for autoregulation. For example, if a region is metabolically active it will require a higher minimum blood flow and correspondingly higher minimum central pressure to maintain acid–base balance and adequate oxygen tension than a region which is quiescent. Given this perspective, a set point is not a central parameter, but a "consensus" among multifarious local autoregulatory regions.

I have described a theory of autonomic regulation differing significantly from the current paradigm, which depends either upon unrealistic interoceptor characteristics or ignores the role of the tonic sympathetic outflow in long-term regulation. Although somewhat unorthodox because it interweaves behavioral and physiological principles, the new theory incorporates only well-established mechanisms with a single exception: it depends upon the applicability of Type II learning to visceral responses. Thus, demonstrating the existence of visceral learning is a necessary first step in verifying the theory and admitting the possibility that learning could participate in some autonomic regulatory paradigms. This would require that learning be considered as a possible mechanism in well-designed physiological experiments.

LEARNING AND LONG-TERM PHYSIOLOGICAL REGULATION

However, actual proof that visceral learning is significant in physiological regulation would require specific analytical experiments in which, for example, the homeostatic consequences of natural visceral regulatory responses were experimentally manipulated (Dworkin & Miller, 1977).

Although not categorical, the demonstration in a paralyzed animal of Type I learning or classical conditioning of a visceral response, such as a change in regional blood flow, and of Type II learning of a skeletal response such as firing a motor nerve, but not Type II learning of the same visceral response, would be strong evidence against a physiologically significant Type II visceral learning, as well as against the regulatory hypothesis presented in this paper.

REFERENCES

BAUM, W. M. (1974). On two types of deviation from the matching law: Bias and undermatching. *Journal of the Experimental Analysis of Behavior, 22*, 231–242.

CHERNIGOVSKY, V. N. (1960). *Interoceptors*. Moscow: State Publishing House of Medical Literature.

DELIUS, W., HAGBARTH, K. E., HONGELL, A., & WALLIN, B. G. (1972). General characteristics of sympathetic activity in human muscle nerves. *Acta Physiologica Scandinavica, 84*, 65–81.

DIAMOND, J. (1955). Observations on the excitation by acetylcholine and by pressure of sensory receptors in the cat's carotid sinus. *Journal of Physiology, 130*, 513–532.

DWORKIN, B. R. (1984). Operant mechanisms in physiological regulation. In T. ELBERT, B. ROCKSTROH, W. LUTZENBERGER, & N. BIRBAUMER (Eds.), *Self regulation of the brain and behavior*. Berlin: Springer-Verlag, pp. 296–309.

DWORKIN, B. R. (1980). The role of instrumental learning in the organization and maintenance of physiological control mechanisms. In G. ADAM, I. MESZAROS, & E. I. BANYAI (Eds.), *Advances in physiological sciences: Brain and behavior* (Vol. 17) Budapest: Akademiai Kiado, pp. 169–176.

DWORKIN, B. R., & MILLER, N. E. (1977). Visceral learning in the curarized rat. In G. SCHWARTZ & J. BEATTY (Eds.), *Biofeedback: Theory and research*. New York: Academic Press, pp. 221–242.

GILMORE, J. P. (1983). Neural control of extracellular volume in the human and nonhuman primate. In J. T. SHEPHERD & F. M. ABBOUD (Eds.), *The handbook of physiology: The cardiovascular system* (Vol. 3, Sec. 2). Baltimore: Williams & Wilkins, pp. 885–915.

GRANGER, H., & GUYTON, A. C. (1969). Autoregulation of the total systemic circulation following distruction of the central nervous system in the dog. *Circulation Research, 25*, 379–388.

GUYTON, A. C. (1977). An overall analysis of cardiovascular regulation. *Anesthesia and Analgesia, 56*, 761–768.

GUYTON, A. C. (1982). *Textbook of medical physiology* (6th ed.). Philadelphia: W. B. Saunders.

GUYTON, A. C., COLEMAN, T. G., & GRANGER, H. J. (1972). Circulation: Overall regulation. *Annual Review of Physiology, 34*, 13–46.

HENRIKEN, O. (1977). Local sympathetic reflex mechanism in regulation of blood flow in human subcutaneous tissue. *Acta Physiologica Scandinavica, Suppl., 101*, 1–48.

HERRNSTEIN, R. J. (1961). Relative and absolute strength of response as a function of frequency of reinforcement. *Journal of the Experimental Analysis of Behavior, 4*, 267–272.

JOHNSON, P. C. (1964). Review of previous studies and current theories of autoregulation. *Circulation Research* (supplement 1), *15*, 2–9.

LOWENSTEIN, W. R., & SKALAK, R. (1966). Mechanical transmission in a pacinian corpuscle: An analysis and a theory. *Journal of Physiology, 182*, 346–378.

LOWENSTEIN, W. R., & MENDELSON, M. (1965). Components of receptor adaptation in a pacinian corpuscle. *Journal of Physiology, 177*, 377–397.

McFARLAND, D. J. (1971). *Feedback mechanisms in animal behavior.* London and New York: Academic Press.

MANNARD, A., & POLOSA, C. (1973). Analysis of background firing of single sympathetic preganglionic neurons of cat cervical nerve. *Journal of Neurophysiology, 36*, 398–408.

MIFFLIN, S. W., & KUNZE, D. L. (1982). Rapid resetting of low pressure vagal receptors in the superior vena cava of the rat. *Circulation Research, 51*, 241–249.

MIRGORODSKY, V. N., & SKOK, V. I. (1969). Intracellular potentials recorded from a tonically active mammalian sympathetic ganglion. *Brain Research, 15*, 570–572.

MORFF, R. J., & GRANGER, H. J. (1982). Autoregulation of blood flow within individual arterioles in the rat cremaster muscle. *Circulation Research, 51*, 43–55.

MOUNTCASTLE, V. (1980). *Medical physiology* (14th ed.). St. Louis: Mosby.

POLOSA, C., MANNARD, A., & LASKEY, W. (1979). Tonic activity of the autonomic nervous system: Functions, properties, origins. In C. BROOKS, K. KOIZUMI, & A. SATO (Eds.), *Integrative functions of the autonomic nervous system.* Tokyo: University of Tokyo Press, pp. 342–354.

RODDIE, I. C. (1983). Circulation to skin and adipose tissue. In J. T. SHEPHERD & F. M. ABBOUD (Eds.), *The handbook of physiology: The cardiovascular system* (Vol. 3, sec. 2). Baltimore: Williams & Wilkins, pp. 397–452.

ROTHE, C. F. (1983). Venous system: Physiology of the capacitance vessels. In J. T. SHEPHERD & F. M. ABBOUD (Eds.), *The handbook of physiology: The cardiovascular system* (Vol. 3, sec. 2). Baltimore: Williams & Wilkins, pp. 285–317.

ROTHE, C. F. (1976). Reflex vascular capacity reduction in the dog. *Circulation Research, 39*, 705–710.

SAGAWA, K. (1983). Baroreflex control of systemic arterial pressure and vascular bed. In J. T. SHEPHERD & F. M. ABBOUD (Eds.), *The handbook of physiology: The cardiovascular system* (vol. 3, sec. 2). Baltimore: Williams & Wilkins, pp. 453–496.

SATINOFF, E. (1978). Neural organization and evolution of thermal regulation in mammals. *Science, 201*, 16–22.

SCHAD, H., & SELLER, H. (1975). A method for recording autonomic nerve activity in unanesthetized, freely moving cats. *Brain Research, 100*, 425–430.

SHEPHERD, J. T. (1983). Circulation to skeletal muscle. In J. T. SHEPHERD & F. M. ABBOUD (Eds.), *The handbook of physiology: The cardiovascular system* (Vol. 3, sec. 2). Baltimore: Williams & Wilkins, pp. 319–370.

SIBBY, R., & McFARLAND, D. (1964). A state–space approach to motivation. In D. J. McFARLAND (Ed.), *Motivational control systems analysis.* London: Academic Press, pp. 1–84.

WEARDON, J. H., & BURGESS, I. S. (1982). Matching since Baum. *Journal of the Experimental Analysis of Behavior, 38*, 339–348.

WIDDICOMB, J. G. (1974). Enteroceptors. In J. J. HUBBARD (Ed.), *The peripheral nervous system.* New York: Plenum Press, pp. 455–485.

8 *Progressive Relaxation Then and Now*

Does Change Always Mean Progress?

PAUL M. LEHRER, ROBERT L. WOOLFOLK,
AND NINA GOLDMAN

I. INTRODUCTION

Edmund Jacobson died on January 7, 1983, at the age of 94. A psychologist and physician by training, he made important early contributions to the fields of psychophysiology, psychosomatics, and bioelectronics. He devised one of the most widely used self-control techniques in the overlapping fields of behavior therapy, behavioral medicine, and self-regulation: progressive relaxation. This chapter was stimulated by reflecting on Jacobson's contributions and evaluating some of his ideas and empirical contributions in light of current concerns and controversies in the various fields in which he worked. In it we shall contrast Jacobson's original progressive relaxation technique with some of the "revised" progressive relaxation techniques that have been developed over the years. We shall argue that some of these methods are so fundamentally different from Jacobson's that they require entirely different rationales, and we shall hypothesize that they have very different effects.

Most of the revised progressive relaxation techniques have been devised by individuals who identify themselves as "behavior therapists" (e.g., Bernstein & Borkovec, 1973; Paul, 1966; Wolpe & Lazarus, 1966). It is probable that the changes were prompted, at least in part, by the populations with which the behavior therapists were working. Thus, when the first author once approached Jacobson to take part in a sym-

---

PAUL M. LEHRER ● UMDNJ–Rutger's Medical School, Piscataway, New Jersey 08854. ROBERT L. WOOLFOLK AND NINA GOLDMAN ● Rutgers—The State University, New Brunswick, New Jersey 08903.

posium on relaxation treatment of anxiety, Jacobson declined, saying that he considered himself to be an internist, not a psychiatrist. The early behavior therapists, on the other hand, worked primarily in the fields of psychiatry and clinical psychology and tended to concern themselves less with the field of psychosomatics than with problems such as phobias, behavioral disorders, and social skills problems. Consistent with this, we shall hypothesize that Jacobson's original method is more appropriate for use with persons suffering from stress-related somatic disorders, whereas the revised techniques may be more appropriate in treating those whose problems might be described as purely emotional. The innovations in technique by the early behavior therapists may have been prompted by the needs of their particular clients, and the advantages brought by these innovations may not generalize to all persons in need of relaxation therapy. This consideration is particularly important in light of changes that have occurred recently in the field of behavior therapy. Many behavior therapists are now working with nonpsychiatric physical disorders in the relatively recent field of behavioral medicine, thus blurring the distinction between Jacobson's applications of progressive relaxation and their own.

Although most behavior therapists working in the area of behavioral medicine are still trained in the revised technique, we predict that they would have better clinical success if they switched to Jacobson's original technique. This may also be true for therapists who treat anxiety disorders in which somatic symptoms predominate (e.g., hyperventilation, panic attacks). Despite Jacobson's disclaimer about being an internist rather than a psychiatrist, many of his published cases are of persons suffering from various anxiety disorders (Jacobson, 1938, 1964, 1970; McGuigan, 1984); and one of his major clinical books includes the word *anxiety* in its title (Jacobson, 1964). The book contains numerous studies of anxious individuals whose symptoms were markedly improved by progressive relaxation. Conversely, we also hypothesize that adherents of Jacobson's original method might improve upon their technique if, for certain patients, they adopted some components of the revised techniques, particularly when cognitive or behavioral symptoms predominate.

Our views have been influenced by the currently widely held theory that somatic, cognitive, and behavioral symptoms of tension are, in part, independent of each other and are most efficiently treated by modality-specific therapies—that is, cognitive symptoms by cognitively oriented techniques, somatic symptoms by somatically oriented techniques, and behavioral symptoms by behaviorally oriented techniques (Davidson &

Schwartz, 1976; Lang, 1971; Lazarus, 1981).[1] This contrasts with Jacobson's theory that progressive relaxation (a somatic therapy) is the path of choice for all tension-related problems; with the theories of the cognitive and dynamic therapists that cognitive-insight therapies are best for all such problems; and with the theory of Benson (1975) and his followers who assert that all relaxation methods (if not all stress-reduction methods in general) are equivalent and that therefore the fastest and simplest methods are universally preferable.

Let us return to the differences between Jacobson's technique and the various modified progressive relaxation techniques used by most behavior therapists. We shall contrast them on the dimensions upon which we believe they differ fundamentally, justifying our belief that they are, in fact, different techniques, containing different procedures and having different effects (Woolfolk & Lehrer, 1984a). The dimensions are as follows:

1. *Pedagogy versus psychotechnology.* We see Jacobson's technique as being oriented more toward teaching a life skill, and the revised techniques more as requiring something to be done to the client in order to produce relaxation, either through a psychological technique or electronic gadgetry.

2. *Emphasis on muscular learning versus on direct modification of cognitions.* Jacobson taught progressive relaxation entirely as a muscular skill. Although dramatic cognitive changes would often occur, Jacobson argued that cognitive and behavioral changes would occur automatically, as individuals reduced their levels of neuromuscular tension, thereby having more energy and a better ability to think clearly about what is rational and what is in their own best interests. The behavior therapists, on the other hand, give specific behavioral and cognitive prescriptions to their patients and attempt to modify directly that which Jacobson saw only as indirect targets of therapy. In Jacobson's mind, the most direct goal of therapy was to teach self-control of muscle tension, and to enable his patients to approach a level of absolutely no tension in the skeletal muscles. Then, he said (Jacobson, 1970, xii), they

---

[1] The reader should note that this theory does *not* postulate complete independence of the three psychobiological systems (cognitive, somatic, and behavioral) in the etiology and/or treatment of stress. The systems undeniably interact with and affect each other, and how they interact with each other is an important avenue of current research and theory (Lang, 1977; Sheehan, 1983; Tyrer, 1976). We are merely asserting that the three modalities are *partially* independent, and, although symptoms in each of these areas may be affected to some extent by almost any form of treatment, nevertheless each problem will respond best to modality-specific treatment.

would become free and energetic enough to see new alternatives in their lives and to change their cognitions and behaviors accordingly.

3. *The use of suggestion.* This category actually overlaps the other two. The behavior therapists use suggestion during progressive relaxation instructions both as a method of producing relaxation automatically (i.e., the psychotechnology approach) and as a method of enlisting the mental and cognitive faculties in the relaxation process. Jacobson rejected suggestion as a vehicle for relaxation training, because he felt that it interfered with the fundamental task of learning exquisite control of skeletal muscle activity. With suggestion, he cautioned, a person might believe relaxation to be present even when it is not.

The relative merits of the various progressive relaxation techniques can of course be decided only by empirical investigation. To date, the empirical data on this issue are sparse. Two studies have directly compared Jacobson's original technique with various of the revised techniques, and both of them contain substantial design problems. Turner (1978) compared Jacobson's technique with various other procedures, including the progressive relaxation techniques described by Paul, 1966, and by Wolpe and Lazarus, 1966, EMG biofeedback, and various control methods. Turner found a small but significant advantage for Jacobson's technique on one paper-and-pencil measure of anxiety and advantages of borderline significance on other paper-and-pencil and physiological measures. A similar study was done by Snow (1977), who found no significant differences between Jacobson's method and other methods. The major problem in both studies is that the authors used normal college students as subjects rather than clinical populations and therefore the clinical implications are at best inferential. Indeed, there is some evidence that the physiological effects of learning a relaxation technique may not be noticeable among a nonanxious population because of a "floor" effect and that therefore even substantial differences in the power of the various techniques might have been obscured in the above studies on college students. To illustrate this problem, Lehrer (1978) found marked physiological differences between progressive relaxation and a no-treatment control among anxiety neurotics, but almost no physiological differences among normal subjects. The results were interpreted as indicating that nonanxious individuals are able to relax to a great extent without special training, even under conditions of mild stress, thus obscuring the effects of progressive relaxation training when it is compared to a no-treatment or self-relaxation control. In a more dramatic illustration of this, Lehrer (1972) administered a series of gradually more intense electric shocks to paid college student volunteers in order to test the effect of muscular relaxation on habituation of the skin potential response elicited by shock. Although subjects in the relaxation group did habituate more quickly than subjects in a group that had been instructed to tense their muscles and a group that had been instructed to hold their levels of muscle tension constant, there were no differences in habituation rate between subjects in the relaxation group and subjects in a group that was given no instruction at all. Indeed, in the latter group, the experimenter had some difficulty in keeping subjects *awake* during the entire procedure. One can easily conclude from this study that normal, nonanxious college students usually have no difficulty relaxing when they are reclining in a comfortable chair in a dimly lit room and are told to relax and that studies of subtle but potentially important differences in relaxation training technique must be done on a symptomatic population.

Thus studies involving direct contrasts between Jacobson's progressive relaxation technique and the revised techniques have until now been inconclusive. Perhaps future investigation will, some day, tell us whether the differences are clinically significant. We offer the following conceptual analysis as a preliminary step in the design and execution of this research.

II. Pedagogy versus Technology

Often one hears the verb *to relax* used transitively, meaning something that a therapist does *to* someone as in the sentence, "The therapist first relaxed the client and then began the desensitization process." In conjunction with this usage the phrase "relaxation exercises" is often used, meaning the method by which the therapist "relaxes" someone. These phrases are alien to Jacobson's method but are not infrequently heard from practitioners of the revised progressive relaxation procedures. According to Jacobson's philosophy, the therapist should do nothing *to* the client other than teach him or her a muscular skill. If the client practices the skill dutifully, he or she will voluntarily be able to relax the skeletal muscles to an extraordinary degree and thereby experience various beneficial physiological and psychological effects. If the client chooses not to use the skill, no such effects will be felt. Indeed, having the client feel relaxed during a training session is, at most, a secondary goal, useful only as a motivator for further practice. Jacobson considered countertherapeutic any attempt to "prompt" clients to feel relaxed in any way other than by learning to recognize very low levels of skeletal muscle tension and by learning to "'switch off" the tension at will. He argued that any attempt to make a person feel relaxed in the absence of actual muscle relaxation would make the client dependent on the therapist for the beneficial feelings and would interfere with motivation to learn the relaxation technique. Thus, after having experimented with them in his own practice, he eschewed the use of such aids as tape recorders and biofeedback instrumentation because, he found, they created dependence on an external machine rather than on internal proprioception and muscle skill.

A. Number of Sessions

Jacobson's method is often characterized as unworkable because of the large number of sessions needed to teach the technique. Indeed, the number of sessions required by Jacobson's method is the reason almost universally cited by those who opt for the adaptations of Jacobson's technique rather than the original. It is true that various treatment manuals written by Jacobson (1964, 1970) do indicate that the technique can only be taught in upwards of twenty sessions. An examination of Jacobson's own cases, however, indicates that he himself often did not adhere to these guidelines. In some instances he reported therapeutic effects in as few as two hours of treatment (Jacobson, 1964, pp. 200–201). Although he believed that thorough training is the preferred treatment for everyone, he understood that, for many practitioners, thoroughness must be sacrificed for clinical expediency. Thus, although on the average most practitioners of the revised procedures may spend less time than Jacobson did in training an individual to relax, this is not a necessary difference between the two approaches.

The research literature is unclear about the importance of lengthy training. In their literature review, Borkovec and Sides (1979) concluded that multiple sessions of training were necessary to insure that progressive relaxation training has a measurable physiological effect, and they found a significantly greater number of sessions devoted to training among studies that found measurable physiological effects as opposed to those that did not. On the other hand, Lehrer (1982) reviewed a voluminous amount of more recent literature and did not find significant differences on this measure, thus casting in doubt the importance of length of training. Even in the review by Borkovec and Sides, however, the number of training sessions in the "effective" studies was not large (with a mean of less than 5).

B. One Muscle at a Time versus All at Once

A characteristic that does differentiate the two techniques quite clearly is the number of muscle groups that are given training in each session. Jacobson tended to restrict each session to training of a single muscle group, or at most to the muscles of a single area of the body (viz., the arms, or the legs, the trunk, the neck, the speech region, or the eye region). Virtually all of the revised procedures involve asking the client to tense and release muscles throughout the body in each session. The difference stems from the contrasting goals of the two techniques: teaching a muscle skill as opposed to having the individual experience relaxation during each training session. There have been no systematic empirical studies of this component of the progressive relaxation technique. Our own clinical experience leads us to predict that focusing on fewer muscle groups per session should produce a greater ability to decrease muscle tension in the particular muscle group(s), whereas presenting training in all muscle groups might lead to a greater subjective sense of relaxation, particularly during early training sessions. One recent empirical study bears on this issue. Sime and DeGood (1977) found that multiple sessions of taped progressive relaxation training of the frontalis muscle alone did produce significant decreases in frontalis EMG. Of the many studies reviewed by Lehrer (1982) of taped progressive relaxation training, this was one of only two that showed a significant physiological effect for this mode of treatment compared with a control group. In the other study (Parker, Gilbert, & Thoreson, 1978) significant results were obtained because of *increased* arousal in the control group. We take the Sime and DeGood study as supporting the theory that repeated focus on an isolated muscle does produce greater ability to relax specific muscles than does simultaneous training in all muscles (which had been offered to subjects in virtually all of the other studies of taped relaxation that Lehrer reviewed).

C. Live versus Taped Relaxation

As just mentioned, Borkovec and Sides (1979) and Lehrer (1982) have both concluded, after extensive literature reviews, that taped progressive relaxation training is ineffective as a method of training people to control physiological activity. There was a subtle difference in the conclusions reached in the two reviews, however. By the time of Lehrer's more recent review, a number of studies had appeared showing, in fact, a physiological effect for taped relaxation training, although the proportion of studies showing at least one significant physiological effect was still greater with live training than with taped training. The superiority of live training was most obvious when *generalization* of the relaxation skill outside the training session was examined. The generalizability of relaxation is, of course, critical for its clinical effectiveness.

Nevertheless, a number of studies have found positive effects of taped progressive relaxation training on *self-report* measures (e.g., Borkovec, Grayson, & Cooper, 1978; Carrington *et. al.* 1980; Edelman, 1970; Gilbert, Parker, & Clairborn, 1978; Haynes, Griffen, Mooney, & Parise, 1975; Russell, Sipich, & Knipe, 1976; Sheridan, Vaughan, Wallerstedt, & Ward, 1977; Townsend, House, & Addario, 1975). It is thus possible that taped training may have important therapeutic use in treating conditions for which self-report or, perhaps, overt behavior is clinically more relevant than is physiological activity. It is also possible that self-report measures are more influenced by placebo or expectancy effects than are physiological measures.

D. Conditioned Relaxation

The induction of relaxation by classical conditioning methods is foreign to Jacobson's method but often used in the revised procedures. This is another form of "inducing" relaxation by external means rather than teaching it as a skill, and Jacobson eschewed all such approaches. Included among techniques for inducing conditioned relaxation are imagining a pleasant scene and "cue-controlled relaxation," a procedure in which the individual learns to say a silent cue word (e.g., "relax") while in the relaxed state, and to use it later when under stress to induce the relaxed state.

Proponents of relaxing imagery have theorized that pleasant and calm feelings are evoked by the associations produced by the relaxing images. Jacobson, on the other hand, theorized that the process of deliberately thinking about a pleasant scene necessarily involves increased tension in the muscles in and around the eyes because, he found, visual imagery is always accompanied by such increases in muscle tension (Jacobson, 1931). By its very nature, according to Jacobson, relaxation is a completely passive experience.[2] Arguing in favor of the use of relaxing imagery, Lazarus (1981) has proposed that it has its greatest beneficial effects on problems involving anxiety-producing imagery. Jacobson observed that when complete muscle relaxation is achieved, particularly involving the muscles of the eyes, *no* imagery takes place. He thus felt that deliberate use of relaxing imagery is counterproductive. No empirical comparisons have yet been reported between Lazarus's

[2] In some ways Jacobson's view of relaxation is similar to descriptions of the deeper stages of Zen or yogic meditation (Patel, 1984; Suzuki, 1979). Actually, however, Jacobson disliked this comparison, feeling that his method was entirely scientific and not at all mystical, as are the Eastern meditative disciplines.

"modality-specific" argument and Jacobson's argument for sticking to muscle reeducation.

A number of studies have appeared evaluating cue-controlled relaxation and comparing it to progressive relaxation. Grimm (1980) extensively reviewed the empirical literature on cue-controlled relaxation and concluded that the method had no advantages over progressive relaxation. Indeed, there is some evidence that progressive relaxation training alone has superior effects (e.g., Holstead, 1978). Although Jacobson never wrote about this technique, it is probable that he would have disapproved of it for reasons similar to those used against relaxing imagery. Imagining a word, he found, necessarily involves tension in the speech area and, being a deliberate muscular act, it necessarily decreases relaxation of the musculature. This reasoning could explain the otherwise seemingly paradoxical findings that one component of a relaxation technique (i.e., progressive muscle relaxation, which is a component of cue-controlled relaxation) might be more powerful than the combined technique. Another possible explanation for this anomaly is that the time demands involved in cue training necessarily detract from the intensity of the progressive relaxation training given during the early stages of this technique, thus diluting its possible beneficial effects.

E. The "Pendulum Effect"

Jacobson's method differs starkly from the revised progressive relaxation methods in its use of deliberate tension and in the theoretical justification for such tension. In Jacobson's method, deliberate tensing of muscles was done during training sessions in order to familiarize people with the sensations of muscle tension and to illustrate how these sensations are produced by *doing* things with particular muscles. Jacobson advised taking great pains to differentiate the feelings of active muscle flexion with other sensations in the muscles and tendons that do not directly reflect active "doing," such as the sensations of passive muscle stretching that occurs when an opposing muscle is tensed and a limb moved, and the sensations in tendons, joints, and ligaments that may occur when a nearby muscle is flexed. The sensations of muscle flexion are extraordinarily subtle, often considerably more so than the sensations of passive stretching or joint sensations, and people who are not very sensitive to muscle sensations often have great difficulty feeling them. Jacobson insisted that these particular sensations be recognized at extraordinarily low levels of flexion, because he found that in many cases of anxiety and tension disorders the degree of muscle tension in the body is nowhere near the level of maximal tension that a person can produce. Although Jacobson did advise his patients to tense each muscle quite severely when first becoming acquainted with its function and with the sensations associated with its flexion, he did not advise extreme tension when attempting to relax. Extreme tension was used only didactically, when first pointing out the things that individuals must *refrain* from doing in each muscle when they want to relax. Thereafter Jacobson advised using the "method of diminishing tensions" (Jacobson, 1938, p. 53), in which the trainee successively tenses as *little* as possible while still remaining aware of the "control" sensations (i.e., the sensations of tension that tell us when we are exerting control over the actions of part of the body, by use of the particular muscle). In each training session, the individual tenses a muscle only a few times and spends most of the time "switching off" the muscle—but each incidence of tension should require progressively less muscle contraction to produce readily perceived control sensations. The goal of training is to enable the individual to develop such exquisite sensitivity to, and control over, the skeletal muscles that he or she can switch off each muscle at any moment, without tensing at all.

In contrast to Jacobson's method, some of the revised progressive relaxation procedures unabashedly advise tensing muscles as a method of inducing relaxation (cf. Bernstein & Borkovec, 1973, p. 20). Individuals are often asked to tense several muscle groups simultaneously, with maximal effort, and then to release them, each time the individual wishes to relax. In the latter case, the sudden release of extreme tension is theorized to produce a decrease in baseline muscle tension, much as a pendulum swings back in the opposite direction past its resting point when it has been lifted and then released.

Jacobson's research specifically argued against the existence of a pendulum effect. He found (Jacobson, 1934,a,b) that in many individuals tension remains high, often for prolonged periods, after release from high levels of deliberate tension. Individuals who have received training in progressive relaxation tend to be able to return to low levels much more quickly than others; and athletes (who presumably devote considerable time and concentration to their muscles and their muscle sensations, and therefore have developed greater sensitivity and control than most people) show a post-tension release that is intermediate between the levels achieved by other individuals who are trained and those untrained in progressive relaxation (Jacobson, 1934b).

Jacobson's results would actually suggest that an egg timer would be a better analogy than a pendulum in describing the effect of tension. When the sand inside is moved to the top, it reaches bottom rather slowly and gradually, and much of it may remain elevated for considerable time. With athletes and those trained in relaxation, the sand in the timer may flow more swiftly, and with untrained individuals suffering from neuromusclular tension the sand may flow more slowly, but in no instance does it reach levels below those at which it had started before the timer was turned over.

We have recently reported the results of a study on this issue from our laboratory. We performed it because, upon reviewing Jacobson's studies of EMG levels following tension release, we noticed that Jacobson did not use tension procedures that are analogous to those used in the revised progressive relaxation procedures. In the latter, tension takes place only for 10–20 seconds, and tension-release cycles are repeated five or more times; whereas in Jacobson's experiments subjects tensed their muscles for one minute or more, and the tension took place only once. In our study (Lehrer, Batey, Woolfolk, Remde, & Garlick, 1985), we attempted to replicate more closely the conditions used in the revised progressive relaxation procedures. We repeatedly asked subjects to tense for 20 seconds and then to release their frontalis and dominant forearem extensor muscles, alternately, and in balanced order. Simultaneously, we measured EMG levels from both sites and asked subjects to rate their levels of tension in the muscles that they were tensing at the time. We found little evidence for a pendulum effect. In both muscle groups, EMG levels remained elevated for a minute or more after subjects were told to release their tension. Although frontal EMG levels did eventually reach levels lower than baseline after tension release, forearm EMG levels appeared to have remained elevated. Self-reported feelings of tension appeared to dissipate relatively slowly in both muscle groups.

An additional objection to the tense-release method of training used in the revised methods was raised by Sime (1982), who pointed out that most of these methods involve tensing several muscle groups at once (e.g., the entire fist and arm at once) and therefore produce so many sensations that the trainee cannot possibly isolate the subtle control sensations. For example, tightening the fist and arm together produces multiple sensations from tendons and ligaments (the feelings of nails digging into the palms, etc.), all superimposed upon each other in a way that makes them almost impossible to discriminate from each other. In most cases, this completely masks the sensations of muscle contraction, which often are much more subtle. If any relaxation is achieved by this method, it certainly would not be by training individuals to make subtle muscle discriminations. Beneficial effects from this procedure, if they occur at all, probably result more from suggestion and expectation, issues that will be discussed in detail below.

Note that, although we call into doubt the procedure of inducing relaxation through tense-release cycles, we are pointedly not denying the usefulness of tensing and releasing muscles during the process of learning to discriminate tension. Indeed, in the treatment of insomnia Borkovec, Kaloupek, and Slama (1975) found that relaxation using tension-release cycles is more useful than simple suggestions to relax (without any deliberate tension, but therefore also without any instruction in recognizing muscular tension). Similarly, the only study that found EMG biofeedback to be more powerful than live progressive relaxation as a method of reducing EMG activity utilized progressive relaxation instructions which consisted only of suggestions to relax each muscle and descriptions of the feelings that should be obtained—without tense-release instructions (Canter, Kondo, & Knott, 1975). These findings support our opinion that tension and release do serve an important role in progressive relaxation training, even if tension-release cycles are not appropriate as methods of *inducing* relaxation. In our view, as in Jacobson's, their proper use is as a training vehicle, not as a form of relaxation technology designed to produce automatic results.

F. The Use of Biofeedback

Actually, Jacobson was one of the first to experiment with EMG biofeedback as an aid to teaching people to relax. According to McGuigan (1984), he rejected the method in the 1950s because he felt it tended to make people dependent on the machines. Jacobson's goal was to teach people to recognize tension in their own muscles. Reliance on an external machine, he felt, was counterproductive.

Parametric studies of relaxation and biofeedback have found that, although not harmful (as predicted by Jacobson), EMG biofeedback is generally not so powerful as progressive relaxation and seems, on the average, to add little to Jacobson's method. In a review of the literature on progressive relaxation and EMG biofeedback, Lehrer (1982) concluded that EMG biofeedback does not add incremental effectiveness when combined with live relaxation instructions and that, when the two techniques are compared with each other, live relaxation instructions are, on the average, superior. More recently, Janssen (1983) found the combination of live relaxation training and biofeedback to be more potent than biofeedback alone but three other recent studies (Nicassio, Boylan, & McCabe, 1982; Pollard & Ashton, 1982; Wilson & Bird, 1981) found no differences between live progressive relaxation training and biofeedback.

When compared and/or combined with taped relaxation instruction, the picture is quite different. On the average, EMG biofeedback tends to be more powerful than taped progressive relaxation instruction (cf. reviews by Lehrer, 1982; Lehrer & Woolfolk, 1984; and recent studies by Bennick, Holst, & Renthem, 1982; Daly, Donn, Galliher, & Zimmerman, 1983; Stout, Thornton, & Russell, 1980; Walsh, Dale, & Anderson, 1977). Also, although the combination of taped relaxation instructions and biofeedback does yield superior results to taped relaxation instructions alone (cf. review by Lehrer, 1982), taped relaxation training probably does not add anything to biofeedback. Two recent studies (Kappes, 1983; Walsh, Dale, & Anderson, 1977) found no differences between biofeedback alone and the combination of biofeedback and taped relaxation instructions.

Nevertheless, EMG biofeedback might still be useful to some individuals. Prager-Decker (1978) found that individuals who score high on a paper-and-pencil measure of external control tend to do better with EMG biofeedback than do other individuals. Two recent studies from Blanchard's laboratory (Blanchard *et. al.*, 1982; Neff, Blanchard, & Andrasik, 1983) also suggest that some individuals who cannot be helped by progressive relaxation might be helped by biofeedback. They found that administering biofeedback produced significant improvements in symptoms among individuals suffering from headaches who did not respond to prior relaxation instruction. Several investigators have argued that biofeedback might be a useless technology because of the high cost of equipment and because it does not appear to be more powerful than relaxation therapy (cf. Furedy, 1984a,b; White & Tursky, 1982). However, Lehrer (1983, 1984a,b) has argued that the price of biofeedback equipment had declined significantly enough to warrant consideration as an inexpensive home aid to relaxation training, or, at times, even a substitute—especially when the alternative is superficial or taped instruction.

III. Differing Views on Cognitive and Somatic Factors in Emotion and in Treatment

In both his clinical approach and in his theoretical view of the nature of mind and body, Jacobson emphasized the importance of the periphery of the body. Emotions and other maladaptive mental processes, he felt, might most effectively be modified by changing a person's use of the skeletal muscles. The post-Jacobson relaxation therapists have tended to give more emphasis to direct modification of cognitions; indeed, the whole field of behavior therapy in recent years has emphasized the importance of cognitive mediation of behavior and of direct treatment of cognitions. Even such a bedrock "somatic" technique as biofeedback has come to be interpreted as being mediated by cognitions and having profound effects upon cognitions (Lazarus, 1977; Holroyd, 1979). One practical corollary of this theoretical direction is the devotion of a relatively greater amount of therapy time to cognitive interventions and rather less to physical relaxation strategies in modern behavior therapy.

Jacobson's theory of emotion is quite similar to that of Gellhorn. Indeed, the two men had great influence on each other. Gellhorn (1958; Gellhorn & Loofbourrow, 1963, Chapter 17) devoted considerable attention to devising a theory explaining the effectiveness of Jacobson's techniques; Jacobson reciprocated by adopting, in large part, Gellhorn's theory (Jacobson, 1967, pp. 149–158). Following Hess (1925), Gellhorn postulated two emotional systems: the ergotrophic and the trophotrophic. These systems are often mutually inhibitory, with ergotrophic activation associated with sympathetic reactivity and the trophotrophic response associated with parasympathetic reactivity. They also, however, work homeostatically, such that overactivation in one system can produce increased reactivity in the opposing system. This can occur through reflexes elicited by blood pressure fluctuations, mediated through baroreceptors in the carotid sinus and aortic arch, and often modulated by cerebral (chiefly hypothalamic) and neurohumoral mechanisms (Gellhorn, 1957; Lacey, 1967). According to Gellhorn (1958), progressive relaxation decreases ergotrophic dominance directly by decreasing proprioception from the striated musculature. He notes that a high proportion of the innervation of the ascending reticular system emanates from skeletal muscle proprioceptors, so that diminished muscular tension would be expected to produce diminished autonomic and emotional reactivity through decreased stimulation of the posterior hypothalamus and cortex from the ascending reticular system. He supported this theory by citing evidence that, in cats, administration of curare (which was thought to block muscular activity at the neuromuscular juncture) produced decreased sympathetic reactivity and slow-wave EEGs similar to those observed in a state of somnolence.

Jacobson believed that anxiety and anxious ideation—indeed, *any* ideation—are impossible when the skeletal musculature is completely relaxed (Jacobson, 1938, pp. 164–189). In his final book, *The Human Mind*, Jacobson (1982) argued that thought *depends* upon proprioception, such that the perception of any thought or feeling would necessarily differ among any organisms that differed physically in the periphery of the body as well as in the brain.

Davison (1966) and Campbell, Sanderson, and Laverty (1964) argued against this peripheralist theory of emotion. They criticized Gellhorn's reliance upon animal studies of curare in order to justify his assertion that muscle relaxation produces relaxation and somnolence, and they cited some human curare studies indicating that people whose muscles are experimentally rendered flaccid by curare can nevertheless remain extremely anxious. McGuigan (1978), in justifying Jacobson's position, however, noted that the humans who allowed themselves to be experimentally curarized were never as deeply curarized as the animals in the studies cited by Gellhorn.

Following Davison's earlier conclusions, Davidson and Schwartz (1976) hypothesized that the positive affective state generated by progressive relaxation and the inhibitory effect of diminished efferent motor activity are the elements in progressive relaxation therapy responsible for its anxiolytic effect. By emphasizing these central effects of relaxation therapy, Davison established the theoretical rationale for the development of cognitive behavior therapy. If relaxation therapy for anxiety has primarily central effects, then it would be quite natural to presume that other procedures affecting the fundamental operation of the central nervous system (e.g., direct modification of cognition) might be expected to have effects that are just as profound as muscular relaxation or even more so.

Although peripheralist theories of emotion have fallen into disrepute, there is a large body of evidence indicating the importance of peripheral events in the generation of emotion. It has been shown that distension of the corotid sinus affects electrocortical activity (Bonvallet, Dell, & Hiebel, 1954). Lacey (1967) argued that these data suggest a mechanism whereby changes in blood pressure might have a direct effect on cortical activity. A study of individuals with spinal cord injuries (Hohmann, 1966) has suggested that the loss of autonomic feedback is associated with a lessened capacity to experience emotion. Tomkins (1970) has hypothesized that feedback from the facial musculature to subcortical centers may cause the latter to influence emotional experience. Some empirical support for this hypothesis was generated in a number of studies (Kraut, 1982; Laird, 1974; Lanzetta, Cartwright-Smith, & Kleck, 1976).

In ascertaining whether a more cognitive approach to relaxation has effects that are superior or inferior to those of Jacobson's progressive relaxation—or simply different kinds of effects –it is instructive to examine the literature on the effects of cognitive therapy. All forms of cognitive therapy have in common the attempt to restructure or modify the client's thoughts, beliefs, or imagery so as to alleviate emotional distress. Although there is some overlap among the different forms of cognitive therapy, each has its distinctive emphasis. Meichenbaum's (1977) method tends to emphasize the systematic alteration of clients' self-verbalizations and the replacement of worry and anxiety-generating self-talk by salutary thinking. Beck's (1976, 1984) approach stresses the identification and alteration of faulty thinking and the cognitive styles that produce anxiety and arousal. This occurs through a "Socratic" dialogue between therapist and patient. Ellis's (1962) approach is a didactic, persuasive effort directed toward the modification of the content of dysfunctional cognitions. It aims to identify and to eradicate "irrational" beliefs and attitudes (especiallly those having to do with moralism and perfectionism) and to replace them with a more "rational" (in Ellisonian terms) outlook on life.

Cognitive techniques often are applied in conjunction with somatic relaxation methods and within a specified sequential program of therapeutic activities. *Stress inoculation training* (Jaremko, 1979; Meichenbaum & Cameron, 1973) is one such cognitive-behavioral package. Its three stages are described at (1) client preparation, (2) skills training, and (3) application training. In the phase of client preparation the patient is taught the relationship between maladaptive thinking and behavior. The client learns a cognitive-appraisal model of stress (cf. Lazarus, 1966) and a rationale that explains the efficacy of cognitive procedures. In the second stage, the client learns and rehearses a variety of skills including cognitive restructuring, coping imagery, modification of self-verbalization, and physical relaxation (usually a version of Jacobson's technique). In the third stage, the client practices and applies the newly learned skills for coping with stress by confronting a graded sequence of stressors, in one or a combination of several ways: imaginally presented, by role playing with the therapist or *in vivo*.

Other forms of combined cognitive and somatic interventions are those related to the widely used technique of systematic desensitization (Wolpe, 1958). This involves slowly exposing oneself to phobic stimuli, either *in vivo* or in imagination, while in a deeply relaxed state. This technique is widely used in the treatment of phobias. Although Wolpe described it as a form of classical conditioning, Wilkins (1971) and Locke (1971) argued that cognitive mechanisms were probably more important than conditioning in producing therapeutic success with the technique. Although this view has not been universally accepted (e.g., Davison & Wilson, 1972), it is unquestionable that some cognitive processes are directly involved in the desensitization technique (e.g., the requirement that the client must build a hierarchy of anxiety-provoking scenes, thus making cognitive judgments about the amount of anxiety that is aroused by each scene). When it is done as described originally by Wolpe, this technique thus involves both somatic (relaxation) and cognitive component. A similar technique is *stress management training*, which is a combination of visuomotor behavior rehearsal and a technique called *anxiety management training*. Anxiety management training takes place in three phases. In the first, clients are given brief training in one of the modified progressive relaxation techniques. During the second phase, they imagine anxiety-producing scenes, in a manner analogous to systematic desensitization, and they are taught to identify the specific physiological or muscular sensations associated with the anxiety they perceive. In the third phase, they learn to utilize a cue word, as is done in the technique of cue-controlled relaxation, and to use it to induce a relaxed state when confronted with an anxiety-provoking situation. In the visuomotor rehearsal phase of stress management training, clients imagine themselves engaging in behaviors that are alternatives to those that generate life stress. Following imaginal rehearsal, these behaviors are practiced *in vivo*.

Cognitive therapies have been proven to be effective treatments for a variety of disorders, including depression, asthma, anxiety, and headaches. For most of these dysfunctions, at least at their present level of conceptualization and measurement, the self-report of distress is the most important and even the defining element of the difficulty. For other syndromes (e.g., hypertension and other somatic complaints) we have little evidence supporting the efficacy of cognitive therapy. The literature to date on cognitive approaches to physiological problems has been sparse. Few studies have evaluated the impact of cognitive interventions on somatic systems. The available literature does suggest that cognitive treatments may carry less impact on behavioral and physiological response systems than do treatments that target these systems more directly. A study by Kremsdorf, Kochanowicz, and Costell (1981) found that cognitive therapy reduces self-reported headache activity but does not reduce actual muscle tension. Conversely, they found, EMG biofeedback appears to reduce muscle tension but not self-reports of headache. Similarly, Biran and Wilson (1981) found that cognitive treatment is ineffective relative to an exposure-based treatment in ameliorating avoidance among phobic patients.

Cognitive therapy has most often been found to be effective with those disorders for which the individual client's phenomenology is either sufficient to its diagnosis or the most salient indication of its presence. Holroyd and Andrasik (1982) found some evidence for superiority of cognitive therapy over EMG biofeedback in the treatment of tension headache. The effectiveness of cognitive techniques in the treatment of clinical pain resulting from various disorders has been demonstrated repeatedly (Turk, Meichenbaum, & Genest, 1983). Cognitive approaches have also been found effective in the treatment of test anxiety (Meichenbaum, 1972), social anxiety (Goldfried, 1979), depression (Beck, Rush, Shaw, & Emery, 1979), and chronic anger (Novaco, 1975).

We recently (Lehrer & Woolfolk, 1984) reviewed the results of empirical studies comparing cognitive with somatic treatments for various stress-related problems, and concluded that cognitive therapy has more powerful effects than somatic relaxation procedures on cognitive symptoms, including cognitive assessments of *somatic* problems (self-ratings of pain, insomnia, etc.). A recent comparative study by Woolfolk and McNulty, 1983, of sleep-onset insomnia found that self-report of sleep latency showed more improvement at a six-month follow–up among subjects who had been given visual imagery training (with or without progressive relaxation) than among those who had been given progressive relaxation alone. Also, Langosch *et al.* (1982) studied patients at a cardiac rehabilitation center and found that, immediately after training, subjects receiving stress management training showed greater decreases in feelings of job responsibility than subjects in the relaxation group. At a six-month follow–up subjects in the stress management training group reported less emotional lability and a greater ability to reduce stress than subjects in the relaxation group, who reported a *decrease* in the latter ability. Although subjects in the relaxation group showed a greater decrease in cardiac complaints than subjects in the stress management training and control groups immediately after training, they also showed the greatest post-test to follow-up *increase* in this measure. The authors interpreted the results as indicating the superiority of stress management training, but the interpretation is clouded by the fact that subjects chose which treatment to receive rather than having been assigned randomly.

Several other recent studies have found greater effects for combined relaxation and cognitive therapies than for relaxation therapy alone, although the combination of techniques may not be superior to cognitive therapy alone when cognitive measures are used to assess outcome. Osberg (1981) studied speech-anxious subjects and found that practicing public speaking, with or without concurrent relaxation training, produced greater decreases in self-rated anxiety than did relaxation training alone. Furthermore, the combined technique produced greater decreases in observer ratings of anxiety than did relaxation training alone. Although perhaps more of a "behavioral" than a cognitive technique, the speech practice condition did include some imaginal and cognitive components, so we classify it as a cognitive technique. Similarly, Miller and DiPilato (1983) compared systematic desensitization with relaxation therapy in treatment of nightmares and found, 25 weeks after the beginning of their six-week treatment program, that subjects reported greater decreases in intensity of nightmares in the desensitization group than in the relaxation group. At the 15th week after therapy onset, however, there had been no differences between the two treatments, and ratings of nightmare frequency did not differ between the two groups at either time period. Finally, Peal, Handal, and Gilner (1981) found greater decreases in two measures of death anxiety after desensitization than after relaxation among death-anxious undergraduates. This is consistent with a large body of earlier literature indicating the systematic desensitization is more effective than progressive relaxation alone in treatment of phobias (cf. Cooke, 1968; Davison, 1968; Lomont & Edwards, 1967). (In these studies self-report and behavioral approach measures were used almost exclusively to assess outcome.)

Three recent studies found no differences on various cognitive measures between relaxation therapy and combined relaxation and cognitive therapies. White, Gilner, Handal, and Napoli (1983) found that systematic desensitization produced the same decreases in death anxiety among high death-anxious undergraduates as did relaxation training alone. Similarly, Philips and Hunter (1981) found that the combination of relaxation therapy and calming images did not differ from relaxation therapy alone in improving pain behavior and self-rated pain experience among psychiatric patients suffering from headaches. Finally, Van Hassel, Bloom, and Gonzales (1982) studied schizophrenic individuals who were given either relaxation training or anxiety management training. They found that both treatments, compared to a control group, produced improvements in self-ratings of generalized anxiety and in therapist ratings of a number of behaviors related to anxiety, emotion, and overall psychiatric status.

The only study comparing cognitive therapy and progressive relaxation therapy using a physiological measure as an outcome variable was reported by Kaplan, Metzger, and Jablecki (1983). They studied 40 adult male patients while they were undergoing a rather painful clinical electromyographic study in a Veterans Administration hospital and compared the effects of four interventions: cognitive reappraisal therapy, progressive relaxation, a combined technique called cognitive behavior modification, and an attention control group. In a *post hoc* analysis, they found lower heart rates in the groups that received relaxation training than in the other two groups. On various self-report measures of emotional distress and on a behavioral rating of stress and discomfort, patients who received training had lower scores than control subjects, but no differences were found among the various treatment conditions. Although not directly relevant to progressive relaxation therapy, dramatic findings from a study comparing cognitive therapy with EMG biofeedback deserve mention because they illustrate the somatic-cognitive treatment–symptom specificity so well. Schandler and Dana (1983) studied students with high scores on paper-and-pencil tests of nervousness, hostility, and depression. They compared frontalis EMG biofeedback with taped training in guided imagery and cognitive desensitization (using relaxing images in place of muscle relaxation in systematic desensitization) and with a self-relaxation control. Only guided imagery produced reliable therapeutic changes in a wide array of self-report measures (including anxiety, hostility, and depression), but only bio-feedback produced reliable decreases in frontalis EMG and heart rate.

Our laboratory, which is one of the few active centers using Jacobson's original relaxation technique, has produced some additional evidence for the somatic specificity of progressive relaxation therapy. Lehrer (1978) found that among anxiety neurotics progressive relaxation training produces decreases in psychophysiological reactivity, but not necessarily in self-report of anxiety—a measure which may be more refractory to change in this population. Also, a recent study of relaxation therapy for asthma found greater effects for relaxation therapy in a somatic measure of asthma (bronchial constriction caused by inhalation of methacholine) than in various self-report measures of asthmatic symptoms (Lehrer, Hochron, McCann, Swartzman, & Reba, in press), although in this study various self-report measures of *anxiety* did show improvement. It is possible that longer follow-up in both of these studies might have shown cognitive changes as well, and future research may prove that the discrepancies we observed resulted from a cognitive lag. Both of these studies were of populations with marked chronic problems, and self-perception of improvement in such conditions may not occur as rapidly as physiological improvement. For the short run, however, data from our research does suggest that progressive relaxation has more reliable somatic than cognitive effects.

In summary, there is considerable evidence for somatic specificity for progressive relaxation and cognitive specificity for cognitive therapy. Relaxation therapy produces more reliable effects on somatic measures and cognitive therapy produces more reliable effects on cognitive measures. Adding cognitive therapy to relaxation therapy tends to strengthen the cognitive effects of the latter, whereas there is evidence from one study that adding relaxation therapy to cognitive therapy does not appear to strengthen such effects. There is as yet no systematic evidence that these therapies have additive effects on physiological outcome variables.

IV. SUGGESTION

Edmund Jacobson was unalterably opposed to the notion that suggestion could be used effectively in teaching people to relax. The danger of suggestion, he said, is that it may make the individual feel that relaxation is taking place even when it is not. The *perception* of relaxation is not so important as actual physical relaxation, according to Jacobson. Therefore, suggestion may be deleterious because a person may stop devoting the time and concentration necessary to learn relaxation if he or she feels relaxed already. Jacobson went to great lengths to eliminate suggestion from his technique. In his clinical technique, when asking a person to tense a particular muscle in order to detect the exact location of muscle tension sensations, Jacobson would not even tell the trainee where the sensations *should* be felt. If the trainee was having difficulty "finding" the sensation of tension in a particular muscle, Jacobson simply asked the trainee to prolong or to intensify the tension, or he applied pressure with his hand to oppose the muscle movement he was asking the trainee to make, in order to intensify the sensations of tension. If the trainee discovered the source of the "control sensations" (i.e., the sensations produced by the muscles when they produce some form of active movement or control over part of the body) without being told where to look for them, Jacobson felt more certain that proprioceptive learning was, in fact, taking place.

In Jacobson's mind, the processes involved in progressive relaxation are radically different from the processes involved in hypnosis, the quintessential form of suggestion. In his classic work, *Progressive Relaxation*, Jacobson (1938, pp. 303–308) enumerated 32 ways in which progressive relaxation differs from hypnosis. Included are the following most notable ways:

1. In the method of relaxation, no technical suggestions are given. For instance, the physician would never suggest, "Now your arm is becoming limp!" or "This will help you be quiet!" He simply directs the patient in the same manner as when prescribing diet or exercise.

2. The physician does not hesitate to interrupt the patient at a moment when he is failing in the attempt to relax and to criticize him vigorously. Such practice is foreign to all suggestive procedures.

3. Relaxation has to be learned step by step with various details of success and failure. It is a learning process by the method of trial and error. It requires the cultivation of the observation skill of the patient, which largely depends upon practice apart from the physician. Hypnosis does not have to be learned at all.

4. The therapeutic effects of suggestion and hypnosis, while brilliant, are likely to be ephemeral. Symptoms disappear to be succeeded by other ones, for the basic nervous hypertension is not treated. On the other hand, re-educative treatment by relaxation tends to be relatively thorough-going and permanent in effect.

5. The individual is generally awakened from hypnosis by some suggestive signal. Occasionally the awakening proves difficult. In contrast with this, there is no difficulty and no special signal of arousal from profound relaxation. If the individual has fallen asleep, he awakes in every respect as from a natural sleep.

6. In suggestion, the doctor designates the symptoms which are to disappear. After learning to relax, the patient often reports disappearance of symptoms never before mentioned.

Jacobson's view of the sharp distinction between skill learning and suggestion is not universally accepted. Edmonston (1981, p. 210) takes the relatively extreme position that hypnosis and relaxation are identical.

He says that "traditional" hypnotic procedures all either specifically use relaxation inductions or have phenomenological and physiological effects that are very similar to relaxation procedures. He cites studies indicating that direct comparisons between hypnosis and various relaxation procedures reveal no important differences between the two procedures. Where differences are found, he explains them away by idiosyncratic problems in individual studies.

Even among those who believe that there are important differences between relaxation and hypnosis, few will doubt that they both involve a number of similar characteristics. Both involve the focusing of attention, and both can produce profound effects on thought processes and levels of physiological arousal. Both can be used therapeutically to help people to control aspects of themselves that appear, in ordinary circumstances, to be uncontrollable. The degree to which these characteristics and effects are emphasized in the various techniques does differ, however. Some hypnotic inductions do not use relaxation at all and seem to depend for their effects almost entirely on the active focus of attention; some relaxation techniques, such as biofeedback and Jacobson's progressive relaxation method, use very little direct suggestion of any mental effects. Also, reasonable people can and do differ about the meaning of various empirical studies comparing relaxation and hypnosis. For example, despite Edmonston's dismissal of the studies finding differences between relaxation and hypnosis, we (Lehrer & Woolfolk, 1984) have interpreted them as valid and important.

Expanding on this view, others have shown that it is almost impossible to eliminate suggestion from any form of psychological treatment. Even before an individual arrives at the office, he or she has already invested the therapist and the therapist's method with the power to influence and change important aspects of personal functioning. The decision to seek out a professional and to pay a fee to have oneself changed already predisposes the individual to change. Frank (1961) has stated that such influence is a hallmark of all psychotherapies. Orne (1982, p. 429) has pointed out that the "placebo" effect is present in all treatments, including drug treatments. Indeed, he could find only one drug study that evaluated the behavioral effects of drugs independently of a placebo effect. In virtually all the other studies, he found, the subjects knew that they were taking a drug; therefore these studies actually evaluate the combination of the drug and the placebo effect, rather than just the drug effect. Virtually no studies of psychological treatment have completely eliminated the placebo effect. So it is with Jacobson's own work; although he tried to minimize suggestion in his technique, he could not totally eliminate it. The most ingenious approach to eliminating the placebo effect in relaxation research was devised by Borkovec and his colleagues (cf. Borkovec & Hennings, 1978), who used "counterdemand" instructions: they told their subjects that no therapeutic effects might be expected until after the first four sessions, so they could measure the therapeutic effects of the technique devoid of placebo contribution *before* the fourth session. This methodology, unfortunately, is much more adaptable to studying the revised techniques than to studying Jacobson's original technique, because the former present training in all the muscle groups right from the beginning, whereas Jacobson's method does not; therefore Jacobson's method may actually have fewer therapeutic effects during early sessions. Unless a suitable method can be found to eliminate suggestion even further from Jacobon's technique, the most we can hope for is comparisons between various relaxation techniques that differ in the amount of suggestion that is deliberately included in the technique, compared with the amount of specific physiological training that takes place.

An approach that comes closer to our own was recently articulated by Clarke and Jackson (1983), who interpret hypnosis primarily as a cognitive technique and progressive relaxation primarily as a somatic technique. In a review of the comparative outcome literature, we concluded that the effects of hypnosis are greater on mental function and on overt behavior than on levels of physiological arousal, and that exactly the opposite is the case with such somatically oriented techniques as progressive relaxation and biofeedback (Lehrer & Woolfolk, 1984). We found that the most dramatic results among studies of hypnosis were obtained on self-report measures or on overt voluntary behavior. Thus, even in studies of ostensibly physiological events such as pain, insomnia, smoking, drug craving or withdrawal, and overeating—all of which are found to yield to hypnotic treatment—the most relevant outcome measure consists of self-report or overt behavior, both of which are directly manipulated by hypnotic suggestion. Although physiological effects also are occasionally obtained with hypnosis, they tend to be weaker, perhaps because the physiological effects are indirect. Exactly the opposite tends to happen with such presumably somatically oriented techniques as progressive relaxation and biofeedback.

Another approach to this problem is to define the hypnotic and relaxation procedures operationally and from an atheoretical perspective to examine the comparative and combined effects of the two forms of intervention. Barber (1984) takes this course and hypothesizes that combining suggestion with relaxation may help both techniques. We, on the other hand, predict that the advantage of adding hypnotic suggestion to relaxation would be seen only when an outcome measure is of a sort that directly reflects cognitive or overt behavioral function. Consistent with this, Barber states that "the goal (of relaxation) is not muscular relaxation per se but a new level of being which is characterized by peace of mind." He thus focuses his prescription of a combined technique to conditions under which the mental state associated with relaxation is the primary goal of therapy. This certainly would not be the case in treating such disorders as hypertension, ulcers, or epilepsy, when a physiological measure would be the logical measure of therapeutic outcome (cf. Jacobson's self-description as a specialist in internal medicine, not psychiatry!).

A study by Friedman and Taub (1977) gives some support to our position. This study found the combination of biofeedback and hypnotic relaxation suggestions to have *worse* results than either technique alone in reducing blood pressure. The interpretation of this study is somewhat questionable because it used nonrandom assignment of subjects to groups; but if these results are borne out by future studies we would be forced to conclude that in the case of a physiological measure like blood pressure the two techniques should not be combined. Previously we (Lehrer & Woolfolk, 1984) explained these results by hypothesizing that "the unrelenting truth of the biofeedback machine may undermine the more flexible 'suggested truth' that must be believed if one is to enter a hypnotic trance; and the hypnotic set may detract from learning the biofeedback task." On the other hand, the fact that the biofeedback and hypnosis groups did not differ from each other does run counter to the prediction that hypnosis should have weaker physiological effects. Other studies also produced results consistent with our position. Stanton (1975) found hypnotic relaxation suggestions to be more effective than progressive relaxation in improving self-reports of sleep latency and awakenings among insomniacs. Conversely, Paul (1969a, 1969b) found progressive relaxation to have greater effects than hypnotic suggestion to relax in lowering various indices of physiological arousal. Holroyd, Nuechterlein, Shapiro, and Ward (1982) reported some results that at first glance appear to give our position some difficulty. In both high and low hypnotizable subjects, faster reductions in EMG levels were achieved with EMG biofeedback than with hypnosis, whereas faster reductions in blood pressure and skin conduction took place with hypnosis than with blood pressure biofeedback. A possible explanation for the latter finding is the ineffectiveness of the blood pressure biofeedback condition. Some *increases* in arousal occurred in this condition.

We are not, of course, claiming that the cognitive and physiological levels of functioning are completely independent of each other. One would then be hard-pressed to explain the effects of progressive relaxation on such obviously mental or cognitive processes as anxiety and depression (Lehrer & Woolfolk, 1984), or the known physiological effects of suggestion (Barber, Spanos, & Chaves, 1974, p. 70; Barber, 1984). Our argument now is only that hypnotic suggestion has a *relatively* greater direct effect on thought and overt action, and that Jacobson's progressive relaxation method has a *relatively* greater direct effect on somatic function.

The voluminous literature on the technique of autogenic training (Luthe, 1969), does appear to produce some problems for our theory about the contrasting natures of hypnosis and relaxation. Autogenic training is a self-hypnotic technique in which individuals give themselves self-hypnotic instruction to affect various physiological functions. The empirical outcome literature shows rather conclusively that it can have profound effects on various psychosomatic problems and that it can affect various measures of somatic function rather substantially. From our perspective, however, autogenic training is much more than simple suggestion, just as a hypnotic technique that employs progressive relaxation as part of the hypnotic induction is more than simple suggestion. Autogenic training involves learning to perceive subtle changes in physiological activity and to control them voluntarily. It is often combined with various forms of biofeedback (cf. Norris & Fahrion, 1984). In our opinion, the most important aspect of the autogenic technique for achieving somatic effects is training in self-monitoring and in understanding of various physiological functions—rather than the suggestive aspects of the technique. In order to evaluate our hypotheses the autogenic training must be "dismantled" using a component control design, (cf. Borkovec, Johnson, & Block, 1984) so that the effects of various aspects of the technique can be studied separately. There are as yet no such dismantling studies, but in our review of studies comparing progressive relaxation with autogenic training (Lehrer & Woolfolk, 1984) we found relatively greater muscular effects for progressive relaxation and relatively greater autonomic effects for autogenic training. This is consistent with the muscular emphasis of progressive relaxation and the relatively greater emphasis on autonomic activity in autogenic training. Clinically, our review found progressive relaxation (often accompanied by EMG biofeedback) to be more effective with problems of muscular origin than autogenic training (often accompanied by surface temperature biofeedback); but for autonomic problems the two techniques appear to be equivalent. This remains consistent with Jacobson's (1938) theory of the central importance of skeletal muscle tension in affecting general physiological arousal. Reducing muscle tension to extremely low levels appears to have profound effects on the autonomic nervous system; however, the combination of suggestion and training in autonomic control does not produce effects that generalize to the musculoskeletal system.

Examining the relationship between hypnotizability and individual differences in response to relaxation therapy is still another way to examine the importance of the hypnotic component in relaxation therapy. One study from our laboratory found no correlation between hypnotizability and response either to progressive relaxation or autogenic training among anxious individuals (Lehrer, Atthowe, & Weber, 1980), whereas another found a *negative* correlation between hypnotizability and response to progressive relaxation among asthmatics (Infantino *et al.*, 1983). Other studies have also found a lack of relationship between hypnotizability and response to biofeedback (Engstrom, 1976; Frischholz & Tryon, 1980; Holroyd *et al.*, 1982). One study found a positive relationship between hypnotizability and self-reported improvement in migraine headaches (Andreychuk & Shriver, 1975), whereas another study found that high hypnotizable subjects do more poorly than low hypnotizable subjects in increasing EEG alpha during biofeedback training (Dumas, 1980).

A measure that has been used in relaxation research that is closely related to hypnotizability is that of absorption. Tellegen and his colleagues define absorption as the capacity to engage in episodes of "total" attention, and they have designed a scale to measure the capacity for it (Tellegen & Atkinson, 1974). Neff *et al.* (1983) reported some rather intriguing results indicating an interaction between response to relaxation versus biofeedback and the capacity for absorption. In a study of headache treatment using either progressive relaxation or EMG biofeedback, they found that "vascular headache patients low in absorption were significantly improved after biofeedback training. Tension headache patients low in absorption did not respond significantly to either form of treatment, while those high in absorption responded significantly to biofeedback training." Qualls and Sheehan (1979) similarly found greater reductions among high absorption subjects in frontal EMG with a no-feedback self-instructed relaxation procedure than with biofeedback, whereas low absorption subjects tended to do better with EMG biofeedback. Roberts, Schuler, Bacon, Zimmerman, and Patterson (1975) found no relationship between absorption and response to skin temperature biofeedback.

All we can conclude from this literature is that the relationship between absorption, hypnotizability, and the ability to relax is quite complex. There is some suggestion from the literature that biofeedback may produce better results among low hypnotizable subjects and relaxation methods (which generally included suggestion in their administration) produce better results with high hypnotizable subjects; but there is some inconsistency in the results, and no definitive conclusion can be made at this time.

We have taken a rather long digression from the original topic of the contribution of suggestion to progressive relaxation. What does the empirical literature say about the facilitative or detrimental effects that suggestion may have on the progressive relaxation technique, if any? We present our conclusions as speculations and hypotheses, rather than as proven fact. As with autogenic training, the progressive relaxation technique has not been systematically and empirically dismantled so that the effects of muscle training and suggestion can be separately evaluated. Indeed, almost no studies actually used Jacobson's original technique, minimizing suggestion; therefore, the effects of the two are confounded in almost all the progressive relaxation research. Our prediction, however, is that adding suggestion to the progressive relaxation technique will be shown to have beneficial effects only on self-report measures and that the muscle training component will be shown to be more important for obtaining somatic effects.

V. CONCLUSION

Jacobson's original progressive relaxation technique differs from the types of progressive relaxation used by many current practitioners in a number of fundamental respects. Jacobson emphasized relaxation as a method of learning to control one's excess muscle tension 24 hours per day. In his mind, progressive relaxation was not a method by which something is done *to* a person. Rather, it is a method by which the individual learns to control his or her own body. Jacobson, therefore, rejected the use of suggestion and of various biofeedback instruments and conditioning techniques that may induce relaxation during a training session. Empirical evaluations of most elements of the two progressive relaxation techniques have not yet been done. Thus, although many studies have compared progressive relaxation with a number of hypnotic, cognitive, and combined somatic-cognitive techniques, no one has dismantled the progressive relaxation technique Jacobson's or modified versions, in order to study the exact contribution of suggestion or cognitive interventions to the modified progressive relaxation technique, or of teaching one muscle at a time. The evidence reviewed above, however, does lead us to hypothesize that Jacobson's original technique would be relatively more effective in producing lasting somatic changes, whereas the revised technique might be more effective in producing cognitive changes or even short-term somatic changes. If these hypotheses are borne out, we predict that for many applications in behavioral medicine Jacobson's original technique will be found to be preferable. This will be especially true for those disorders which cannot be assessed by asking the patient how he or she feels but must be evaluated

210   PAUL M. LEHRER, ROBERT L. WOOLFOLK, AND NINA GOLDMAN

physiologically (e.g., hypertension and various cardiac arrythmias, where the patient may sometimes even feel worse when the problem is controlled than when it is not).

In the "big picture" of therapy, of course, the distinctions between the two techniques may be overshadowed by such overriding issues as whether relaxation therapy is even *relevant* for the individual. We have extensively discussed this issue elsewhere (Woolfolk & Lehrer, 1984b), but we reemphasize here that we see relaxation training as a specific method for overcoming definable problems and not as a panacea nor as a way of life. Nevertheless, we believe that the various approaches to the progressive relaxation technique are sufficiently different, both in practice and in philosophy, that we would do well to evaluate these differences in a rigorous fashion.

ACKNOWLEDGMENTS

The authors are indebted to John Atthowe for his helpful suggestions in the section about hypnosis.

REFERENCES

ANDREYCHUK, T., & SKRIVER, C. (1975). Hypnosis and biofeedback in the treatment of migraine headache. *International Journal of Clinical and Experimental Hypnosis, 23.* 172–183.

BARBER, T. X. (1984). Hypnosis, deep relaxation, and active relaxation: Data, theory, and clinical applications. In R. L. WOOLFOLK & P. M. LEHRER (Eds.), *Principles and practice of stress management.* New York: Guilford.

BARBER, T. X., SPANOS, N. P., & CHEVES, J. F. (1974). *Hypnosis, imagination, and human potentialities.* New York: Pergamon.

BECK, A. T. (1976). Cognitive therapy and the emotional disorders. New York: International Universities Press.

BECK, A. T. (1984). Cognitive approaches. In R. L. WOOLFOLK & P. M. LEHRER (Eds.), Principles and practice of stress management. New York: Guilford.

BECK, A. T., RUSH, A. J., SHAW, B. F., & EMERY, G. (1979). *Cognitive therapy of depression.* New York: Guilford.

BENNICK, C. D., HOLST, L. L., & BENTHEM, T. A. (1982). The effects of EMG biofeedback and relaxation training on primary dysmenorrhea. *Journal of Behavioral Medicine, 5,* 329–341.

BENSON, H. (1975). *The relaxation response.* New York: Morrow.

BERNSTEIN, D. A., & BORKOVEC, T. D. (1973). *Progressive relaxation training: A manual for the helping professions.* Champaign, IL: Research Press.

BIRAN, M., & WILSON, G. T. (1981). Treatment of phobic disorders using cognitive and exposure methods: A self-efficacy analysis. *Journal of Consulting and Clinical Psychology, 49,* 886–899.

BLANCHARD, E. B., ANDRASIK, F., ARENA. J., AHLES, T. A., JURISH, S. E., PALLMEYER, T. P., BARRON, K. D., & RODICHOK, L. D. (1982). Biofeedback and relaxation training with three kinds of headache: Treatment effects and their prediction. *Journal of Consulting and Clinical Psychology, 50,* 562–575.

BONVALLET, M., DELL, P., & HIEBEL, G. (1954). Tonus sympathique et activité électrique corticale. *Electroencephlography and Clinical Neurophysiology, 6,* 119–144.

BORKOVEC, T. D., & HENNINGS, B. L. (1978). The role of physiological attention-focusing in the relaxation treatment of sleep disturbance, general tension, and specific stress reaction. *Behaviour Research and Therapy, 16,* 7–19.

BORKOVEC, T. D., GRAYSON, J. B., & COOPER, K. M. (1978). Treatment of general tension: Subjective and physiological effects of progressive relaxation. *Journal of Consulting and Clinical Psychology, 46,* 518–528.

BORKOVEC, T. D., JOHNSON, M. C., & BLOCK, D. L., (1984). Evaluating experimental designs in relaxation research. In R. L. WOOLFOLK & P. M. LEHRER (Eds.), *Principles and practice of stress management.* New York: Guilford.

BORKOVEC, T. D., KALOUPEK, D. G., & SLAMA, K. (1975). The facilitative effect of muscle tension-release in the relaxation treatment of sleep disturbance. *Behavior Therapy, 6,* 301–309.

BORKOVEC, T. D., & SIDES, K. (1979). Critical procedural variables related to the physiological effects of progressive relaxation: A review. *Behaviour Research and Therapy, 17,* 119–126.

CAMPBELL, D., SANDERSON, R. E., & LAVERTY, S. G. (1964). Characteristics of a conditioned response in human subjects during extinction trials following a single traumatic conditioning trial. *Journal of Abnormal and Social Psychology, 68,* 627–639.

CANTER, A., KONDO, C. Y., & KNOTT, S. R. (1975). A comparison of EMG biofeedback and progressive muscle relaxation in anxiety neurotics. *British Journal of Psychiatry, 127,* 470–477.

CARRINGTON, P., COLLINGS, G. H., JR., BENSON, H., ROBINSON, H., WOOD, L. W., LEHRER, P. M., WOOLFOLK, R. L., & COLE, J. W. (1980). The use of relaxation-meditation techniques for the management of stress in a working population. *Journal of Occupational Medicine, 22,* 221–231.

CLARKE, J. C., & JACKSON, J. A. (1983). *Hypnosis and behavior therapy: The treatment of anxiety and phobias.* New York: Springer.

COOKE, G. (1968). Evaluation of the efficacy of the components of reciprocal inhibition psychotherapy. *Journal of Abnormal Psychology, 73,* 464–467.

DALY, E. J., DONN, P. A., GALLIHER, M. J., & Zimmerman, J. S. (1983). Biofeedback applications to migraine and tension headaches: A double blinded outcome study. *Biofeedback and Self-Regulation, 8,* 135–152.

DAVIDSON, R. J., & SCHWARTZ, C. E. (1976). Psychobiology of relaxation and related states. In D. MOSTOFSKY (Ed.), *Behavior modification and control of physiological activity.* Englewood Cliffs, NJ: Prentice Hall.

DAVISON, G. C. (1966). Anxiety under total curarization: Implications for the role of muscular relaxation in the desensitization of neurotic fears. *Journal of Nervous and Mental Disease, 143,* 443–448.

DAVISON, G. C. (1968). Systematic desensitization as a counterconditioning process. *Journal of Abnormal Psychology, 73,* 91–99.

DAVISON, G. C., & WILSON, G. T. (1972). Critique of "Desensitization: Social and cognitive factors underlying the effectiveness of Wolpe's procedure." *Psychological Bulletin, 78,* 28–31.

DUMAS, R. A. (1980). Cognitive control in hypnosis and biofeedback. *International Journal of Clinical and Experimental Hypnosis, 28,* 58–63.

EDELMAN, R. I. (1970). Effects of progressive relaxation on autonomic processes. *Journal of Clinical Psychology, 26,* 421–425.

212 PAUL M. LEHRER, ROBERT L. WOOLFOLK, AND NINA GOLDMAN

EDMONSTON, W. E. (1981). *Hypnosis and relaxation: Modern verification of an old equation.* New York: Wiley.

ELLIS, A. (1962). *Reason and emotion in psychotherapy.* New York: Lyle Stuart.

ENGSTROM, D. R. (1976). Hypnotic susceptibility, EEG alpha, and self-regulation. In G. E. SCHWARTZ & D. SHAPIRO (Eds.), *Conciousness and self-regulation: Advances in research.* New York: Plenum Press, pp. 173–221.

FRANK, J. D. (1961). *Persuasion and healing.* New York: Shocken Books.

FRIEDMAN, H., & TAUB, H. A. (1977). The use of hypnosis and biofeedback procedures for essential hypertension. *International Journal of Clinical and Experimental Hypnosis, 27,* 335–347.

FRISCHHOLZ, E. J., & TRYON, W. W. (1980). Hypnotizability in relation to the ability to learn thermal biofeedback. *American Journal of Clinical Hypnosis, 23,* 53–56.

FUREDY, J. (1984a). Booers, beware of biofeedback boosting. *Contemporary Psychology, 29,* 524.

FUREDY, J. (1984b). Specific vs. placebo effects in scientific vs. snake oil medicine. *Contemporary Psychology, 29,* 599.

GELLHORN, E. (1957). *Autonomic imbalance and the hypothalamus.* Minneapolis: University of Minnesota Press.

GELLHORN, E. (1958). The physiological basis of neuromuscular relaxation. *Archives of Internal Medicine, 102,* 392–399.

GELLHORN, E., & LOOFBURROW, G. N. (1963). *Emotions and emotional disorders.* New York: Harper & Row.

GILBERT, G. S., PARKER, J. C., & CLAIRBORN, C. D. (1978). Differential mood changes in alcoholics as a function of anxiety management strategies. *Journal of Clinical Psychology, 34,* 229–232.

GOLDFRIED, M. R. (1979). Anxiety reduction through cognitive-behavioral intervention. In P. C. KENDALL & S. D. HOLON (Eds.), *Cognitive-behavioral interventions: Theory, research, and procedures.* New York: Academic Press, pp. 117–152.

GRIMM, L. G. (1980). The evidence for cue-controlled relaxation. *Behavior Therapy, 11,* 283–293.

HAYNES, S. N., GRIFFIN, P., MOONEY, D., & PARISE, M. (1975). Electromyographic biofeedback and relaxation instructions in the treatment of muscle contraction headaches. *Behavior Therapy, 6,* 672–678.

HESS, W. R. (1925). *On the relations between psychic and vegetative functions.* Zurich: Schwabe.

HOHMAN, G. W. (1966). Some effects of spinal cord lesions on experienced emotional feelings. *Psychophysiology, 3,* 143–156.

HOLROYD, K. A. (1979). Stress, coping, and the treatment of stress-related illness. In J. R. McNamara (Eds.), *Behavioral approaches to medicine: Application and analysis.* New York: Plenum Press.

HOLROYD, K. A., & ANDRASIK, F. (1982). Do the effects of cognitive therapy endure? A two-year follow-up of tension headache sufferers treated with cognitive therapy or biofeedback. *Cognitive Therapy and Research, 6,* 325–333.

HOLROYD, J. C., NUECHTERLEIN, K. N., SHAPIRO, D., & WARD, F. (1982). Individual differences in hypnotizability and effectiveness of hypnosis or biofeedback. *The International Journal of Clinical and Experimental Hypnosis, 30,* 45–65.

HOLSTEAD, B. N. (1978). Cue-controlled relaxation: An investigation of psychophysiological reactions to a stressor film (doctoral dissertation, University of Mississippi) *Dissertations Abstracts International,* 1978, *39,* 2987B. (University Microfilms No. 78-05,763)

INFANTINO, A. T., SWARTZMANN, L. C., KARLIN, R. A., LEHRER, P.M., McCANN, B., & HOCHRON, S. (1984). *Hypnotizability: Its relationship to outcome in the behavioral treatment of asthma.* Paper presented at the annual meeting of the Association for the Advancement of Behavior Therapy, Washington, DC.

JACOBSON, E. (1931). Electrophysiology of mental activities. *American Journal of Psychology*, 44, 677–694.

JACOBSON, E. (1934a). Electrical measurements concerning muscular contraction (tonus) and the cultivation of relaxation in man: Studies on arm flexors. *American Journal of Physiology*, 107, 230–248.

JACOBSON, E. (1934b). Electrical measurements concerning muscular contraction (tonus) and the cultivation of relaxation in man: Relaxation times of individuals. *American Journal of Physiology*, 108, 573–580.

JACOBSON, E. (1938). *Progressive relaxation*. Chicago: University of Chicago Press.

JACOBSON, E. (1964). *Anxiety and tension control: A physiologic approach*. Philadelphia: Lippincott.

JACOBSON, E. (1967). *Biology of emotions*. Springfield, IL: Charles C Thomas.

JACOBSON, E. (1970). *Modern treatment of tense patients*. Springfield, IL: Charles C Thomas.

JACOBSON, E. (1982). *The human mind*. Springfield, IL: Charles C Thomas.

JANSSEN, K. (1983). Differential effects of EMG-feedback vs. combined EMC-biofeedback and relaxation instructions in the treatment of tension headache. *Journal of Psychosomatic Research*, 27, 243–253.

JAREMKO, M. E. (1979). A component analysis of stress inoculation: Review and prospectus. *Cognitive Therapy and Research*, 3, 35–48.

KAPLAN, R. M., METZGER, G., & JABLECKI, C. (1983). Brief cognitive and relaxation training increases tolerance for a painful clinical electromyographic examination. *Psychosomatic Medicine*, 45, 155–162.

KAPPES, B. M. (1983). Sequence effects of relaxation training, EMG, and temperature biofeedback on anxiety, symptom report, and self-concept. *Journal of Clinical Psychology*, 39, 203–208.

KRAUT, R. E. (1982). Social presence, facial feedback, and emotion, *Journal of Personality and Social Psychology*, 42, 853–863.

KREMSDORF, R. B., KOCHANOWICZ, N. A., & COSTELL, S. (1981). Cognitive skills training versus EMG biofeedback in the treatment of tension headaches. *Biofeedback and Self-Regulation*, 6, 93–102.

LACEY, J. I. (1967). Somatic response patterning and stress: Some revisions of activation theory. In M. H. APPLEY & R. TRUMBULL (Eds.), *Psychological stress*. New York: Appleton Century Crofts.

LAIRD, J. D. (1974). Self-attribution of emotion: The effects of expressive behavior on the quality of emotional experience. *Journal of Personality and Social Psychology*, 29, 475–486.

LANG, P. J. (1971). The application of psychophysiological methods to the study of psychotherapy and behavior change. In A. E. BERGIN & S. L. GARFIELD (Eds.), *Handbook of psychotherapy and behavior change: An empirical analysis*. New York: Wiley

LANG, P J (1977). Imagery in therapy: An information processing analysis of fear. *Behavior Therapy*, 8, 862–886.

LANGOSCH, W., SEER, P., BRODNER, G., KALLINKE, D., KULICK, B., & HEIM, F. (1982). Behavior therapy with coronary heart disease patients: Results of a comparative study. *Journal of Psychosomatic Research*, 26, 475–484.

LANZETTA, J. CARTWRIGHT-SMITH, J., & KLECK, R. (1976). Effects of nonverbal dissimulation on emotional experience and autonomic arousal. *Journal of Personality and Social Psychology*, 33, 354–370.

LAZARUS, A. A. (1981). *The practice of multimodal therapy*. New York: McGraw-Hill.

LAZARUS, R. S. (1966). *Psychological stress and the coping process*. New York: McGraw-Hill.

LAZARUS, R. S. (1977). A cognitive analysis of biofeedback control. In G. E. SCHWARTZ & J. BEATTY (Eds.), *Biofeedback: Theory and research*. New York: Academic Press.

LEHRER, P. M. (1972). Psychophysiological effects of relaxation in a double blind analog of desensitization. *Behavior Therapy, 3,* 193–208.

LEHRER, P. M. (1978). Psychophysiological effects of progressive relaxation in anxiety neurotic patients and of progressive relaxation and alpha feedback in nonpatients. *Journal of Consulting and Clinical Psychology, 46,* 389–404.

LEHRER, P. M. (1982). How to relax and how not to relax: A re-evaluation of the work of Edmund Jacobson. *Behaviour Research and Therapy, 20,* 417–428.

LEHRER, P. M. (1983). Biofeedback boosters beware. *Contemporary Psychology, 28,* 824–825.

LEHRER, P. M. (1984a). Yes: A cautious (and limited) boost for biofeedback. *Contemporary Psychology, 29,* 524.

LEHRER, P. M. (1984b). Biofeedback: Not penicillin but not snake oil. *Contemporary Psychology, 29,* 599.

LEHRER, P. M. & WOOLFOLK, R. L. (1984). Are stress reduction techniques interchangeable, or do they have specific effects?: A review of the comparative empirical literature. In R. L. WOOLFOLK & P. M. LEHRER (Eds.), *Principles and practice of stress management.* New York: Guilford.

LEHRER, P. M., ATTHOWE, J., & WEBER, E. S. P. (1980). Effects of relaxation and autogenic training on anxiety and physiological measures, with some data on hypnotizability. In F. J. MCGUIGAN, W. SIME, & J. M. WALLACE (Eds.), *Stress and tension control.* New York: Plenum Press.

LEHRER, P. M. BATEY, D., WOOLFOLK, R. L., REMDE, A., & GARLICK, T. (1985). The effect of repeated tense-release cycles on EMG and self-report of muscle tension. Submitted for publication.

LEHRER, P. M., HOCHRON, S., MCCANN, B., SWARTZMAN, L., & REBA, P. (In press.) Relaxation decreases asthma in asthmatic subjects with large-airway constriction. *Journal of Psychosomatic Research.*

LOCKE, E. (1971). Is "behavior therapy" behavioristic? An analysis of Wolpe's psychotherapeutic methods. *Psychological Bulletin, 76,* 318–327.

LOMONT, J. F., & EDWARDS, J. E. (1967). The role of relaxation in systematic desensitization. *Behaviour Research and Therapy, 5,* 11–25.

LUTHE, W. (1969). *Autogenic therapy* (Vols. 1–6). New York: Grune & Stratton.

MCGUIGAN, F. J. (1978). Imagery and thinking: Covert functioning of the motor system. In G. E. SCHWARTZ & D. SHAPIRO (Eds.), *Consciousness and self-regulation: Advances in research and theory* (Vol. 2). New York: Plenum Press.

MCGUIGAN, F. J. (1984). Progressive relaxation: Origins, principles, and clinical applications. In R. L. WOOLFOLK & P. M. LEHRER (Eds.), *Principles and practice of stress management.* New York: Guilford.

MEICHENBAUM, D. (1972). Cognitive modification of test anxious college students. *Journal of Consulting and Clinical Psychology, 39,* 370–380.

MEICHENBAUM, D. (1977). *Cognitive behavior modification: An integrative approach.* New York: Plenum Press.

MEICHENBAUM, D., & CAMERON, R. (1973). *Stress inoculation: A skills training approach to anxiety management.* Unpublished manuscript, University of Waterloo.

MILLER, W. R., & DiPILATO, M. (1983). Treatment of nightmares via relaxation and desensitization: A controlled evaluation. *Journal of Consulting and Clinical Psychology, 6,* 870–877.

NEFF, D. F., BLANCHARD, E. B., & ANDRASIK, F. (1983). The relationship between capacity for absorption and chronic headache patients' response to relaxation and biofeedback treatment. *Biofeedback and Self-Regulation, 8,* 177–183.

NICASSIO, P. M., BOYLAN, M. B., & MCCABE, T. G. (1982). Progressive relaxation, EMG biofeedback, and biofeedback placebo in the treatment of sleep-onset insomnia. *British Journal of Medical Psychology, 55,* 159–166.

NORRIS, P. A., & FAHRION, S. L. (1984). Autogenic biofeedback in psychophysiological therapy and stress management. In R. L. WOOLFOLK & P. M. LEHRER (Eds.), *Principles and practice of stress management.* New York: Guilford.

NOVACO, R. W. (1975). *Anger control: The development and evaluation of an experimental treatment.* Lexington, MA: Heath.

ORNE, M. T. (1982). Perspectives in biofeedback: Ten years ago, today, and. . . . In L. WHITE & B. TURSKY, *Clinical biofeedback: Efficacy and mechanisms.* New York: Guilford, pp. 422–437.

OSBERG, J. W. (1981). The effectiveness of applied relaxation in the treatment of speech anxiety. *Behavior Therapy, 12,* 723–729.

PARKER, J. C., GILBERT, G. S., & THORESON, R. W. (1978). Reduction of autonomic arousal in alcoholics: A comparison of relaxation and meditation techniques. *Journal of Consulting and Clinical Psychology, 46,* 879–886.

PATEL, C. (1984). Yogic therapy. In R. L. WOOLFOLK & P. M. LEHRER (Eds.), *Principles and practice of stress management.* New York: Guilford.

PAUL, G. L. (1966). *Insight vs. desensitization in psychotherapy.* Stanford, CA: Stanford University Press.

PAUL, G. L. (1969a) Inhibition of physiological response to stressful imagery by relaxation training and hypnotically suggested relaxation. *Behaviour Research and Therapy, 7,* 249–256.

PAUL, G. L. (1969b) Physiological effects of relaxation training and hypnotic suggestion. *Journal of Abnormal Psychology, 74,* 425–437.

PEAL, R. J., HANDAL, P. J., & GILNER, F. H. (1981). A group desensitization procedure for the reduction of death anxiety. *Omega, 12,* 61–69.

PHILIPS, C. & HUNTER, M. (1981). The treatment of tension headache:—II. EMG "normality" and relaxation. *Behaviour Research and Therapy, 19,* 499–507.

POLLARD, G., & ASHTON, R. (1982). Heart rate decrease: A comparison of feedback modalities and biofeedback with other procedures. *Biological Psychology, 14,* 245–257.

PRAGER-DECKER, I. J. (1978). The relative efficacy of progressive muscle relaxation, EMG biofeedback and music for reducing stress arousal of internally versus externally controlled individuals (Doctoral dissertation, University of Maryland). *Dissertations Abstracts International, 1979, 39,* 3177B. (University Microfilms No. 79-00,924.

QUALLS, P. J., & SHEEHAN, P. W. (1979). Capacity for absorption and relaxation during electromyograph biofeedback and no-feedback conditions. *Journal of Abnormal Psychology, 88,* 652–662.

ROBERTS, A. H., SCHULER, J., BACON, J. G., ZIMMERMANN, R. L., & PATTERSON, R. (1975). Individual differences and autonomic control: Absorption, hypnotic susceptibility, and the unilateral control of skin temperature. *Journal of Abnormal Psychology, 84,* 272–279.

RUSSELL, R., SIPICH, J., & KNIPE, J. (1976). Progressive relaxation training: A procedural note. *Behavior Therapy, 7,* 566–568.

SCHANDLER, S. L. & DANA, E. R. (1983). Cognitive imagery and physiological feedback relaxation protocols applied to clinically tense young adults: A comparison of state, trait, and physiological effects. *Journal of Clinical Psychology, 39,* 672–680.

SHEEHAN, D. (1983). *The anxiety disease.* New York: Scribner.

SHERIDAN, C. L., VAUGHAN, K. S., WALLERSTEDT, M. J., & WARD, L. B. (1977, March). *Electromyographic biofeedback and progressive relaxation compared: Interactions with gender and type of dependent measure.* Paper presented at the annual meeting of the Biofeedback Society of America, Orlando, Florida.

SIME, W. (1982). Review of *Principles and practice of progressive relaxation* by E. JACOBSON & F. J. MCGUIGAN. *Stress and Pain Manager Newsletter, 3,* 1,3–4.

SIME, W. E., & DeGOOD, D. E. (1977). Effect of EMG biofeedback and progressive muscle relaxation training on awareness of frontalis muscle tension. *Psychophysiology, 14,* 522–530.

SNOW, W. G. (1977). The physiological and subjective effects of several brief relaxation training procedures. (Doctoral dissertation, York University, Canada, 1977). *Dissertations Abstracts International, 1984, 40,* 3458B.

STANTON, H. E. (1975). The treatment of insomnia through hypnosis and relaxation. *Terpnos Logos, 3,* 4–8.

STOUT, C. C., THORNTON, B., & RUSSELL, H. L. (1980). Effects of relaxation training on students' persistence and academic performance. *Psychological Reports, 47,* 189–190.

SUINN, R. M. (1975). The cardiac stress management program for Type A patients. *Cardiac Rehabilitation, 5,* 13–15.

SUZUKI, S. (1979). *Zen mind, beginner's mind.* New York: Weatherhill.

TELLEGEN, A., & ATKINSON, G. (1974). Openness to absorbing and self-altering experience ("absorption"), a trait related to hypnotic susceptibility. *Journal of Abnormal Psychology, 83,* 268–277.

TOMKINS, S. S. (1970). Affect as the primary motivational system. In M. B. ARNOLD (Ed.), *Feelings and emotions.* New York: Academic Press.

TOWNSEND, R. E., HOUSE, J. F., & ADDARIO, D. (1975) A comparison of biofeedback-mediated relaxation and group therapy in the treatment of chronic anxiety. *American Journal of Psychiatry, 132,* 598–601.

TURNER, P. E. (1978). A psychophysiological assessment of selected relaxation strategies (Doctoral dissertation, University of Mississippi). *Dissertations Abstracts International, 1978, 39,* 1010B. (University Microfilms No. 78-24,063).

TURK, D. C., MEICHENBAUM, D. H., & GENEST, H. (1983) *Pain and behavioral medicine: A cognitive-behavioral perspective.* New York: Guilford.

TYRER, P. (1976). *The role of bodily feelings in anxiety.* London: Oxford University Press.

VAN HASSEL, J. H., BLOOM, L. J., & GONZALEZ, A. M. (1982). Anxiety management with schizophrenic outpatients. *Journal of Clinical Psychology, 38,* 280–284.

WALSH, P., DALE, A., & ANDERSON, D. E. (1977). Comparison of biofeedback of pulse wave velocity and progressive relaxation in essential hypertensives. *Perceptual and Motor Skills, 44,* 839–843.

WHITE, L., & TURSKY, B. (1982). *Clinical biofeedback: Efficacy and mechanisms.* New York: Guilford.

WHITE, P. D., GILNER, F. H., HANDAL, P. J., & NAPOLI, J. G. (1983). A behavioral intervention for death anxiety in nurses. *Omega, 14,* 33–41.

WILKINS, W. (1971). Desensitization: Social and cognitive factors underlying the effectiveness of Wolpe's procedure. *Psychological Bulletin, 76,* 311–327.

WILSON, V. E., & BIRD, E. (1981). Effects of relaxation and/or biofeedback training upon hip flexion in gymnasts. *Biofeedback and Self-Regulation, 6,* 25–34.

WOLPE, J. (1958). *Psychotherapy by reciprocal inhibition.* Stanford, CA: Stanford University Press.

WOLPE, J., & LAZARUS, A. A. (1966). *Behavior therapy techniques.* New York: Pergamon.

WOOLFOLK, R. L., & LEHRER, P. M. (1984a). Clinical stress reduction: An overview. In R. L. WOOLFOLK & P. M. LEHRER (Eds.), *Principles and practice of stress management.* New York: Guilford.

WOOLFOLK, R. L., & LEHRER, P. M. (1984b). Clinical applications. In R. L. WOOLFOLK & P. M. LEHRER (Eds.), *Principles and practice of stress management.* New York: Guilford.

WOOLFOLK, R. L., & McNULTY, T. F. (1983). Treatment of insomnia: A component analysis. *Journal of Consulting and Clinical Psychology, 51,* 495–503.

Author Index

Abrams, S., 125
Ach, N., 2
Adair, J. R., 58
Adams, J. E., 88, 94
Addario, D., 190
Ader, R., 97, 98
Akaike, A., 94
Akil, H., 88, 89, 90, 93
Alexander, F., 131
Allport, D. A., 13, 14
Amir, S., 89, 90, 92
Amit, Z., 89, 90, 92
Anderson, D. E., 194, 195
Andrasik, F., 195, 199
Andreychuk, T., 208
Anisman, H., 100
Antonis, B., 13, 14
Antrobus, J. S., 31
Antrobus, T. S., 30, 42
Appleton, J., 21
Archer, R. L., 130
Ascough, J. C., 146
Ashton, R., 194
Atkinson, G., 157, 208
Atthowe, J., 208
Azami, J., 94

Baars, B., 16
Bacon, J. G., 208
Bain, A., 19, 24
Baker, J., 138
Ball, G., 153
Barber, T. X., 205, 206
Barchas, J. D., 89, 90
Bardo, M. T., 97
Barrett, J., 33
Barrios, B. A., 109
Bartoshuk, A. K., 38

Basbaum, A. I., 88, 89, 94
Basmajian, J. V., 43
Batey, D., 193
Battit, G., 74
Baum, W. M., 174
Baxter, R., 146
Beahrs, J. O., 149
Beck, A. T., 197, 199
Beck, E. C., 74
Bekesy, G. V., 119
Bellman, K., 4
Bennett, D. H., 148
Bennett, G. J., 88, 90
Bennick, C. D., 194
Benson, H., 185
Bentov, I., 80
Bering, E. A., 80
Berka, C., 67
Berman, J. S., 130
Berman, W. H., 140
Bernstein, D. A., 183, 192
Bernstein, G. L., 141
Bhatnagar, R. K., 97
Binder, R., 128
Biran, M., 199
Birch, L., 21
Bird, E., 194
Birren, J., 67, 77
Birzis, L., 61
Bissell, L. E., 69
Black, A. H., 68
Blackburn, R., 126
Blanchard, E., 148, 156, 195
Bleecker, E. R., 147, 157
Block, D. L., 207
Bloom, F. E., 93
Bloom, L. J., 201
Bloomfield, H. H., 44, 45

Blouin, D., 158
Bock, J. C., 142, 144
Boden, M., 6
Bodnar, R. J., 89, 90, 92, 100
Bonvallet, M., 58, 197
Boon, C., 130
Borkovec, T. D., 183, 188, 189, 190, 192, 193, 204–205, 207
Botwinick, J., 67
Boylan, M. B., 194
Branch, B. J., 97
Brener, J., 68, 138–139, 140, 141, 142, 153, 156
Brown, B. B., 30
Brown, H. O., 21
Brucker, B. S., 147, 152, 157
Buchsbaum, M., 69
Buck, R. W., 127
Burgess, A. W., 128
Burgess, I. S., 174
Buss, A., 116

Cacioppo, J. T., 49, 50, 63, 64, 68
Cain, M. P., 44
Callaway, E., 67, 69
Cameron, R., 198
Campbell, D., 196
Campos, J., 67
Cannon, J. T., 89, 09, 92, 93
Cannon, W., 55, 56, 57
Canter, A., 194
Cardon, P., 67
Carmon, A., 74
Carrington, P., 190

217

Cartwright-Smith, J., 27, 197
Castiglioni, A. J., 88
Chan, B., 89, 90
Chance, W. T., 89, 90, 92, 93, 94
Chang, K.-J., 92
Chaves, J. F., 206
Chernigovsky, V. N., 163, 166, 167
Chesher, G. B., 89, 90
Chew, C., 122
Choiniere, M., 88
Chudler, E. H., 92
Clairborn, C. D., 190
Clanton, C. H., 89
Clarke, J. C., 205
Clarke, M. A., 142, 144
Cleckley, H., 125
Clemens, W. J., 138, 146
Cobb, S., 109, 118
Cobelli, D. A., 92, 94
Cohen, B. H., **19**, 24, 34, 38, 50
Cohen, M. J., 146
Cole, R. A., 48
Coleman, T. G., 173
Coleridge, H. M., 59
Coleridge, J. C. G., 59
Conrad, M., 131
Cooke, G., 201
Coon, D. J., 90
Cooper, K. M., 190
Corner, M. A., 80
Costell, S., 199
Cox, D. J., 140
Crane, L. A., 94
Crowley, W. R., 100
Crowne, D. P., 116, 126
Curzon, G., 94
Cuthbert, B. N., 33–34

Dale, A., 194, 195
Daly, E. J., 194
D'Amour, F. E., 90
Dana, E. R., 201
D'Andrade, R., 16
Davidson, L. A., 56
Davidson, R. J., 116, 126, 184–185, 197
Davies, M., 126

Davison, G. C., 196, 197, 198, 201
Deckert, G. H., 30
DeDoux, J. E., 77
DeGood, D. E., 189
Delfini, L., 67
Delius, W., 172
Dell, P., 58, 197
Dennis, S. G., 88, 90
Denny-Brown, D., 10
Derouesne, J., 9
Dewey, W. L., 93
Diamond, B., 67
Diamond, J., 166nl
DiCara, L. V., 68
Diliberto, E. J., Jr., 92
Dince, W. M., 142
DiPilato, M., 200
Ditto, W. B., 147
Donchin, E., 74
Donn, P. A., 194
Doxey, N., 142, 144
Dumas, R. A., 208
Duncan, J., 13
Dunlap, K., 21
Dustman, R. E., 74
Dworkin, B. R., **163**, 174, 179, 181
Dyk, R. B., 56

Edelman, R. I., 190
Edmonston, W. E., 203, 204
Edmundson, E. D., 148
Edwards, J. E., 201
Egger, M. D., 152
Ehrlichman, H., 33
Ekman, P., 19
Elliot, R., 67
Ellis, A., 197
Ells, J. G., 13
Ellsworth, P., 19
Emery, G., 199
Engel, B. T., 146, 147, 157
Engstrom, D. R., 208
Eriksen, C. W., 126
Evarts, E. V., 21

Fahrion, S. L., 207
Farnell, S. K., 57
Farrell, T., 141

Fattuson, H. F., 56
Fechner, G., 25
Fenigstein, A., 116
Festinger, L., 118
Fields, H. L., 88, 94
Folkman, S., 132
Forgy, C., 4
Forster, A., 59
Fowles, D. C., 121, 125
Frank, J., 130, 204
Freud, S., 120, 131, 132
Fridlund, A. J., 19, 50
Friedman, H., 206
Friesen, W., 19
Frischholz, E. J., 208
Furedy, J. J., 137, 195
Fuster, J. M., 10

Gadzhiev, 9
Gahery, Y., 59
Galambos, R., 75, 77
Galliher, M. J., 194
Garlick, T., 193
Gazzaniga, M. A., 149, 150
Gebhart, G. F., 97
Geisser, S., 31
Gellhorn, E., 196, 197
Genest, H., 199
Gershon, E., 146
Gibson, J. J., 120
Giesler, G. J., 88, 90
Gilbert, G. S., 189, 190
Gilmore, J. P., 168n2
Gilner, F. H., 200, 201
Glass, D., 116
Glass, G. V., 130
Glick, S., 94
Glusman, M., 90
Goldband, S., 141
Goldfried, M. R., 199
Goldman, Nina, **183**
Goldstein, K., 9
Goleman, D., 116
Gombus, G. M., 74
Gonzales, A. M., 201
Goodell, J., 108
Goodenough, D. R., 56
Goodman, L. S., 21
Gough, H. G., 125
Gowen, A., 141, 142, 146, 147

Author Index

Graf, V., 67
Graham, K. R., 30
Granger, H., 169, 170, 171, 173, 174
Gray, J., 120–121, 129
Grayson, J. B., 190
Greene, W. A., 146
Greenhouse, S. W., 31
Greenwald, A. G., 5
Griffen, P., 190
Grimm, L. G., 191
Grudin, J., 16
Guillemin, R., 91, 92, 93
Guyton, A. C., 169, 170, 171, 173

Hagbarth, K. E., 172
Handal, P. J., 200, 201
Hansen, J. C., 76
Hardyck, C. D., 47
Hare, R. D., 63, 125
Hasher, L., 151
Hayes, R. L., 89, 90, 94
Haynes, S. N., 190
Hazum, E., 92
Hebb, D. O., 23, 24
Hefferline, R. F., 23
Helson, H., 11
Hennings, B. L., 204–205
Henriken, O., 171
Hentall, I. D., 94
Hernandez-Peon, R., 119
Herrnstein, R. J., 174
Herz, A., 92
Hess, W. R., 196
Hiebel, G., 58, 197
Hilgard, E. R., 149
Hillyard, S. A., 75, 76
Hinton, G., 16
Hirst, W., 13
Hobbs, W., 140
Hochron, S., 202
Hoffer, J. L., 59
Hohmann, G. W., 197
Hökfelt, T., 89
Holmes, D. S., 148
Holmes, T., 109, 110
Holmstrom, L. L., 128
Holroyd, B. N., 208
Holroyd, J. C., 206
Holroyd, K. A., 195, 199

Holst, L. L., 194
Holstead, B. N., 191
Holt, V., 92
Hongell, A., 172
Hoover, C. W., **107**
Horowitz, M. J., 130
Hosobuchi, Y., 88
House, J. F., 190
Howard, J. L., 39
Hughes, J., 89
Huli, C. L., 119, 155
Humphrey, D. R., 60
Hunter, M., 201
Hutcheson, J. S., 59
Hutchinson, P., 158
Hutson, P. H., 94

Ikemi, Y., 61
Iker, H., 110
Imiolo, D., 141
Inanaga, K., 61
Infantino, A. T., 208
Ingvar, D. H., 61, 69
Isenhart, R., 61
Izard, C. E., 19, 50

Jablecki, C., 201
Jackson, J. A., 205
Jackson, R. L., 90
Jacobson, E., 22, 23, 44, 45, 52, 183, 184, 185, 186, 187, 188, 189, 190, 191, 192, 193, 194, 195, 196, 197, 202, 203, 204, 205, 206, 207, 209
Jaffe, D. T., 44
James, W., 2, 15, 25, 31, 39, 40, 55, 56, 57, 80
Janssen, K., 194
Jaremko, M. E., 198
Jarrell, M. P., 158
Johnson, M. C., 207
Johnson, P. C., 174, 175
Jonas, C., 34
Jones, H. E., 126
Jourard, S. M., 120, 130
Joy, M. D., 58
Judy, W. V., 57
Jutai, J. W., 74

Kagan, J., 63
Kahneman, D., 2, 5

Kaiser, D. N., 67, 68
Kaloupek, D. G., 193
Kamin, L. J., 152
Kaplan, R. M., 201
Kappes, B. M., 195
Karp, S. A., 56
Katkin, E. S., 138, 141
Keefe, F. J., 140
Keele, S. W., 13, 16
Kelley, H. H., 120
Kelly, B., 146
Kelly, D. D., 90
Kennedy, J. L., 80
Kibler, G., 30
Kilpatrick D. G., 129
Kimmel, H. D., 146, 147
Kissen, D. M., 126
Kleck, R. E., 127, 197
Klein, M. V., 96
Klivington, K. A., 77
Knipe, J., 190
Knott, S. R., 194
Kobasa, S., 109
Koch, E., 57
Kochanowicz, N. A., 199
Kokka, N., 97
Komisaruk, B. R., 100
Kondo, C. Y., 194
Konorski, J., 120
Krantz, D., 116
Krausz, H. I., 75
Kraut, R. E., 197
Kremsdorf, R. B., 199
Krynock, G. M., 89, 93
Kubiak, E. W., 148
Kunze, D. L., 163
Kuramoto, S., 61

Lacey, B. C., 39, 60, 63, 67
Lacey, J. I., 39, 60, 63, 67, 196, 197
Lacroix, J. M., **137**, 140, 141, 142, 143, 144, 145, 146, 147, 148, 153, 156, 157
Laird, J. D., 127, 197
Lang, P. J., 33–34, 185
Lange, A. F., 30
Langosch, W., 200
Lanzetta, J. T., 127, 197

AUTHOR INDEX

Laskey, W., 172
Laudenslager, M. L., 100
Laverty, S. G., 196
Lavis, S., 144
Layne, R., 67, 69
Lazarus, A. A., 183, 185, 186, 190
Lazarus, R. S., 56, 120, 132, 195, 198
LeDoux, J. E., 149, 150
Lee, W., 16
Lehrer, P. M., **183**, 185, 186, 188, 189, 193, 194, 195, 199, 202, 204, 205, 206, 207, 208, 210
Lenox, J. R., 20
LeShan, L. L., 110
Leuba, C., 21
Levene, H. I., 146
Levenson, R. W., 127, 146–147
Levy, S. M., 98
Lewis, J. W., **87**, 88, 89, 90, 91, 92, 93, 94, 95, 96, 98, 99
Lewis, K., 13
Lhermitte, F., 9
Libby, W. L., Jr., 39, 63
Liebeskind, J. C., **87**, 88, 89, 90, 91, 92, 93, 94, 95, 96
Light, K. C., 59
Linchitz, R., 88
Liu, S. H., 97
Livingston, R. B., 87
Llewelyn, M. B., 94
Locke, E., 198
Lomont, J. F., 201
Long, J., 16
Loofbourrow, G. N., 196
Lovaas, K. M., 96
Lowenstein, W. R., 166
Luria, A. R., 8, 9, 28
Luthe, W., 207
Lynn, M., 10

MacLenna, A. J., 92
Madden, J., 90, 93
Maier, S. F., 90, 99
Maixner, W., 93
Malmejac, J., 57

Mandler, G., 16
Mannard, A., 172
Manning, J. W., 58
Marks, D. F., 33
Marley, N. J., 89
Marlin, R. G., 141, 153
Marlowe, D., 116, 126
Marsden, D. C., 10
Mason, K. A., 98
Matin, E., 30
Matin, L., 30
Matus, I., 153
Maudsley, H., 19
Mayer, D. J., 88, 89, 90, 92, 94
McCabe, T. S., 194
McCann, B., 202
McCanne, T. R., 57, 63, 67
McCarthy, 9
McClelland, J. L., 3
McCubbin, J. A., 59
McDermott, J., 4
McFarland, D. J., 163, 174, 179
McFie, J., 9
McGivern, R. F., 100
McGuigan, F. J., 21, 23, 28, 48, 50, 184, 194, 196
McLean, J. P., 11
McLeod, P. D., 13, 16
McNulty, T. F., 200
McPeek, B., 74
Meichenbaum, D. H., 140, 197, 198, 199
Melton, A. W., 120
Melzack, R., 88, 90, 119
Mendelson, M., 166
Metzger, G., 201
Miczek, K. A., 100
Mifflin, S. W., 163
Millan, M. J., 92, 93
Miller, N. E., 142, 147, 152, 157, 174, 181
Miller, T. I., 130
Miller, W. R., 200
Milner, B., 9
Mirgorodsky, V. N., 172
Monguillot, J. E., 158
Mooney, D., 190
Mordkoff, A. M., 56

Morell, M. A., 141
Morff, R. J., 174
Moss, H., 63
Mountcastle, V., 163
Murray, E. N., 138
Mycielska, K., 2, 12

Nakazawa, T., 94
Napoli, J. G., 201
Naranjo, C., 44
Neff, D. F., 195, 208
Neisser, U., 13, 120
Nelson, H., 9
Nelson, L. R., **87**, 97, 98
Newlon, P. G., 89, 90
Newsome, H. H., 92
Nicassio, P. M., 194
Nicholson, R. A., 130
Nisbett, R. E., 118, 149
Nolan, J. M., 64
Norman, D. A., **1**, 2, 3, 12, 27–28
Norris, P. A., 207
Notarius, C. I., 127
Novaco, R. W., 199
Neuchterlein, K. N., 206

Obrist, P. A., 39, 59, 68, 147
Obrist, W. D., 69
Offutt, C., 157
O'Halloran, J. M., 61
O'Heeron, R. C., 130
O'Keefe, J., 89
Oleson, T. D., 89
Oliveras, J. L., 88
Orne, M. T., 121, 125
Ornstein, R. E., 44
Osberg, J. W., 200

Pappas, B., 67, 77
Parise, M., 190
Parker, J. C., 189, 190
Patel, 190n2
Patrick, R. L., 90
Patterson, R., 208
Paul, G. L., 183, 186, 206
Pavlov, I., 119
Peal, R. J., 200
Pearce, D., 30
Pearce, J. W., 60

Author Index

Pearson, J. A., 146
Pedigo, N. W., 93
Pennebaker, J. W., **107**, 108, 109, 110, 116, 122, 130, 149
Penner, E. R., 95
Perera, T. B., 23
Persson, B., 59
Pert, A., 89
Peters, L. J., 98
Peterson, L. H., 60
Petrides, 9
Petrinovich, L. F., 47
Petty, R. E., 49, 50, 64, 68
Pew, R. W., 8
Philips, C., 201
Phillips, S., 67
Picton, T. W., 75, 76
Pillsbury, W. B., 15, 19, 25
Pollard, G., 194
Polosa, C., 172
Ponte, JU., 61
Pope, K. S., 40, 41
Posner, M. I., 2, 13
Prager-Decker, I. J., 195
Prieto, G. J., 94
Przewlocki, R., 92
Purves, M. J., 61, 74

Qualls, P. J., 153, 157, 208
Quy, R. J., 148

Rahe, R., 109, 110
Randich, A., 93
Reason, J. T., 2, 12
Reba, P., 202
Reeves, J. L., 64
Remde, A., 193
Renthem, T. A., 194
Rescorla, R. A., 120
Resick, P. A., 129
Reynolds, D. V., 88
Reynolds, P., 13, 14
Ribot, T. A., 19, 26
Richardson, D. D., 88
Riley, D. M., 137
Risse, 149
Roberts, A. H., 208
Roberts, H. H. T., 94

Roberts, L. E., 141, 147, 148, 153, 156, 158
Robbins, T. W., 10
Roddie, I. C., 172
Rodier, W. I., III, 28
Rodriguez-Sierra, J. F., 100
Rogers, M. C., 74
Rosecrans, J. A., 89, 90, 93
Rosenthal, F., 59
Ross, A., 138, 141
Ross, N., 125
Rossier, J., 93
Rothe, C. F., 171
Rubenstein, C., 110, 112, 115
Rudy, T. A., 89
Ruemlhart, D. E., 3, 16
Rush, A. J., 199
Russell, H. L., 194
Russell, R., 190
Rylander, G., 9, 10

Saari, M., 67, 77
Sagawa, K., 165
Sahaikian, B., 10
Sanderson, R. E., 196
Sandman, C. A., **55**, 56, 57, 61, 63, 64, 65, 67, 68, 69, 71, 73, 74, 76, 77, 81
Satinoff, E., 165
Satoh, M., 94
Schad, H., 170, 172
Schandler, S. L., 201
Scheier, M., 116
Schenkenberg, T., 74
Schmale, A. H., 110
Schmidt, R. A., 8
Schneider, W., 1, 2, 40, 151
Schober, R., 147
Schuler, J., 208
Schwartz, G. E., 116, 126, 146, 147, 184–185, 197
Schwartz, J. C., 94
Scott, R. E., 148
Seligman, E. P., 100
Seller, H., 170, 172
Selye, H., 91, 119, 128

Shallice, T., **1**, 9, 13, 27–28
Shapiro, D., 64, 146, 147, 206
Shattock, R. J., 146
Shavit, Y., **87**, 98, 99, 100
Shaw, B. F., 199
Shaw, W. A., 22
Sheehan, D., 185nl
Sheehan, P. W., 153, 157, 208
Shepherd, J. T., 172, 176
Sheridan, C. L., 190
Sherman, J. E., 91, 92
Shiffrin, R. M., 1, 2, 40, 151
Shriver, C., 208
Shulman, A. G., 5
Shulman, G. L., 11
Shuster, L., 100
Sibby, R., 174
Sides, K., 188, 189
Signoret, J.-L., 9
Silver, R. L., 130
Sime, W., 189, 193
Singer, J. L., 30, 31, 40, 41, 42
Sipich, J., 190
Sipprelle, C. N., 146
Skalak, R., 166
Skinner, B. F., 120
Sklar, L. S., 100
Skok, V. I., 172
Slama, K., 193
Smith, D. L., 90
Smith, M. L., 130
Smith, M. O., 19
Smith, R. E., 60
Smith, S. M., 21
Snow, W. G., 186
Snyder, M., 116
Sotaniemi, K. A., 69
Spanos, N. P., 206
Speisman, J. C., 56
Spelke, E., 13
Spence, K. W., 119
Sperry, R. W., 20, 21
Stapleton, J. M., 88
Steger, J. A., 11
Steiner, S. S., 90, 142
Stern, M., 146

Stilson, D. W., 153
Stone, T. W., 59
Stones, M. H., 130
Stout, C. C., 194
Stoy, E. G., 33
Striker, 31
Surwit, R. S., 140
Sutterer, J. R., 39
Suzuki, S., 190n2
Svensson, T. H., 59
Swartzman, L., 202

Tachibana, S., 61
Takagi, G., 94
Taub, H. A., 206
Taylor, A. N., 97
Taylor, J., 126
Tellegen, A., 157, 208
Terman, G. W., **87**, 91, 92, 93, 94, 95, 96
Terrace, H. S., 120
Thompson, F. J., 60
Thompson, L. W., 67
Thompson, M. L., 100
Thoren, P., 59
Thoreson, R. W., 189
Thornton, B., 194
Todd, D., 74
Toman, J. E. P., 21
Tomkins, S. S., 197
Torda, C., 97
Tordoff, M. G., 92
Totten, E., 23
Tournade, A., 57
Townsend, R. E., 190
Trasler, G., 125
Treisman, A. M., 2, 11
Tricklebank, M. D., 94, 96
Tryon, W. W., 208

Turk, D. C., 140, 199
Turner, P. E., 186
Tursky, B., 146, 147, 195
Twombly, D. A., 89
Tyrer, P., 185nl

Urca, G., 89, 90

Valins, S., 118
Van Hassel, J. H., 201
Van Twyver, H. B., 146, 147
Vaughan, K. S., 190
Veronen, L. J., 129
Vigier, D., 59
Visintainer, M. A., 100
Viveros, O. H., 92
Volpicelli, J. R., 100

Waid, W. M., 121, 125
Wallerstein, H., 38
Walsh, K. W., 8, 9, 10
Walker, B. B., 63, 64, 67, 68, 69, 71, 73, 77, 81
Walker, J. M., 81
Wallerstedt, M. J., 190
Wallin, B. G., 172
Walsh, P., 194, 195
Walter, M., 89
Ward, F., 206
Ward, L. B., 190
Washburn, M. F., 19, 22
Watkins, L. R., 88, 90, 92, 94
Watson, S. J., 89, 92
Weardon, J. H., 174
Webb, R. A., 39
Weber, E. S. P., 208
Weimer, W. B., 20

Weinberg, V. E., 89
Weinberger, D. A., 126
White, A. C., 89, 93
White, L., 195
White, P. D., 201
White, T. W., 148
Widdicomb, J. G., 163
Wilkins, W., 198
Williams, R. J., 141
Williamson, D. A., 158
Willison, J. R., 77
Wilson, S. P., 92
Wilson, D. H., 149
Wilson, D. T., 149
Wilson, G. T., 198, 199
Wilson, V. E., 194
Winstead, C. L., JR., 23
Wirth, H. G., 146
Wise, J. A., 141
Witkin, H. A., 56
Wolff, H. G., 108
Wolpe, J., 183, 186, 198
Wood, A., 144
Woody, C. D., 176
Woolfolk, R. L., **185**, 193, 194, 199, 200–204, 205, 206, 207, 210

Yaksh, T. L., 89
Yanagisawa, N., 10
Yeung, J. C., 89
Young, L. D., 148
Young, M., 48
Young, R. F., 88

Zacks, R. T., 151
Zimmerman, J. S., 194
Zimmerman, R. L., 208
Zorman, G., 94

Subject Index

Action, 1–2
Activation values, 6
Adrenal hormones, 92
Affect
    consciousness and, 56–57
    inhibition and, 126–127
    progressive relaxation and, 195–202
Alcohol exposure, 97–98
Amphetamines, 10
Anxiety, 196
Attention, 1–18
    action selection and, 13
    cardiovascular system and, 63–64
    conscious control and, 14–16
    modulating role of, 10–12
    motor theories of, 24–26
    motor theory of voluntary thinking
        and, 38–40, 42
    neuropsychological evidence and, 8–
        10
    perception and, 1
    tasks and, 2–3, 13–14
    theory and, 3–7
Auditory evoked potentials, 74–77
Autogenic training, 207
Automaticity
    conscious control and, 14–15
    definitions of, 1–2
    theory and, 3
Awareness, 1–2. *See also* Attention

Baroreceptor system
    blood pressure and, 164–165
    cardiovascular physiology and, 57–63
Basal ganglia, 10
Behavior
    brain and, 159–151
    cardiovascular system and, 63–67
    learning theory and, 139

Biofeedback, 137–162
    learning theory and, 138–147
    motor theory of voluntary thinking
        and, 47–48
    progressive relaxation and, 194–195
    questions in, 137–138
    two-process theory in, 152–158
    verbal interface, 147–152
See also Feedback
Biosyntonic therapy, 64–67
Blood, 173–176
Blood pressure
    baroreceptor system and, 59, 60, 164–
        165
    biofeedback and, 147
    kidney and, 169–170
    spinal anesthesia and, 171
Brain
    baroreceptor system and, 58–59
    behavior and, 150–151
    cardiovascular system and, 69–80
    contention scheduling and, 10
    frontal lobe lesions, 9
    information-processing systems in,
        149
    motor theories and, 21
    motor theory of voluntary thinking
        and, 26, 40
    physiological regulation and, 163
    prefrontal lesions, 8–9
    reality experience and, 55–56
    sensory information and, 87
Bulimia, 109

Cardiac afferent influences, 55–85
Cardiac output
    regulation factors in, 169, 174
    tonic sympathetic control of, 171
    See also Heart

223

SUBJECT INDEX

Cardiovascular system
  baroreceptor physiology and, 57–63
  behavior and, 63–67
  brain and, 69–80
  consciousness and, 67–68
  See also Heart
Central nervous system
  interoceptors and, 176–178
  physiological regulation and, 173
  sensory perception and, 87
  See also Brain; Spinal cord
Cerebral blood flow, 61
Chemical regulation, 173–176
Child molestation. *See* Pedophilia
Cognition
  confiding and, 130–131
  consciousness and, 56–57
  inhibition and, 120
  learning theory and, 139
  motor theory of voluntary thinking
    and, 42–43
  progressive relaxation and, 184–185,
    195–202
Conditioned relaxation, 190–191
Confiding
  cognition and, 130–131
  inhibition and, 128–129
  trauma and, 118–129
Conflict resolution, 4, 5–6
Conscious control
  neuropsychology and, 8
  slips of action and, 12
  speed of activity and, 11
  supervisory attention system and, 14–16
Consciousness
  biofeedback and, 155
  cardiac afferent influences on, 55–85
  cardiovascular system and, 67–68
  cognition/emotion and, 56–57
  motor theory and, 20–21
Contention scheduling, 5–6
  action theory and, 3–5
  neuropsychology and, 8, 10
Creativity, 43
Curare studies
  motor theory, 21
  motor theory of voluntary thinking
    and, 21, 42
  progressive relaxation and, 196–197

Dopaminergic system, 10

Eating disorders, 109
Electroencephalography (EEG)
  heart/brain relationship, 69–74
  progressive relaxation and, 208
Electromyography (EMG)
  biofeedback and, 142–144, 147
  motor theories and, 22, 23
  motor theory of voluntary thinking
    and, 47–48, 49–52
  progressive relaxation and, 189, 193,
    208
Emotion. *See* Affect
Endocrine system, 91–93
Ergotrophic emotional system, 196
Error correction, 9. *See also* Slips of
  action
Evoked vascular responses, 74–77
Experience
  action and, 1–2
  reality and, 55
Eye. *See* Vision

Face, 50
Feedback
  confiding and, 118
  motor theories and, 21, 23
  motor theory of voluntary thinking
    and, 43–44
  See also Biofeedback
Feedforward processes, 153–155
Frontal lobe lesions, 9
Frontal syndrome, 9

Guilty knowledge test, 108, 121–124

Hand temperature data, 144–145
Heart
  cardiac output regulation, 169
  motor theory of voluntary thinking
    and, 39
  See also entries under Cardiac;
    Cardiovascular system.
Heart rate control, 141, 146–147
Horizontal thread
  action theory, 4
  model aspects of, 8
  supervisory attentional system, 6–7
Hypertension
  biofeedback and, 147
  See also Blood pressure
Hypnosis, 203–204, 205–209

SUBJECT INDEX 225

Ideo-motor acts, 2
Inhibition
  contention scheduling and, 5
  definition of, 119–120
  failure to confide as, 128–129
  personality considerations and, 124–127
  psychodynamic views of, 131–132
  psychotherapy and, 130
Interoceptive stimuli, 139–140
Interoceptors
  central nervous system and, 176–178
  physiological regulation and, 165–166, 167–168

Kidney, 169–170
Kinesthetic imagery, 22–23, 28

Language
  brain and, 150
  visual imagery and, 32
Learning, 163–182
Learning theory
  biofeedback and, 138–147, 152–158
  brain and, 149–150
  physiological regulation and, 176, 178

Meditation, 43–45
Migraine headache, 144–145
Motivation, 7
Motor systems, 139, 140
Motor theory
  attention and, 24–26
  cognition and, 22–24
  consciousness and, 20–21
Motor theory of voluntary thinking
  (MTVT), 19–54
  attention (spontaneous) and, 39–40
  attention (voluntary) and, 38–39
  central assertion of, 45–46
  defining of, 26–38
  motor theories and, 20–26
  research implications of, 46–52
  stream of thought regulation and, 40–45
Muscle. See entries under Motor

Naloxone, 89, 90
Natural relaxation, 41–43
Nervous system. See Brain; Central
  nervous system; Spinal cord

Neurotransmitters, 93–94
Nucleus raphe magnus, 94

Operant autonomic conditioning
  biofeedback and, 138, 147, 156
  verbal interface and, 148

Pain perception, 87–106
  endocrine system in stress analgesia,
    91–93
  endogenous analgesia system
    activation, 89–90
  endogenous control mechanisms, 88–89
  immunosuppressive and tumor-
    enhancing effects of stress, 98–99
  independent opioid forms of stress
    analgesia, 95–96
  neuroanatomy of stress analgesia, 94–95
  neurotransmitters in stress analgesia,
    93–94
  opioid and nonopioid mechanisms of
    stress analgesia, 91
  prenatal alcohol exposure and, 97–98
  spinal cord and, 87–88
  See also Perception
Parkinson's disease, 10
Pedophilia, 64–67
Pendulum effect, 191–194
Perception
  attention and, 1–18
  cardiovascular system and, 63–64
  consciousness and, 56–57
  motor theory and, 20
  See also Pain perception
Physiological regulation, 163–182
Pituitary hormones, 91–92
Prefrontal lesions, 8–9
Progressive relaxation, 183–216
  behavior therapy and, 183–184, 185–186
  cognitive/somatic factors in, 195–202
  origin of, 183
  pedagogy versus technology in, 187–195
  suggestion and, 202–209
  See also Relaxation
Psychotherapy, 130

Reality, 55
Refractory period, 5

226   SUBJECT INDEX

Relaxation
  biofeedback and, 142–144
  motor theory of voluntary thinking
    and, 41–45
  See also Progressive relaxation
REM sleep
  motor theory of voluntary thinking
    and, 42–43
  tonic skeletal muscle vasoconstriction
    during, 172
Repression, 125–126
Response image, 139

Selective attention, 11
Self-disclosure. *See* Confiding
Sensory processes, 59
Skin, 171–172
Skin conductance tests, 141
Sleep
  motor theory of voluntary thinking
    and, 42–43
  progressive relaxation and, 200
  tonic skeletal muscle vasoconstriction
    during, 172
Slips of action, 12
Smell, 34
Socialization
  affect and, 126
  inhibition and, 125
Somatic factors, 195–202
Speech, 23, 28–29
Speed of performance, 11–12
Spinal cord
  blood pressure and, 171
  pain perception and, 87–88
  sensory perception and, 87
  See also Brain; Central nervous system
Stimulation-produced analgesia, 88–89
Stream of consciousness, 40–45
Stress
  cognition and, 132
  confiding and, 119, 131
  immunosuppressive and tumor-
    enhancing effects of, 98–99
  pain perception and, 88
  progressive relaxation and, 198, 199,
    200

Stress analgesia
  activation of system in, 89–90
  endocrine system and, 91–93
  neuroanatomy of, 94–95
  neurotransmitters in, 93–94
  opioid and nonopioid forms of, 95–96
  prenatal alcohol exposure and, 97–98
  two independent opioid forms of, 95–
    96
Stroop phenomenon, 11
Suggestion, 186, 202–209
Supervisory attentional system, 6–7
  action selection and, 13
  conscious control and, 14–16
  modulating role of, 10–12
  motor theory and, 27–28
  neuropsychological evidence of, 8–10
Sympathectomy, 171–172

Taped relaxation techniques, 189–190
Task competition, 13–14
Tasks, 2–3
Taste, 34
Thinking. *See* Cognition
Transcendental meditation, 44–45
Trauma, 107–136
  confiding and, 118–119
  health and, 109–118
Triggers, 3–5, 6
Trophotrophic emotional system, 195

Vasomotor control, 171–172
Verbal processing, 147–152
Vertical thread influences, 6
Vision
  motor theory and, 20, 23–24
  motor theory of voluntary thinking
    and, 29–34
Volition. *See* Will

Will, 2
  motor theory of voluntary thinking
    and, 26–28
  supervisory attention system and, 14–
    16